HOW TO
SELL
$
S
RE
F!

Pro
Tha

D1507242

Dearborn™
Trade Publishing
A **Kaplan Professional** Company

This publication is designed to provide accurate and authoritative information in regard to the subject matter covered. It is sold with the understanding that the publisher is not engaged in rendering legal, accounting, or other professional service. If legal advice or other expert assistance is required, the services of a competent professional person should be sought.

Vice President and Publisher: Cynthia A. Zigmund
Acquisitions Editor: Michael Cunningham
Senior Managing Editor: Jack Kiburz
Interior Design: Lucy Jenkins
Cover Design: James Bell
Typesetting: the dotted i

Published by Dearborn Trade Publishing
A Kaplan Professional Company

Printed in the United States of America

05   06   07   10 9 8 7 6 5 4 3 2 1

Library of Congress Cataloging-in-Publication Data

Smith, Steve (Steve Paul), 1947-
    How to sell more stuff : promotional marketing that really works / Steve Smith
with Don E. Schultz.
        p.   cm.
    Includes index.
    ISBN 0-7931-9331-1 (pbk.)
    1. Sales promotion.   I. Schultz, Don E.   II. Title.
HF5438.5.S635 2004
658.8′2—dc22

                                                                        2004014748

Dearborn Trade books are available at special quantity discounts to use for sales promotions, employee premiums, or educational purposes. Please call our Special Sales Department to order or for more information at 800-621-9621, ext. 4444, e-mail trade@dearborn.com, or write to Dearborn Trade Publishing, 30 South Wacker Drive, Suite 2500, Chicago, IL 60606-7481.

DEDICATION

To Karen for her inspiration; Tania, Todd, and Chelsea for their toleration; and Lorene and Gerald for their dedication *and* their entrepreneurial spirit that launched Smith Radio's Collect & Get 45 RPM Record Club

Contents

When Steve Smith first called me about working with him on a book about sales promotion, my first reaction was "Been there, done that." In the 1980s, Bill Robinson of the William A. Robinson Agency (now Robinson-Maites) and I coauthored two of the first books in what we liked to call "the modern era of sales promotion." By modern era, we simply meant those books treated sales promotion as a sophisticated, focused business development tool that could compete alongside traditional media advertising, salesforce efforts, and the like to build sales and profits. The approach was a structured method for developing definable sales promotion programs and activities, based on proven and consistent planning models that included measurable outcomes against clearly defined sales goals.

That approach was, at that time, a big change from the historical way sales promotion had been considered both inside and outside the marketing organization. For years, promotion managers had been focused on sourcing gizmos, that is, purchasing and distributing buttons and banners and in-store signs and logo-emblazoned trinkets. Now, there's nothing wrong with these things if used properly, but simply distributing them to any and everybody didn't really make use of the inherent capabilities of sales promotion.

The books Bill and I wrote were "cutting edge" back in the 1980s. In fact, some were revised and updated even into the mid-1990s. But today, sales promotion is much more sophisticated, strategic, and important to all types of marketing organizations. That's certainly true, if the investment in sales promotion by marketing organizations is any indicator. Sales promotion budgets continue to climb, shifted from other types of marketing activities. New concepts, ideas, and approaches continue to be developed in all types of businesses around the world. Sales promotion really has come of age today, much more than Bill Robinson and I would ever have imagined years ago.

But looking back doesn't do much to move the business ahead today. And that is what this book is all about: *moving the business ahead through sales promo-*

tion. In fact, this is one book that is really true to its title by showing you how to sell more stuff.

So why am I involved in this book? Frankly, I had a real itch to get back into the fray as sales promotion continues to evolve and expand. Sales promotion is an exciting area, focusing on one of the most important aspects of any business today: how to sell more stuff and make more money.

Then Steve called. I was intrigued because he approaches sales promotion like a craftsman. That is, he's not as interested in the analytical, theoretical, or nifty algorithms as I am. He's much more focused on concisely explaining how to do sales promotion programs in exquisite detail; how to bring sales promotion programs to market; how to implement them successfully; and how to "cover off" on all the details so that the all-too-common glitches don't jeopardize the entire program.

I'm a conceptualizer. Steve is a practical implementer. So we complement each other. This complementary approach sets the stage for this book. At the beginning of each chapter, I'll do my stuff . . . some relevant research, basic concepts, and the like. Steve then follows with an extensive "how to." But you'll find a few other things we think are important in this book that you likely won't find in others. Here's what we have done to differentiate this text from others:

- *This is a workbook.* This isn't a book you read, think a bit about, and then put on the shelf. Instead, it's designed as a handbook of how to do all types of sales promotions. We think you'll be using this book over and over again.

- *This is a book for everyone.* Many sales promotion books are one of two kinds. One kind consists of esoteric, scholarly research reports filled with lambdas and gammas and equations in language you can't cut through with a knife. That's fine if you're planning on writing a doctoral dissertation, but it's not much help if you're on the firing line, putting together a promotion that will sell more stuff next month. The other type of sales promotion text tends to be discussions on big-budget, complex programs written with lots of four-color photos and seemingly developed more for the trade press than for the company's business. There's nothing wrong with studying those glitzy promotions either, but, generally, they are totally out of the smaller marketer's reach and the reach of more limited area marketers operating on a day-to-day promotional schedule. Yes, you can learn much from either of these kinds of books, but you likely can't do much with what they provide. This book is for the day-to-day promotional marketer who doesn't have the time, big bucks, or unlimited resources that the big guys use.

- *Plain English.* We've made this book as clear, concise, and complete as possible. And we've used business English so you won't have to constantly scurry to a dictionary. We've broken complex issues into bite-size pieces so you don't choke on the information. We've also included a glossary to clarify the jargon of the business. Even if you're wet behind the ears, the glossary will have you sounding like a seasoned pro.

- *Lots of examples.* Typically, sales promotion is visually focused, so we've illustrated concepts with graphics to let you grasp the concepts. But you won't find four-color, pop-up pages with loads of impressive illustrations and little text. Our premise is that you bought this book to learn how to do sales promotion better, not to be entertained by our art director.

- *A bit of theory to impress you and your boss.* A lot of theory underlies our methods and approaches, but it isn't "in-your-face," sophisticated jargon that's so popular today. Instead, we've added just enough "meat" at the beginning of each chapter to make you comfortable with our approaches to the programs you're developing. We've thrown in these introductions so you can impress your boss and maybe some of your coworkers. (Note: If you want more theoretical concepts, send us a note and we'll suggest some really esoteric books for you to ponder.)

- *What to avoid.* A unique feature of this book is our treatment of items that can get you in trouble. It's the little things that cause most of the problems. That's why each section describes what not to do, what to avoid, and what hazards exist. Remember, Hoover almost went bankrupt because it didn't think through a promotion that gave away airline tickets with the purchase of a vacuum cleaner. Setting up protective walls is sometimes as important as having a great idea.

- *The true joy of seeing a promotion work.* Unlike advertising, public relations, or even direct marketing, sales promotion can be observed. You can watch customers bring coupons to the store, see people wearing your premium T-shirts, and watch people head for your display and pick up your product. That's the key element of sales promotion. It impacts behavior so people do things they might not have done without it—encouraging them to buy things earlier than planned, to go to stores they hadn't previously considered, to find new and different ways of using products and services. In short, sales promotion impacts consumer behavior. We have titled this book *How to Sell More Stuff* because we believe that is what marketing and sales promotion are all about . . . selling more stuff.

I started this introduction by explaining why I am the coauthor and why I am so pleased that Steve Smith thought of me when he conceived this book. It is a book I know is important. It is a book I know you will find useful, helpful, and valuable. Most of all, I am sure it's a book you will use and reuse. And if you use it as much as Steve and I hope you will, you'll wear this one out and have to buy another. And that's what makes happy customers and happy authors.

So get started. It's time to sell more stuff!

1

HELP!

"**H**elp! Our sales are down 15 percent heading into the third quarter! What can I do? Help! I promised the franchisees a Super Bowl sweepstakes! How do I do it? Oh my! I need a tie-in partner! Who and how? Yikes! We've got a warehouse of industrial sprayers, and we're introducing a new line. Hmm. That loyalty idea of mine sounded easy at the time—I'm clueless where to start! Do'h! It's already November, and I need to motivate Thanksgiving Friday traffic! No, no! The competitor just cut its abrasive roll costs $10 a pallet! How can I match that value? Umm, what's a dangler?"

If you want to study a lot of theory, graphs, irrelevant industry figures, and rose-colored case histories and memorize test questions, don't buy this book! This book is for people with a lot to do and not much time to waste—people who need to know what direction to take, how to do it, and how to avoid the pitfalls in the process.

If you're ready for a comprehensive crash course in designing and executing a sales promotion, just get a highlighter and Post-it flags. This is information you can use—ideas, actions, and how-tos to help your company sell a lot more stuff through tried-and-true promotional marketing techniques.

For every informative page in this book, we may well have reviewed over 100 reference pages. That's because 99 percent of the published information out there isn't usable. So this book can save you reading thousands of pages of information you can't use.

It might even save your job, because it also tells you the pitfalls and risks. Most promotional marketing books dwell on successes, real or not. (I've personally received calls from panicked agencies trying to dump Ninja Turtle overstocks, Olympic lapel pins, and "hit" videos from promotions that failed, some of which were award winners.)

In short, this book cuts to the quick so you can develop a well-planned promotion from concept through completion.

WHAT IS PROMOTIONAL MARKETING?

Promotional marketing used to go by the less distinguished name of "sales promotion." It simply referred to extra ways and means of promoting sales, from sales incentives to price-off signs. As Don Schultz's introduction points out, marketers began to realize there was more to promotion than a pure sales function. Like advertising, direct marketing, and similar disciplines, promotional tactics are effective marketing tools that help to extend the brand image, target consumer segments, support strategic planning, and, of course, promote sales. In fact, promotional marketing accomplishes objectives less achievable with other marketing disciplines, such as continuity, qualified traffic, multiple purchase "loading," sampling, and "bounce-back" purchases. Promotional marketing is a term of broad scope for several disciplines and an integral part of any successful marketing plan.

Briefly put. *Promotional marketing* ("sales promotion") is the marketing discipline that utilizes strategic motivational tactics to encourage a predetermined action(s) by the sales, distribution, trade, end-user, and/or consumer target(s).

Action! Sales promotions generate an immediate action. Advertising viewers may flip the page or continue watching the game. Public relation events may make people feel good about the product. But promotion motivates people to do something—clip a coupon, enter a sweepstakes, purchase a value-added offer, collect another stamp, reach a sales quota, open a new account, and other strategic activities.

Strategic tactics. Sales promotion relies on motivational tactics derived from marketing and sales strategies. Each tactic has a subset of variations. This book describes 135 varieties of 12 strategic tactics.

Measurable results. Well, somewhat measurable. If you drop a coupon, for example, you'll learn how many were redeemed, and that's measurable. But other factors are always at work—advertising levels, competitor activities, the economy, the product itself, even the weather.

Promotion results vary greatly by industry and tactic. A popular grocery brand may consider a 2 to 3 percent coupon redemption good. Meanwhile, nearly half of marketers target incremental sales gains from 15 to 20 percent through their various promotions.

Advertising versus Promotion

You might say advertising opens the sale, whereas promotion closes it. Advertising creates awareness and positions a product in terms of its image, benefits, and uniqueness. Promotion encourages direct action through motivational tactics, from discounts to bonus offers to sales incentive programs. Ideally, it also reinforces the brand and advertising.

2003 Spending per Discipline

Consumer promotion	30.6%
Trade promotion	26.6%
Advertising	37.6%
Other	5.2%

Source: *PROMO* Promotion Trends Report 2003.

Marketing Allocations by Type—2004

Sales promotion	14.8%
Event marketing	10.5%
Direct marketing	22.3%
Trade promotion	19.2%
Consumer advertising	22.8%
Public relations	7.3%
Other	3.1%
Total marketing budget:	**100%**

Source: "Industry Trends Report," *PROMO* magazine
(http://www.promomagazine.com), a Primedia publication.

Promotional marketing crosses over into a few of the above allocations. For example, direct marketing may include a sweepstakes or refund promotion. As a rule of thumb, yearlong marketing expenditures break down to one-third for advertising, one-third for promotional marketing, and one-third for trade promotion. However, a smaller packaged good brand may devote as much as 90 percent to trade promotion.

Sales Promotion Is Executed through a Chain of Links

Promotion addresses the product pipeline. For packaged goods, manufacturing creates special packaging with custom delivery schedules. Sales is trained and motivated to deliver the program to distributors, who deliver it to the trade, which executes the program in-store. The consumer is the last link in the chain. The world's greatest promotional idea may be doomed if the chain breaks.

Objectives, Strategies, and Tactics

These three terms, which can overlap, are often confused with one another. Beyond business objectives (i.e., sales), promotional objectives might be the following:

- Increased distribution outlets
- Increased shelf space
- Increased in-store presence
- Expanded selling season
- Increased purchase frequency
- Increased usage occasions
- Increased transaction size
- Trial

Strategies and tactics often become confused with one another. Here's a simple *and* promotional differentiation:

- *Strategies* are the plans by which you'll achieve your objectives.
- *Tactics* are the actions you'll take *as you define where you spend your money* to achieve your strategies (an ad with a coupon, a sweepstakes prize, a free on-pack, etc.).

How Should You Plan Your Promotion?

Promotion lives and dies on execution. Sales has to understand the promotion and sell it in to their business customers. Buyers have to approve it and alert the system. The point-of-sale kit has to be self-contained and simple, including easy instructions. Someone has to receive the kit without shoving it to the back of the warehouse. And someone, possibly a teenage stock person, has to assemble the display—all right on schedule. Remember that different tactics require different lead times. And every program's first question should be: "When does sales have to sell it into the trade (or business-to-business target)?"

In a nutshell, be sure to perform each of the following 21 steps:

1. Review your business on every front. See the following section: "Step One—Identify Yourself."
2. Review the extended index, which lays out all the promotional possibilities. Get an idea of what strategies and tactics to explore based on your business review.
3. Establish the objectives that will have the greatest impact on your business—with the most achievable execution demands.
4. Establish the strategies to achieve your objectives and then the tactics for those objectives. (Again, tactics are where you start spending money.)
5. Start your plan and budget, taking the following areas into consideration:
   - Manufacturing
   - Operations
   - Distribution
   - Sales
   - Trade
   - Consumers
   - Retailers and business to business—map your pipeline
6. As you plan, review the relevant chapters of this book, noting the advantages, pitfalls, guidelines, and checklists. (Again, review "Step One—Identify Yourself.")
7. Establish your criteria for success: not just sales but sales and trade participation levels, display penetration, and so on.
8. Create a checklist and assign the people best qualified to address each point.

9. Create a flow chart, critical path, Gant chart, or whatever your business calls a "schedule," with every department, participant, and target accounted for. And allow for these things:
   - Lead times for every item and execution from creative development to approvals, sell-in process, warehousing, and shipping—everything
   - Communication materials for all parties
   - Executional tasks—who does them, when, and how
   - How-to sheets for every participating party from phone operators to teenage store clerks
   - Anything you can think of
10. Put a low-maintenance/cost backup plan and/or program in place in case something falls through.
11. Perform reality checks, running your plan past as many participants as possible, including every party you want to motivate.
12. Advise the system a promotion is coming and what will be expected.
13. Set up various meetings to introduce the plan and all its elements to every group involved.
14. Have sales introduce and sell the program to its respective targets—distributors, businesses, retail accounts, or franchise operations.
15. Obtain as much participation feedback as possible—even enrollment forms if appropriate—so you can project all the quantities.
16. Order and monitor warehouse receipts of all materials.
17. Ship the materials, launch the program, and bird-dog every angle constantly via the phone, the fax, e-mails, and newsletters; and bird-dog even in the field. *Execution is everything.*
18. Track everything so you can evaluate the total program later.
19. Create an evaluation, including comments from a sampling of everyone involved. Include recommendations for future programs.
20. Distribute thanks to everyone involved through letters, certificates, or simple novelties. Small gestures mean a lot, because you've probably put everyone through a lot. Let them know their efforts were noticed and appreciated.
21. Schedule a vacation for when it's all over!

STEP ONE—IDENTIFY YOURSELF

"If anything can go wrong, it will." To avoid this popular prophecy as well as maximize your program's results, consider every angle in your planning. Before you even begin to develop ideas, make sure you take into account the items in the following "Brand Background Document." You don't need to address everything it lists, but use it as a checklist to make sure you don't neglect any important considerations. It will help in all your subsequent planning efforts, including a "SWOT" analysis (strengths, weaknesses, opportunities, threats).

Brand Background Document

Note: This broad-based questionnaire should be adapted according to the brand's category: retail, packaged goods, service, and so on.

PRODUCT/SERVICE
Brand objectives
Products included in this assignment
Product description
Range of models/levels
Quality, price, and the like compared with the competition
Features versus the competition's features

CONSUMER/END-USER MARKET
Age
Income
Gender
Demographics
Psychographics
Region
Database
Levels of loyalty/usage
End-user profile (Also, see distribution.)

COMPETITION
Who?
Activities
Comparison of sales and distribution structure
Respective shares
Point(s) of difference
Strengths/weaknesses
Share of market
Advertising, promotion, and collateral samples

ADVERTISING
Positioning
Unique selling proposition
Image
Slogan
Media
Advertising samples

PROMOTION HISTORY
Types of promotions
Consumer offer and requirement
What does/does not work
What was rejected
Channels
Sales, distribution, and trade sell-in
Redemption/participation
Timing and duration
Evaluation criteria
Samples

PACKAGING
Configurations
Packout
Samples
In-pack/on-pack capability
Packout capability (self-shippers, pallet package, etc.)
Print on package? Where and how much space?
Other manufacturing capabilities/limitations

SALES
Unit
Dollar
Share (and competitors' share)
By channel
Growth/decline trends

SEASONALITY/REGIONALITY
Sales percentage by period
Sales percentage by region
A, B, C, D county
Key sales periods

PRICING/BUDGET
Suggested retail price and everyday price
Competitors' suggested retail prices and everyday prices
Margin
Turn rate—heavy versus moderate consumer
Typical coupon/discount value
Retailer and wholesaler profitability
Promotional allowance funding and usage
Promotional marketing budget per item

DISTRIBUTION
Sales channels—consumer, industrial, commercial, for example
Retail channels—grocer, drug, mass, hardware, mom-pop, services, for example
Dedicated salesforce? Whom do they sell to? Hierarchy?
Salesforce
   Broker/distributor salesforce? Number of reps and other products they
      rep? Hierarchy?
   Importance of brand—share of interest
   Incentives and how they compare with other lines
   Compensation
Warehouse (storage and delivery?)
Store-door?
Frequency of visits/calls and by whom
Market penetration—ACV, number of outlets

BUSINESS-TO-BUSINESS BUYER

Who buys/authorizes at different levels?

Who are end users? Do they influence buyer?

What buyer *expects:* allowance, in-ad, slotting, and degree and manner of
advertising

What buyer/business *needs:* employee incentive, traffic, referrals, direct mail
list/program, awareness beyond advertising medium, trial, push-pull,
goodwill, publicity, flyer participation, other (Can you contribute to any
of these needs?)

Scenario of sales/buyer meeting at each level

ALLOWANCES/INCENTIVES

Overall allocations: customer headquarters, customer locations, distributors,
sales, for example

New products

Slotting

Display

Advertising

Personnel allocations: sales/distribution incentives—managers to route people

Trade/distribution: types (case, promotional, rebate, spiffs, etc.)

Required performance(s) and allocation for achievement

How promotional allowances to be used—best to worst cases

POINT-OF-SALE CONSIDERATIONS

Store sections

Configuration—shelf, pegboard, floor, end cap, bunker, stack, for example

Shelf life

Average number of facings

Turn rate

Who maintains: stock boy, route salesperson, crew, floor salesperson,
merchandiser

DISPLAYS/SIGNAGE

Types: shelf talker, stacker card, floor/pole sign, shelf/easel, self-shippers,
end aisle, decal, ceiling, permanent/semipermanent

Samples

Number of units by channel

Price per unit

Who sells in to chain
Who places: route salesperson, merchandiser, broker rep, retail employees
Longevity
Criteria for getting display: loader, case allowance, promotional allowances, event tie-in, favored cause, creative/graphics, advertised promotion, flyer in-ad, in-store sampling, other

TIMING, LOGISTICS, AND MATERIALS
Internal sell-in
Sales sell-in (sales meeting?)
Distributor sell-in
Distributor materials
Trade sell-in (trade show?)
Materials to distribution center
Materials to trade
In field
Lead times for packaging, product, POS, shipping, other

BUDGET
How allocated and to what areas

WISH LIST
Anything you may want to set your sites on for the future, even if you can't achieve it now

CRITERIA FOR SUCCESS
Make sure all items and considerations are measurable and can serve as benchmarks for future programs. Start to build a learning curve.

EVALUATION
Review the criteria for success.
(Sales are not the only benchmark. If the retailer places the display to receive the self-liquidating premium, it doesn't matter how many consumers ordered the premium—the display got up. And if the product still didn't sell, the display objective was nevertheless successful.)
What will be measured to evaluate the program and how will it be measured?

2

SWEEPSTAKES AND CONTESTS

INTRODUCTION:
MAKING SWEEPSTAKES CONSUMER RELEVANT

Based on *PROMO* magazine's Industry Trends Report (2004), the use of sweepstakes and their companion technique, contests, has not been growing when compared with other types of sales promotion activities. Yet sweepstakes and contests are still very important tools for sales promotion managers. And as we explain in the following chapter, they can be even more important in the future. But increased use and market performance can come only if the sweepstakes and contests are properly developed and employed in the marketplace.

Several reasons explain the lack of growth in sweepstake and contest usage. Obviously, the huge monetary payouts now offered in various state-sponsored lotteries have made traditional prize packages that can be offered by individual marketing organizations seem paltry by comparison. A $1 million grand prize just doesn't mean much anymore in the face of multi-million-dollar payouts by the lottery folk.

But it's likely the sweepstakes and contest structures of traditional promotional programs are equally to blame. Today, customers and consumers want instant satisfaction and gratification. Marketers want instant sales and profits. So whereas sweepstakes and contests can be designed to deliver on the sales portion of the equation, the immediacy issue is more difficult. It just takes time to develop a sweepstakes promotion. Time to plan and implement. Time to generate the entries. Time to select and notify the winners. That's part of the reason we've seen the rapid growth of so-called instant sweepstakes promotions. Those are the sweepstakes and other promotional programs that are now widely used by the fast-food chains, such as the Monopoly game developed by McDonald's and the instant win promotions being offered on products ranging from shaving cream to batteries. These quick reward programs are structured to provide the possibility of winning a major prize instantly, clearly an attempt to overcome the delay in winner selection and notification generally found in traditional sweepstakes promotions. Consumers sometimes win even major prizes instantly, and marketers get the almost instant sales boost they are seeking. Looks like a win-win combination.

Sweepstakes and contests can be effective promotional activities if the sales promotion manager keeps four key strategic-planning issues in mind.

1. A sweepstakes or contest is great for calling attention to a product or service for which there is nothing new to advertise or promote. If properly developed, a sweepstakes can differentiate and raise interest in what is otherwise a commodity product, service, or even business proposition. So if the product or service needs a short-term shot in the arm with consumers, channel members, the salesforce, or whomever, a properly designed sweepstakes can often provide a boost or can at least raise the product or service out of the mass in a crowded marketplace.

2. A corollary to getting attention is the ability to tie the product or service to such current events as golf tournaments, NCAA football, or the World Series—events that enjoy limited time, but do have consumer interest. All offer ways for the brand to take advantage of the inherent consumer attention to these events and generate interest and excite-

ment for the brand. Of course, the key element here is that the event or activity should have some relationship to the product or service being promoted.

3. Sweepstakes and contests are not normally thought of as strategic brand-building techniques, but with the proper planning, they can be. For example, the ongoing sweepstakes conducted by Publishers Clearing House (PCH) have become a cultural icon in American business as has the Pillsbury Bake-Off and the variations of the Bud Bowl for Budweiser tied to the Super Bowl. And under-the-cap sweepstakes and reward programs have built value for brands and organizations ranging from Pepsi-Cola to motor oil. So sweepstakes *can* build brands and can build them over time.

4. A sweepstakes or contest, if properly developed and clearly communicated to participating customers, can be a relatively inexpensive way to build a customer or prospect database. By having customers identify themselves through entries in the sweepstakes or contest, the marketer can gain valuable information on the profiles of those consumers who enter and, by implication, those who are, or might be, logical prospects or customers for brand sales now and into the future. Given the critical nature of customer identification, a sweepstakes can be an efficient way to gain that knowledge.

The biggest challenge for the promotion manager is designing a sweepstakes that helps build brand value over time. That brand building comes from setting clear promotional objectives for the sweepstakes program. And setting objectives starts with identifying which or what kind of customers or prospects the sweepstakes should attract. For example: Is the sweepstakes program designed to reward present customers for their loyalty or to encourage new customers to try the product or service? A different type of program can be designed to do either. Is the structure of the sweepstakes planned to get "off-the-shelf" promotion in a crowded retail aisle or to encourage customers to visit a specific retail location? Different promotional approaches are needed to accomplish those goals. Is the sweepstakes designed to involve the channels or retailers with some sort of matching prize, or is it designed only for the end users? It's asking these types of strategic questions that helps the promotion manager develop an effective sweepstakes or contest.

Sweepstakes and contests are more than just finding a neat prize and putting together a drawing. It's the strategy behind the sweepstakes development that really matters. Indeed, often a $100,000 prize package can be enhanced so that it appears to be worth millions to the right customer or the right audience. But that takes planning and thought—both key elements in developing effective sweepstakes or contest programs. —Don E. Schultz

OVERVIEW

A sweepstakes can be one of the most economical promotions because the prize cost is spread across all the *nonwinners*. Most participants receive nothing, as opposed to a coupon or discount, where every redemption costs. And the prize cost is fixed.

This chapter reviews the various types of sweepstakes, detailing each one's objectives, advantages, and disadvantages. It reviews legalities and provides sample documents. It also outlines principles, applications, suggestions, and cautions so your sweepstakes leaves nothing to chance.

DEFINITION

Three factors determine whether it's a sweepstakes, a contest, or a lottery:

1. Prize: You get (or *may* get) something.
2. Chance: You may or may not get the prize based on an element of luck.
3. Consideration: You have to pay or do something "exceptional" to qualify for the prize.

Legally, you can have two of the above but *not all three:*

- A sweepstakes is a *chance* promotion in which a participant can *win* a prize (through luck). There is no "consideration" because participants cannot be required to purchase to enter.
- A contest is a *skill* promotion, in which a participant may *earn* a prize through a demonstrable skill. "Consideration" (payment to enter) is

legal because there's no element of chance but rather an element of skill. (Like a recipe contest.)

- A *lottery* has all three elements: a prize, consideration (pay to enter), and chance (luck). That's gambling, and it's not allowed!

Sweepstakes and contests are exempt from illegal lottery status, because each meets only two of the three criteria that constitute a lottery. If you run a contest and require a purchase, be sure you hire a sweepstakes attorney to make sure you comply with various state regulations. You may need to include a purchase requirement disclosure in some states, and a few may not allow you to require a purchase based on the nature of the "skill." State regulations frequently change, so make sure the statutes are current.

OBJECTIVES BY CATEGORY

Packaged Goods

Typical objectives:

- Awareness
  - Borrowed interest through prize
  - Theming and image enhancement
  - Involvement (for example, write a slogan on an entry form or say "Supersize Surprise" to the cashier)
- Seek product (such as match game piece to display and win)
- Impulse purchase/trial (such as in-pack instant win announcement)
- Tiebreaker in purchase decision
- Continuity purchase (such as collect and win game)
- Display placement—retail participation
- Information (such as "Write product attribute on entry form")
- Data capture (through entry forms)

Retail

Typical objectives:

- Awareness
  - Borrowed interest through prize

- Theming and image enhancement
- Entry's involvement tactic (match ad's entry number to display number or collect and win, for example)
- Traffic (instant win announcements)
- Cross-store traffic (entry devices in key locations)
- In-store destination (i.e., featured item or display)
- Salesperson interaction (such as "See salesperson for entry")
- Transaction size (such as everyone wins family meal discount, or the more items you buy, the more chances)
- Staff performance (incentive contest)
- Staff retention (ongoing incentive)
- In-store excitement—customer and staff
- Goodwill—PR
- Data capture (through entry forms)

Performance Incentive—Sales, Service, Distribution
(See Chapter 12, "Performance Programs," page 311.)

Performance/incentive programs typically are contests; however, they can also incorporate sweepstakes with entries earned for performance.

Typical objectives:

- Sales performance
- Focus on new product launch
- New distribution goals
- Display/signage placement
- Program/product learning
- Purchase by distributor/end user
- Employee performance
- Employee retention

COMMON SWEEPSTAKES OBJECTIVES BY TACTIC

(See also, itemized tactics below, plus objectives listed above.)

TACTIC	OBJECTIVES
Drawing— entry form	Awareness; package/store visit for entry form; ease of execution
Program learning/ data entry	Added awareness of specific product benefits; added data capture; ease of execution
In-store sweepstakes	Display placement; retailer involvement; in-store excitement and traffic
Match display	Display placement and traffic
Match package	Package placement; package registration; traffic; package interaction
In-pack/on-pack winner announcement	Purchase; package attention; display placement
Watch/listen and win	Media tie-in impact/economies; media merchandising; program learning; awareness; retailer participation (advertised promotion); purchase (depending on tactic)
Radio call-out/ call-in	Media tie-in impact/economies; media trade-outs; program learning; awareness; retailer participation; purchase (sometimes)
Coupon/refund entry	Purchase; data capture
Collect and win	Continuity purchase; visit or performance
Game structure	Awareness; involvement; continuity purchase; program learning; immediacy/ excitement
Mystery shopper	Involvement; awareness; on-site performance; program learning; field survey/ activity
800/900#	Immediacy; involvement; impact; program learning; data capture; purchase (depending on tactic)
Internet code number	Involve consumers with Web site; motivate purchase for code number; tie-in with other Web partners; economize through digital

ITEMIZED TACTICS

I. DRAWING—ENTRY FORM

Definition   Winner selected by random drawing of entries

Advantages
- Variety of turnkey applications
- Data capture capability
- Product learning (request product attribute be written on entry)

Disadvantages
- Entry requires considerable involvement
- Delayed winner announcement—less immediacy and motivation to participate
- Mail-in entry requires postage and effort—reduces participation
- Entrants fear junk mail
- No purchase incentive
- No performance requirement (other than product learning capability)
- Narrower market—only profiles who fill out entries
- Entry box requires valuable space plus staff execution
- Professional/hobbyist entrants (such as retirees and charitable organizations) send alternative entry 3x5 cards
- Media-delivered, mail-in entry form excludes any product involvement or store visit

2. PROGRAM LEARNING/DATA ENTRY

Definition   Entry requests product (or personal) information, thus educating entrant (or gathering entrant data)

Advantages
- Builds awareness of key product attributes
- Captures consumer data
- Motivates applicants to submit forms
- May qualify entrants—those who are interested and participate are targets
- Can generate product trial in "demo entries" ("Visit our site, navigate, and win")

Disadvantages
- Consumer data do not represent a cross section
- Additional effort reduces participation
- Requires expense and task of organizing and evaluating data
- Entrants fear junk mail
- Limitations on how much entrants will do also limits value of the information received
- Requires more space and clutter in communication materials—lost readership

3. IN-PACK INSTANT WIN (ALSO, ON-PACK)

Definition
Participants informed immediately if they won through an announcement in (or on) the product.

"No purchase necessary." Write-in alternative to receive free game piece (In some states, retailer must stock alternative entries.)

Advantages
- Encourages impulse purchase
- Tiebreaker among competitors
- Custom seeding winners only (versus nonwinning announcements) to ease manufacturing concerns
- Minimal consumer effort encourages participation
- Adds product excitement
- Accountability: finite number of winning pieces
- Package announcement reaches all shoppers—not reliant on point-of-sale
- Turnkey for retailer
- On-pack or in-pack entry can also deliver product message or offer

Disadvantages
- On-pack entries may be violated, particularly by retailer, if everybody wins a coupon; removing announcement should deface package
- Shoppers may open pack or tear off announcements without purchase, but weigh the odds of isolated cases against overall benefits
- Food-safe inks required for food packaging
- Announcements with glue, rub-off area, or other should be tested for unique applications (such as freezer, product reaction, hot trucks, etc.)

- Winning announcement should avoid fraud through:
  - Using different typeface and size for different prize levels—minor prize winners may forge major prize announcement typeface
  - Coding winners with invisible fluorescent ink signatures or secret symbol
  - Assurance that winning game pieces cannot be deciphered by holding them up to daylit window, computer-generated sequential patterns, printer employees, and so on
- In-packaging/on-packaging machinery may inhibit production and can be costly
- Advertising and signage timing must match product distribution
- May require suffix code and system to control distribution so promotional packs don't arrive in ineligible regions or countries

4. COUPON/REFUND ENTRY (DRAWING)

Definition

Discount device, such as coupon or refund, doubles as sweepstakes entry

Advantages

- Can increase redemption of coupon or refund
- Draws additional attention to discount offer
- Participant carries physical reminder of promotion
- Combines costs of two elements: coupon/refund and entry
- Data capture—name and address on entry
- Program learning (request product information on entry)
- Turnkey for retailer

Disadvantages

- Lead time—from retail redemption through clearinghouse to drawing—allowing at least three months from coupon drop to drawing date
- Marketers often prefer slippage over high refund redemption
- Requires added involvement to participate
- Delayed winner announcement—less motivating than instant win
- Narrower market: only profiles who fill out forms
- Some may be confused by dual tactic coupon or fear getting junk mail

5. MATCH AND WIN

Definition   Participant must match game piece's number, logo, or other symbol to a separate matching vehicle, such as a display, package symbol, TV/radio announcement, and the like, and if symbols match, participant wins

Advantages
- Directs participant to point-of-sale, product package, TV ad, or other
- Traffic potential encourages retailer to participate in vendor display program
- Participant carries reminder of promotion (i.e., game piece)
- Instant win announcement increases participation
- No winner if winning entry is held by nonplayer, which is very likely (Allows second-chance drawing that can be positioned as a separate event at minimal cost)
- Accountability: finite number of winning entries
- Turnkey at retail (if winning claims are processed by mail)

Disadvantages
- Limitations in seeding winning entries:
  - Extra steps to print magazine page with winning symbol; the rest with nonwinners
  - Some vehicles, like daily newspapers, cannot seed winning symbol
- Requires two elements: entry and matching vehicle
- Extra security steps as winning symbol appears on display (or other)
- May be confusing to consumers—clearly demonstrate how to play
- Nonwinners may claim/believe their entry is a winner—have written policy and consolation announcements
- In-store shoppers (without media-delivered entries) cannot participate—consider in-store drawing entry possibly for unclaimed prizes

6. WATCH/LISTEN AND WIN (also see "BROADCAST CALL-OUT/CALL-IN" below)

Definition   Participant must match game piece's number, phrase, or other symbol to a separate broadcast-delivered (or Internet) announcement (Same principle as "Match and Win" above)

Example: You received lucky number 85, and if you see that number during the Acme Movie broadcast, you win

Advantages
- Draws attention to broadcast sponsorship, advertising, and so on
- Excellent outreach and impact, such as on-air winner announcements
- Extends frequency and impact of media advertising (may negotiate media and prize contributions)
- Program-learning potential—player must acknowledge product attribute/slogan
- Adds human interest with live interaction of players on radio/TV
- Encourages retailer to participate, particularly with media mentions
- Participant carries reminder of promotion if game piece is used
- Instant win announcement increases impact and participation
- Does not necessarily require game piece security

Disadvantages
- Requires significant and coordinated media campaign
- Media often limited to one station and/or network program—narrows reach
- May not drive traffic to package or display as with other match and win alternatives
- Limitations in seeding winning entries (in match and win version—see previous tactic)

7. SCRATCH AND WIN (OR OTHER REVEAL DEVICE)

Definition
Game piece reveals winner (or nonwinner) announcement when participant scratches off or opens announcement area

Advantages
- Fun, involving, player-friendly tactic that increases participation
- Can draw additional attention to coupon
- Can increase traffic
- Can be structured as a game (see "Game" below)
- May be positioned as everybody wins game if players get coupons or offers
- Accountability: finite number of winning game pieces
- No winner if winning entry is held by nonplayer (Allows second-chance drawing that can be positioned as a separate event at minimal cost)
- Can be turnkey at retail (if winning claims are processed by mail)

Disadvantages
- Additional production cost for game pieces
- Requires secure distribution of game pieces
- Execution often neglected or abused by retail staff—may not hand out cards or hand out too many per patron
- Susceptible to misredemption with staff rubbing off numerous cards (everybody wins offers)
- Not necessarily tied to purchase

8. COLLECT AND WIN

Definition
Participants win by collecting game pieces to complete a word, row, puzzle, and so on; often has excellent odds for low-level prizes, but only one major prize-winning symbol is distributed

Advantages
- Continuity of purchase and/or traffic and/or performance
- Vests consumers as they near achieving a reward
- Program learning—collectible words, phrases, or pictures communicate message
- In-pack/on-pack game pieces motivate purchase
- Participant retains reminder of promotion—game pieces and collector card
- Ability to achieve minor prize in short time increases participation
- Players may group together, trading game pieces and thus add participation and awareness
- No winner if winning game piece is held by nonplayer, which is very likely. (Allows second-chance drawing that can be positioned as a separate event at minimal cost)

Disadvantages
- Limited to frequently purchased products/services
- Considerable effort to play, possibly limiting participation
- Requires distribution and retention of considerable materials
- Considerable production costs
- Added logistics distributing two elements—game piece and collector card
- Susceptible to being open-ended, so print finite number of winning pieces
- Shoppers may open pack or tear off game pieces without purchase
- Food-safe inks required for food packaging

- Pieces with glue, rub-off area, or other should be tested for unique applications (such as freezer, cola reaction to in-can inks, hot trucks, etc.)
- Winning game piece should avoid fraud (see "Match and Win" section above)

9. GAME

Definition	A sweepstakes with game elements, such as bingo spin-offs, trivia, slot machine spin-offs, and the like. Instant winner pieces also frequently incorporated
Advantages	• Game aspect adds fun, involvement, and increased awareness of both the promotion and the product • Game and collector tactic builds continuity of traffic and/or purchase • Vests consumers as they near achieving a reward • Program learning—word, phrase, or picture communicates message • In-pack/on-pack game pieces motivate purchase • Participant retains reminders of promotion—game pieces and board • Instant win overlay capability increases impact and participation • No winner if winning game piece is held by nonplayer, which is very likely (Allows second-chance drawing that can be positioned as a separate event at minimal cost)
Disadvantages	• Collector tactic limited to frequently purchased product • Can be confusing, requiring participant to study rules and lose interest • Effort intensive, possibly discouraging participation (though "Monopoly" is McDonald's most successful sweepstakes promotion) • Production costs of multiple or elaborate game pieces • Requires distribution and retention of considerable materials • Added logistics if distributing two elements—game piece and board • Susceptible to being open-ended, so print limited number of winning pieces • Shoppers may open packages or remove on-pack game pieces without purchase • Food-safe ink required for food packaging

- Pieces with glue, rub-off area, or other should be tested for unique applications (such as freezer, cola reaction to in-can inks, hot trucks, etc.)
- Winning game piece should avoid fraud (see "Match and Win" section above)
- Nonwinners may claim/believe their entry is a winner, so have written policy and consolation announcements prepared

10. IN-STORE (ON-PREMISE)

Definition

A sweepstakes conducted by and in the store (though often underwritten by a packaged goods vendor)

Advantages

- Tie-in benefits for packaged good and retail partners
- Packaged good partner may secure floor display as retailer shares spotlight
- Retailer can drive program and solicit several vendor partners to fund it
- In-store excitement
- Goodwill and PR—drawing can be an event
- Opportunity for salesperson to interface with customer
- Can drive traffic to store plus desired department
- Data capture (through write-in entries)
- Program learning (request product attribute be written on entry)
- Participation—better odds of winning in one store and prize immediate

Disadvantages

- Labor intensive
- Vendor program may be left unsupervised by retailer and staff
- Not cost efficient compared with national programs
- May not provide incentive to purchase
- May not provide performance requirement
- Narrower market—only those in store who fill out forms
- In-store entry box requires space
- Prize small compared with national programs—less motivating
- See comments under "Drawing" tactic (page 20)

11. PRIZE BOARD

Definition
A board with secured pull tabs (or other device) that reveal prizes when pulled; typically, one of the pulls is a major prize
Player earns pull through performance or drawing entry

Advantages
- Involving, fun game tactic
- Exceptional tactic for on-premise incentive programs and in-store sweepstakes minievent
- Board allows impactful graphics and theme
- Pull occasions can be events
- Effective incentive tactic with:
  - Defined performance objectives to earn pulls
  - Finite accountability—each board is worth a fixed value that can only be redeemed with qualifying performance
  - Game board on wall is program reminder
  - Remote site execution with systemwide control (each board represents one accountable budget)
- Continuity game

Disadvantages
- Often cost, time, and labor intensive:
  - The qualifying sweepstakes to earn pulls
  - The prize board event
- Qualifying sweepstakes' delayed reward may lessen impact and participation
- Pull-tab board production costs
- Prize offering limited to the number of pulls on the board
- If one of first participants pulls the grand prize, the remainder of the program loses momentum

12. MYSTERY SHOPPER (SPOTTER)

Definition
Winner spotted/announced through personal contact, either by identifying a mystery person or by being identified by one
Minor performance may be required (e.g., "If we spot your car with our bumper sticker, you win," or "If you spot our person and say, 'Acme is best,' you win")

Advantages	• Can reach all targets and locations directly—consumer, trade, employee, purchasing agent, end user, and so on • On-location spotters offer additional capabilities, such as handouts or PR • On-site employee incentive, as workers anticipate spotter visit (Random, *isolated* IRS audits motivate *all* taxpayers through this principle.) • Program learning—require that participant say phrase to qualify • Radio spotter extends broadcast media excitement • Enables vendor to tie in with retailer • Publicity extensions
Disadvantages	• Time, cost, and labor intensive • Potential for nonparticipation by those who (1) believe odds are against their personally encountering mystery shopper (2) or feel awkward approaching a stranger who may or may not be the mystery shopper • Less reach than other sweepstakes entry vehicles • Potential for mistrusting mystery shopper—a stranger • Requires exceptional communication to alert people how to win and remember details • Broadcast execution is limited to station's audience

13. BROADCAST CALL-OUT/CALL-IN

Definition	Broadcast medium receives call from, or makes call to, entrant to announce winner or do on-air quiz
Advantages	• Exceptional awareness through broadcast media with an entertaining deejay versus a "canned" announcer • Leverages media advertising • Vendor can tie in retailer • Involvement, both by entrant and vicarious listener/viewer • Program-learning capability—participant must identify slogan and so on • Can require visit to product/location for entry • Can motivate purchase with in-pack/on-pack entry distribution • Tie-in and prize trade-out opportunities

Disadvantages
- Time and labor intensive—numerous elements, details, and partner negotiations
- Requires media commitment on market-by-market basis
- Broadcast medium is limited to single station's audience
- Clutter potential amid numerous "cash call" programs
- Not necessarily a sales motivator, unless entry can be tied to visit or product purchase (which may be too labor intensive)

14. 800/900 NUMBER

Definition
Participant phones in to:
- Discover winning number/word (match and win)
- Punch in Touch-Tone code to see if it wins
- Provide name and address for entry

Advantages
- Opportunity for interactive messaging
- Easy entry and instant win announcement capability increases participation
- Effective data capture technique

Disadvantages
- Toll-free number and reply system costly
- Potential for unwanted repeat callers, such as children enjoying Santa
- Difficult to motivate purchase or performance
- Limitations in seeding match and win entries

15. INTERNET CODE NUMBER (AND OTHER INTERNET TACTICS)

Definition
Participants receive code number, visit sponsor's Web site, and enter code to see if they win
(Note: Internet can offer several sweepstakes tactics, including games.)

Advantages
- Motivates purchase if code is delivered via product
- Involves participants with brand's Web site
- Can be an interactive game format—entry earns game play
- Internet partners can provide prizes, including downloads and discounts

- Can be a continuity tactic
- Instant win tactic can increase participation
- Easily tracked by hits and capable of building database with entry data requests
- Can be cost efficient through paperless medium

Disadvantages
- May drive participant to Web site instead of the store
- Setting up system is costly
- Internet clutter, including sweepstakes
- Surfers fear getting spam
- Hackers may break prize code system
- Each entry code must be hidden from common view
- Limits audience to proactive Internet users
- Requires considerable effort, including being at a computer, on the Internet, even remembering to enter, which lowers participation
- Hard copy instant win games are more compelling

16. CONTEST

Definition
Requires skill to win and, as such, may require purchase to enter
Many marketers do not require purchase to enter contests
Technically, skill may be to calculate (*guess*) the number of jelly beans in a jar, or skill may also be subjectively judged, as in recipes, photos, or beauty contests (Note: Definition of skill may vary by state.)
Ties must be run off
(Note: Some states may not allow a purchase requirement in some instances, so consult a sweepstakes lawyer.)

Advantages
- Can require purchase
- Can reinforce product positioning or usage, such as a recipe or photo contest
- Program-learning capability
- Involving, particularly with easy challenge, such as calculating number of jelly beans in jar (anyone can guess)
- May encourage point-of-sale placement, as with recipe contest and grocery products
- Sales/performance incentive

- Publicity with winner setting example of product usage or superiority

Disadvantages
- Requires exceptional effort to participate, thus limiting participation
- Expensive—judging and evaluation of *every* entry. Also a runoff in case of a tie
- Labor intensive for marketer
- Market may be limited to those who are sufficiently skilled and prone to enter competition
- Possible discontent of nonwinners
- Some states may not allow a purchase requirement in some instances. Consult a sweepstakes lawyer.

17. LONG SHOT (ALSO HOLE-IN-ONE)

Definition
A $1 million+ prize may be funded for substantially less through difficult, low-odds skill requirement and insurance policy.

Skill may be a golf hole in one, basketball half-court free throw, solving difficult problem in limited time, and so on.

Typically, a qualifying sweepstakes is conducted to select a finalist—for example, the sweepstakes winner may receive a trip to the Final Four (a great prize) *and* a chance to shoot a million-dollar basket

Advantages
- Offers exceptional prize value, increasing excitement, and participation at nominal cost
- Excellent publicity event
- Can leverage sponsorship of the long shot event (Final Four, PGA, etc.)
- Can reinforce product positioning
- Prequalifying *contest* can require purchase or performance
- Prequalifying sweepstakes/contest is a promotion in itself
- Exciting topspin to otherwise traditional sweepstakes—win a car *and* chance to win a car a year for life!

Disadvantages
- Additional costs and tasks, such as securing insurance, location clearances, staging the event, and so on
- Twofold nature adds expense and effort (prequalifying sweepstakes/contest and hole-in-one event contest)

- Contest version expensive—judging and evaluation of *every* entry (if prequalifying contest is utilized)
- Market may be limited to those who are sufficiently skilled to enter— others then feel unqualified

"INSTANT WIN" DOESN'T MEAN INSTANT WIN (BUT OFTEN MEANS INSTANT SALES)

The accepted meaning of *instant win* is that the participant *learns* he or she won instantly (with a scratch-off card, for example) but may receive the prize later. Instant win typically enjoys greater participation than delayed-winner tactics. Put an instant win announcement in a candy wrapper and you'll sell a lot more candy bars than you'll sell with an entry form. In a 2003 IMI International study published by *PROMO* magazine, 53 percent of respondents said instant win sweepstakes influenced their purchasing decisions.

Source: "Industry Trends Report," *PROMO* magazine, April 2003 (http://www.promomagazine.com), a Primedia publication.

Considering that two-thirds of grocery store purchases are made on impulse, the instant win tactic can sway a lot of new purchase decisions that other tactics may not influence.

HAVE A SECOND CHANCE SWEEPSTAKES AT MINIMAL COST

The odds of having a winner in some sweepstakes are low. If 20 percent of customers participate in a collect and win game, there's an 80 percent chance the single grand prize winning piece will be handed to a nonparticipant who'll toss it in the trash.

So offer a "second chance" sweepstakes for unclaimed prizes and enjoy what amounts to a second sweepstakes at very little additional cost. This can be a simple drawing. You can run a match and win sweepstakes with the game piece delivered in print media. Then offer a mail-in sweepstakes at retail for any unclaimed prizes. That way, you'll reach both your media target (building traffic) plus any in-store shoppers who never saw your print ad.

PRIZES

Cash, cars, and travel are the most popular prizes. Cash is king but not the best choice for marketers for these reasons:

- It's the most expensive. Other prizes are available at wholesale at the same time you boast the retail value. You can also negotiate tie-ins, for example, swapping media mentions for prizes. (Sometimes a discount warehouse can match the price you paid for merchandise, so the "perceived value" benefit is lost.)
- Cash is spent and forgotten. Incentive program studies reveal cash winners often don't remember what they purchased with their cash, whereas virtually everyone remembers the specifics behind their merchandise rewards. (However, if the premium fades or falls apart, it's a bad reflection on your brand.)
- Merchandise may be selected to thematically reinforce your product's image or benefit. Cash cannot. Merchandise can even carry your brand logo.

Cash can be effective if it's a huge sum, such as $100,000 or $1 million. A long-shot sweepstakes (above) lets you offer a prize you can't really afford. However, it may not reinforce your brand, and the long shot's difficult challenge may not be motivating.

Merchandise doesn't enjoy the universal appeal of cash; it's subject to personal taste, and the consumer may already own the item. (A premium-based reward program should consider a range of rewards.) A shopping spree prize at a tie-in retailer can deliver cash, merchandise, and tie-in benefits. Ideally, prizes should be aspirational—things we'd love to own but don't allow ourselves to indulge in. It's one thing to win a kitchen appliance but quite another to win the appliance *plus* an Eating Lite Island Cruise with Emeril.

Two Philosophies: Lots of Prizes versus a Hero Prize

Should you focus on one humongous prize or increase everyone's odds with lots of lesser prizes? Ideally, both, otherwise focus on the major prize. Even non-

---

I *n s i g h t*

Don't make the prize so elaborate you can't describe it in a quick headline.

lottery players play when the prize soars. Conversely, research reveals people participate in fast-food sweepstakes partially because they know their odds are good at winning a simple food prize—*and* they might just win the big prize. You might offer lots of low-level prizes with unique appeal, like commemorative coins or baseball cards in one out of ten boxes. The collector aspect adds appeal.

If you want to offer 100 (or less/more) secondary prizes, make them fun and indulgent items that reinforce your brand.

Not everyone wants a butler. Research often reveals surprising, but consistent, insights. For example, heartland cooking moms don't want "millionaire" lifestyle prizes—no maid service, butlers, limousines, even fancy cars. Likewise, middle-Americans tend to prefer domestic travel prizes, not exotic foreign locations (in pre–9/11 studies).

Partner Prizes

You may negotiate free or discounted prizes through "trade-outs." An auto maker may provide a free car if sufficient, targeted advertising and point-of-sale supports the sweepstakes. See "Negotiating Advertising for Prizes or Rewards" on page 296 in Chapter 11, "Tie-ins."

Taxes

Prizes are taxable and the responsibility of the winner. Taxes on a major prize are considerable, and winners should be advised. If nothing else, issue a 1099 to winners of prizes valued $600 or over (retail value). Also, consider adding extra cash to a noncash prize to help the winner pay taxes. (However, the extra cash is taxable.)

Cash Alternatives

Cash alternatives are especially good if the winner can't afford the noncash prize's taxes. However, consider the wholesale price you negotiated versus the retail value the winner expects. (See the cash prize comments above.)

Unclaimed Prizes

Many winning game pieces are unwittingly discarded by nonparticipants, so many prizes go unclaimed. Some states require all prizes be awarded, if necessary to alternative winners. See "Have a Second Chance Sweepstakes at Minimal Cost" on page 33.

Other Prize Considerations

- Consider the winner's ability to use the prize. Urban apartment dwellers can't use a swimming pool. Southerners don't need snowmobiles.
- "Everyone wins" increases participation and good vibes—they didn't lose. A free cola-with-combo-meal-purchase coupon gives you a repeat customer. (However, don't send consumers a "You're a Winner" announcement for this kind of "everyone wins." Numerous states prohibit misleading announcements that make the consumer think he or she is a select winner.)
- How will the prize be delivered? For example, how does a rural winner get to the major airport? How does the car get to the winner from the factory? If there's a tie-in retailer, are there stores in all regions? If secondary prizes are free Dairy Queen treats, has every franchise signed off with the promotion?
- Is the prize safe and reputable?
- If a secondary prize is to be fulfilled by the retailer, that retailer may want full retail, not wholesale, reimbursement. Otherwise, the prize represents a lost sale.
- If a prize is not of significant value, some regulations may not be applicable. Check with a sweepstakes lawyer for prizes over $600. These require filing a 1099 tax form with the retail or market value.

Insight

If you're targeting kids with a sweepstakes, say, "You *could* win . . ." For adults you may be OK with "Win . . ."

THE WINNERS

Notification

At drawings, the winner typically need not be present to win, which increases entries and goodwill. However, in trade shows, sales meetings, and other "limited-to" events, you might require the entrant's presence. It helps draw a crowd to the booth and drawing. (See Chapter 12, "Performance Programs," page 311.)

Publicity

In ongoing or yearly sweepstakes, featuring winners communicates that winning is possible and real. It also promotes goodwill.

Names of major prize winners must be made available to the public through mail-in requests. (See details in rules section on page 48.)

Restrictions

Consider restrictions on who can win; for example, exclude minors from automobile prizes. The sponsor's employees should not be eligible. Winners must typically be residents of the United States (or the continental United States) and may be restricted to your limited trade area. Release of liability should be required in the event there's an accident involving the prize. (See the rules section on page 52.)

Affidavits

See forms that begin on page 49 through the end of the chapter.

PARTICIPATION AND RESULTS

Ongoing studies reveal that roughly one-third of the people polled participate in sweepstakes.

I *n s i g h t*

"Skill" in a contest that requires purchase is subject to interpretation. Guessing how many jelly beans are in a jar is not skill. Calculating them through mathematical clues may be.

A Few Dynamics at Work

There is no way to isolate what elements make a given sweepstakes successful, because too many variables are interacting. Consider:

- Sweepstakes tactic, such as drawing entry versus match and win versus instant in-pack win, and so on

- Sweepstakes tactic as it relates to the product, packaging, distribution, traffic patterns, turn rate, point-of-sale presence, and so on
- Prize value
- Prize appeal (varies by region and target)
- Number of prizes
- Collect to win versus single purchase
- Environment—fast food versus hardware, or soft drink versus apple juice
- Ease or difficulty of participating
- Execution throughout system
- Timing
- Category performance
- Competitive activities
- Advertising support
- Advertising creative effectiveness
- Target market's propensity to participate
- Weather

In-Pack Announcements

In-pack packaged goods sweepstakes can deliver a 10 to 15 percent sales increase, occasionally 30 percent with TV advertising support. Soft drinks may reach 10 percent with TV advertising support. Soft drink studies indicate six out of seven promotion participants play "under-the-cap" (UTC) games— 35 percent of carbonated soft drink users. Participants under the age of 25 tend to be frequent players with a 50 percent male/female breakdown.

Match and Win

According to several marketers, adding a match and win element to a coupon can increase redemption 20 to 30 percent. (The same results are reported in coupons that double as drawing entries.)

Watch and Win

Similar sweepstakes techniques can feed off each other, maybe because when they all emerge at the same time, they mutually educate consumers on how to participate. Watch and win hit a peak of activity in the 1990s, like the following example:

- *Tactic:* Get game piece at a major mass merchandiser and in circulars. Compare number with numbers announced regularly during TV program premiers.
- *Prizes:* 12 minivans, dream Hollywood vacations, TVs, and VCRs; millions of logo mugs
- *Results:*
  - Premier episode ratings up 28 percent versus year ago
  - A 39 percent awareness of *Major Dad* the day before it premiered
  - Repeat viewing of new shows 43 percent versus 37 percent viewership for rivals' networks
  - Mass merchandiser sales up 6 percent during promotion versus same period previous year, though the promotion was half as long

800# Telephone, and Now the Internet

The 800-number promotions were once a rage, but they may have been the case where too much participation is bad. Many marketers found them too costly; and simply calling a marketer and hearing their pitch didn't translate to sales.

At this writing, similar Internet techniques are popular. They may cost less, but again they may suffer clutter and less selling impact than do point-of-sale programs. Studies also show that surfers fear spam.

Caution!

Estimate conservatively, especially if you're projecting results based on another marketer's rosy results released in a trade magazine. Most companies aren't eager to share the knowledge they gained through the hard work, heavy investments, and considerable risk they took executing their sweepstakes promotion. Why should they inform their competitors? Question those who do. Also, companies don't boast losing promotions. All too often an ambitious spokesperson inflates a promotion's results for his or her self-promotion.

A Ninja Turtle fast-food promotion was a national award winner whose premiums had to be liquidated because the award committee wasn't informed the company overprojected the demand. An Olympic lapel pin program won Best Promotion of the Year honors, but a soft drink company that based projections on the award winner's numbers failed miserably because the results had been inflated, and the pins had to be liquidated. Prominent point of sale drove the sales, not demand for the pins. And the retailer charged participating brands for the pins, so it suffered no losses.

One pizza brand manager banned sweepstakes because "they don't work." Meanwhile, the upscale sister brand successfully ran a series of match and win sweepstakes. Perhaps the first brand manager used a write-in entry, which had far less impact.

A motor oil brand claimed sweepstakes didn't work because its scratch and win sweepstakes failed. But how do you deliver a scratch and win card on a motor oil package? The brand subsequently ran an under-the-cap sweepstakes, which worked so well it repeated the promotion in subsequent years.

Consider all the dynamics at the beginning of the "Participation and Results" section on page 37.

Incentive program sweepstakes. See Chapter 12, "Performance Programs," page 331.

GUIDELINES AND CAUTIONS

AMOE: Don't Require Purchase to Claim a Prize

Sweepstakes prizes cannot require purchase either to enter or to claim a prize. With in-pack sweepstakes, for example, provide an alternative means of entry (AMOE). Post rules with an address or phone number to receive a free game piece in the mail. *Important:* one stamped envelope per request.

Control Your Media and Distribution

If your sweepstakes is not available everywhere, be sure your media plan and promotional communication don't include those unavailable states.

Advertising and Communication

- Typically, the prize should receive greater emphasis than should the product, because greed and borrowed interest drive the results. The theme and prizes, however, should reinforce your product and image.
- In-pack instant win packaging should clearly announce: "Instant winner game piece inside!" It can be the tiebreaker on the shelf that ensures your product stands out even if the display doesn't get up.
- Official rules or abbreviated rules should appear in all sweeps announcements (see "Official Rules" section on page 47). A "NO PURCHASE NECESSARY" announcement should be prominent with instructions for entering in lowercase.
- Entry-pad backings should have "Sorry" copy in case entries run out. It may simply state entries have run out or detail an address or Web site to enter.

Creative Challenge

Sweepstakes require exceptional creative to keep so many requirements clean and simple. Typically, you have to devote prominent space to the following:

- Headline *(Win this . . .)*
- Sweepstakes title
- Major prize graphic
- Secondary prizes
- Brand's product
- Official rules (lots of space, though you may be able to use abbreviated rules)
- How to enter—your desired action
- Entry or game piece
- Current advertising slogan
- Logo

Deadline Guidelines

- *Bonding* (in states requiring bonding): Two to three months prior to sweepstakes, but some sweepstakes' legal firms may be able to significantly expedite this process.

- *Sweepstakes announcement to trade, salesforce, and so on:* Allow time to book orders and displays; base it on the lead times your company's system typically requires.
- *Typical sweepstakes' entry duration:* One to two months—allow a grace period of one or two weeks for late entries.
- *Entry drawing:* After entry deadline and grace period. (If a coupon doubles as entry, allow three or more months for the drawing since the coupon has to be processed through grocer and clearinghouse systems.)
- *Winner notification:* Three weeks from sweepstakes' close date to the notification letter receipt. Allow two more weeks for winner to reply.
- *Public notification of winners list:* Six weeks after first winner is drawn (allowing time if first winner is somehow disqualified).
- *Prize redemption:* At least four weeks, preferably six weeks after first winner is drawn, allowing time for verification and alternate winner selection (if necessary). *Note:* Vacation prizes should allow winner time to schedule vacation.

Fraud and Security

If a fraudulent entrant happens to win, you may never know. It's unfortunate that an honest entrant didn't win, but the business results should remain unaffected. Nevertheless, do everything you can to give every honest participant a fair shot.

Sweepstakes clubs share sweepstakes information through newsletters and Web sites. Members are legal participants trying to win prizes through an alternate-entry requirement. They look for sweepstakes with high odds (such as restrictive entry requirements or rule mistakes) and then enter the alternative write-in drawing. Rules should include "Only one entry per household" plus "Only one entry per stamped envelope." If you're collecting a database, sort out any repeat addresses (many judging houses don't bother).

Prior to distribution, the winning instant win entries should be coded. Use signatures or exclusive emblems in invisible ink. Also print major prize announcements in different type sizes and/or faces than for lesser prizes. That way a minor prize winner cannot forge his or her winning typeface to match a major prize's typeface.

Use a bona fide, insured sweepstakes printer with these precautions:

- Shuffle game pieces as they are printed, obscuring where winning entries will be stacked and shipped.
- Avoid predictable patterns of winning numbers/symbols.
- Use thick paper to prevent "candling"—holding the game piece up to light to reveal the announcement inside.
- Consider emptying the facility of all unauthorized personnel when a winning press run is under way.
- Confirm that the foreman understands the details.

Test a sampling of game pieces. Examine them in sunlight and test glues or peel-offs the same day and several days later. Will your game piece survive freezing or hot temperatures and humidity? Will the product react with the print? Will the entry feed through mailing or packaging equipment? Will game pieces be crushed in the packaging process? Will an in-pack or on-pack entry slow down production? Duplicate every condition your entry will go through.

Make sure that removing an on-pack entry also defaces the package to discourage printing and retail workers from removing entries. Make your entry difficult to duplicate, especially if it's match and win. Ask the printer for advice.

The printer or agency should have errors and omission insurance to cover any print production or typographical errors and other unforeseen problems. Consider insuring your company as well. Have your lawyer review the printer's policy.

Make sure the policy covers accidentally printing too many winners. (Have a backup PR plan with consolation rewards and possibly a drawing to win an even greater prize than the original.)

Insight

The Florida Glitch. Florida's reputation may be lacking in presidential elections, but the state is very strict about sweepstakes. You may consider a separate ad printing just for Florida. (You can compromise your national ad to meet Florida's requirements.) To avoid printing complete rules on your half-page ad, consider such non-specific phrases as, "Watch for our promotion on specially marked packages." (If you show the prize, you may have to print all the rules.) Also, you need to file a bond prior to the sweepstakes.

Avoid an open-ended sweepstakes in which the number of winners is not finite. For example, don't offer prizes to everyone who predicts an upcoming sporting event's score.

Hire an outside judging agency, thus relieving you of the responsibility.

Consider limits on free entries—one per visit; one visit per day; one entry per stamped, self-addressed envelope.

Don't rely on independent distributors or store personnel to distribute game pieces. Those entries may wind up in a bowl at customer service where anyone can grab a handful.

Review the official rules requirements detailed below:

Safety

- Use food-safe inks for entries where necessary.
- Kid prizes must be kid-safe, including passing through the "choke test" and others.
- Consider age restrictions.
- Don't offer potentially dangerous prizes—nothing sharp for kids.
- Make sure Release from Liability forms are signed by major prize winners.

BUDGETING

Sweepstakes sound more expensive than they are because most participants lose and receive nothing. There is no formula for how much a sweepstakes will cost, but there are known factors to consider. Calculating your sweepstakes' potential boils down to the following, which is based on funding your sweepstakes strictly through incremental profits:

- What are your *incremental sales* goals?
- What are the profits those incremental sales will generate?
- What percentage of those profits can you allocate to a sweepstakes?
- Reality check 1: Use the "Materials and Services List" on page 46 to project a rough idea of the sweepstakes cost. Will the budget from incremental sales' profit pay for it?
- Reality check 2: Use the best historical information and research you can to determine if your particular sweepstakes tactic will generate the sales. Remember, simply getting a display up or increasing store traffic

I *n s i g h t*

Once upon a time a farmer could only afford a mule to plow with. But the mule couldn't plow all the fields in time for planting. So the farmer set up a pricey Kool-Aid stand, and each expensive serving came with a drawing entry to win gardening equipment. Soon, he had enough money for a down payment on a tractor. Then he awarded the "gardening equipment" prize: the old mule. "Wasn't everybody upset?" his wife later asked. "Nope, just the winner, and I gave him his money back."

can boost sales dramatically, and if the sweepstakes accomplishes that, you win.

Establish Criteria

- What are your objectives—display placement? employee activities? traffic? trial? repeat visits? shopper attention? new product/feature awareness? Are your prize and entry requirement sufficient to meet these objectives?
- What are your base sales without a promotion and how much can you invest to increase those sales and profits? (See list in previous section.)
- How will the event be communicated to the field and buyers? Costs?
- Can part of your budget come under the advertising budget?
- What measurable criteria can be used for an evaluation of the sweepstakes?

Payout

- What are your incremental sales/profit objectives?
- What percentage of the above can be allocated to the promotion?
- Project the sweepstakes' incremental sales, based on:
  - Past experience—similar tactic/program
  - Consideration of all dynamics—timing, display placement, competitor activities, overlays, pricing, and so on
  - Whether the projected cost of the sweepstakes meets the budget (See "Materials and Services List" below.)
  - Whether the projected incremental sales/profits minus cost meet the goal

Materials and Services List

- Prizes and fulfillment
- Legal and judging
- Insurance
- Bonds (in applicable states)
- Official rules sheets
- Winners' list
- Affidavits (see below)
- Advertising and media
- Sales communication materials and presentations
- Program communication materials:
  - How-to sheets for field, stores, salespeople, and so on
  - Brochures—trade, sales, and consumer
  - Newsletters
- Displays and signage—header cards, shelf talkers, counter cards, table tents, banners, and so on
- Detail people, if necessary, to place signage
- Entries—tear pad, in-pack, handout, scratch and win, fill out and mail, and so on
- On-pack announcements
- Ad kits and slicks
- Buttons, flags, balloons, and so on
- Dealer loaders
- Warehousing, cartoning, packing, and shipping of prizes (See "Premium Programs," Chapter 10, for guidelines.)
- Post office box
- 800 number and/or Web site
- Alternate entry receipt and processing (for "No Purchase Necessary" mail-ins)
- Requests for winners list (postage and typewritten sheets)
- Requests for official rules/regulations (postage and typewritten sheets)
- Business reply permit (for returning affidavits to your firm)
- Any database you may want to collect, process, and evaluate
- Employee time to orchestrate and administer the above materials and services

OFFICIAL RULES AND RELATED DOCUMENTS

Note: Certain states have their own sweepstakes requirements, which may be covered in the following all-encompassing checklist. However, state regulations change, so have a sweepstakes legal firm scrutinize your rules.

Sweepstakes Official Rules Checklist

Don't input your official rules verbally to a writer or lawyer. Before contacting an expensive lawyer, type an itemized document that explains how to enter, prize descriptions, who's qualified, and so on, so that everything is clear. That way you only pay to have the legal firm rephrase your document in legal terms. Use this checklist of 25 items as a guideline:

_____ How to enter

_____ How and when winners will be determined

_____ No purchase necessary (alternate means and limitations, such as one stamped envelope per entry)

     _____ One entry per stamped entry; one entry per household

     _____ Requests must be received by ___

_____ Limitations: age, region, U.S. citizen, and so on

_____ Independent judging agency whose decision is final

_____ All properly claimed prizes will be awarded (if desired)

Second-chance opportunity for unclaimed prizes (where applicable)

     _____ "If winner has not responded in 15 days, another winner will be drawn."

     _____ Second drawing may be conducted

     _____ Request for entry (such as scratch-off card) may be made by mail—one per stamped, self-addressed envelope)

     _____ Postage not required in some states

_____ How to redeem prize: normally, certified mail, return receipt requested

Claim by _____

How winner will be notified: "Winners will be notified within 21 days of close of sweepstakes."

_____ Not responsible for lost, stolen, late, or misdirected mail

_____ Prizes nontransferable—no cash or substitution of other prizes (option)

One prize per family, organization, or address

_____ Open to U.S. residents—*(or whichever states you select)*—except for employees, immediate families, agencies, affiliates, carriers, and manufacturers of sweepstakes materials

Must be 18 years old or older to enter (optional)

_____ Winner required to sign affidavit of eligibility and release from liability

_____ Winner(s) required to sign release for right to use photo for promotional considerations without compensation

_____ Void where prohibited or restricted by law (federal, state, and local laws apply) Consult a sweepstakes lawyer for individual state regulations

_____ Void if entries are tampered with, forged, mechanically altered, or in any way irregular

No facsimiles accepted

_____ All entries become the property of _____

_____ Not responsible for printing, typographical, or other errors

Liability for irregular game piece limited to issuance of a replacement game piece (if applicable)

Note: If you distributed hundreds or thousands of instant win announcements, you may want to include: If by reason of a printing or other error, more prizes are claimed than the number set forth in these official rules, all persons making valid claims will be included in a random drawing to award the advertised number of prizes available. No more than the advertised number of prizes will be awarded

_____ Total number of prizes, value of prizes, approximate odds of winning major prize (either calculated based on entries distributed or add "Odds dependent upon number of entries received")

_____ To receive major prize winner list, write _____ after _____ and before _____

_____ Taxes are sole responsibility of winner

_____ Sweepstakes ends _____

Entries must be received by ___

_____ Entries become property of sponsor

_____ Sponsor's right to amend, modify, or terminate promotion

_____ No Internet liability (regarding fraud, faulty transmission, damage, etc.)

_____ Internet entry is deemed made by holder of e-mail account (Internet)

_____ Times and time zones policy (Internet)

Drawing Entry Example

(SWEEPSTAKES TITLE)

Official Entry Form

Complete this Official Entry Form and send it to: (Address—P.O. Box)

_____
(Name)

_____
(Address)

_____
(City)   (State)   (Zip)

_____
(Phone)

NO PURCHASE NECESSARY: Entry must be received by _____. See Official Rules on back of this entry.

[Optional program-learning element: To win an additional $1,000, complete this phrase: Acme Widgets are the only widgets with patented _____.]

"SORRY COPY": Appears at base of tear pad when entries run out

SORRY!

There are no entries left. To enter the _____ Sweepstakes by mail, send a stamped, self-addressed 3×5" card to:

_____ Sweepstakes
   (P.O. Box)
   (City, State, Zip)

Or visit our Web site at _____.

Hurry! Entries must be received by _____.

SWEEPSTAKES WINNER FORMS—MAJOR PRIZES

Winner Announcement—Sample   *Purpose:* To notify mail-in entrant he or she has won prize and how to claim prize.

(Date)

(Name)

(Address)

(City, State, Zip)

Dear (Name):

CONGRATULATIONS!

Your entry has been drawn as the (prize description) prize winner in the (sweepstakes name), sponsored by (company).

Attached are three forms: (1.) Consent and Release; (2.) Waiver of Liability; and (3.) Affidavit of Eligibility and Tax Assignment. You must complete and return these forms to us within 15 days of this letter's date. Your prize cannot be awarded without completing and signing these forms. Accordingly, please execute the enclosed documents and return them to us in the enclosed preaddressed and prestamped envelope.

Upon receipt of the forms, we will contact you again with instructions on how to claim your prize.

On behalf of (company), we thank you for participating.

Sincerely,

(Name)

(Title)

Enclosures: Consent and Release Form
             Waiver of Liability Form
             Affidavit of Eligibility and Tax Assignment Form

Affidavit of Eligibility and Tax Assignment—Sample   *Purpose:* To assure that person receiving the prize meets the criteria and to protect company from any related complaints.

AFFIDAVIT

DATE _____

STATE OF _____

COUNTY OF _____

I, _____, being duly sworn say:
   (Name: First, middle initial, last)

My Social Security number is _____. I reside at

_____, _____, _____, _____
(Street Address)   (City)   (State)   (Zip)

I am submitting this affidavit with the understanding that it will be relied on to confirm my eligibility in the (promotion name) sponsored by (company name).

I represent that I am not an employee of (company name) nor its contractors, affiliates, suppliers, distributors, and advertising, promotion, or judging agencies). I am not a member of the immediate family of any such employee or person nor am I connected with them in any way.

I understand that I am solely responsible for applicable income or other taxes or fees on any prize.

SIGNED _____   WITNESSED _____
        (Contestant signature)   (Witness signature)

Date _____

_____   If winner is under the age of 18,
(Birthdate: Month/Day/Year)   a parent or guardian must also sign

_____   _____
(Area code/Home phone number)   (Signature of parent or guardian)

_____
(Area code/Occupation phone number)

Waiver of Liability—Sample *Purpose:* To protect company from liability and resultant lawsuits should a winner suffer damages associated with the prize, including damage claims by third parties against the winner.

WAIVER OF LIABILITY

In accepting the (sweepstakes title) prize of a (prize), I hereby acknowledge the following:

1. That I for myself, my minor children _____,
                                     (Name)

   _____, and _____, my heirs, executors,

   (Name)   (list additional children on back of this page)

   and administrators, hereby waive, release, discharge and agree to hold harmless (company name) and (agency) and their respective officers, directors, employees, agents, successors and assigns, and anyone authorized by any of them, from any and all losses, damages, costs, expenses, rights, claims, demands and actions which I, my minor children, my heirs, executors or assigns may have arising from my participation in and/or my use of the prize awarded to me in the (sweepstakes title) promotion, including but not limited to personal injuries, death, disability, property damages, and attorneys' fees and expenses for litigation and settlement. I and my minor children also agree to indemnify and hold harmless (company) and (agency) and their respective officers, directors, employees, agents, successors and assigns or anyone authorized by any of them from any and all losses, damages, costs, expenses, rights, claims, demands and actions which any other party may have against me arising out of my participation in and/or use of the prize awarded to me in said promotion, including but not limited to personal injuries, death, disability, property damages, attorneys' fees and expenses of litigation and settlement and that I further shall hold (company) harmless from any taxes or other assessments imposed on me as a result of my ownership and use thereof.

2. That I hereby agree that (company) and (agency) have neither made, nor are in any manner responsible or liable for, any warranty, representation or guarantee, expressed or implied, in fact or in law, relative to any prize, including but not limited to its quality, fitness for particular purpose, or mechanical condition.

3. That I understand the activity of travel (or specify other prize/activity) involves risks and dangers and I am cognizant of such risks and dangers. I warrant that I am a licensed driver and that I am fully capable of participation in motor travel and I willingly assume all risk of injury as my responsibility. (Preceding assumes car is prize or vacation includes rental car—modify according to actual prize.)

4. That I am of legal age and have every right to contract in my own name.
5. That I have read or have had read to me each and every word of the foregoing prior to its execution and am fully familiar with the contents thereof.

PRINT FULL NAME _____

SIGNATURE _____

ADDRESS _____

CITY _____ STATE _____ ZIP_____

SOCIAL SECURITY # _____

Subscribed and sworn to before me this _____ day of _____

_____

(Witness)

Consent and Release—Sample   *Purpose:* To allow the company to advertise and publicize the prize winner without paying rights or fees. It also protects the company from any complaints or actions by third parties resulting from making public the winner's name.

WINNER CONSENT AND RELEASE

I hereby give (company), its successors and assigns, and those acting under their permission and upon their authority, the right to take photographs of me; and the right to use my voice, name and other likenesses based thereon, with or without my name, for business, trade or any other lawful purpose whatsoever as it pertains to the promotion of their (sweepstakes name) and the right to copyright the same. I waive all right of inspection and release (company), its successors and assigns from any and all liability arising out of the use of my name and likeness pursuant to this Consent and Release.

PRINT FULL NAME _____

SIGNATURE _____

ADDRESS _____

CITY _____ STATE _____ ZIP_____

SOCIAL SECURITY # _____

Subscribed and sworn to before me this _____ day of _____

_____
(Witness)

Parental/Guardian Consent and Release—Sample *Purpose:* Same as above Consent and Release in situations where a minor is the winner.

PARENTAL/GUARDIAN CONSENT AND RELEASE

I, the undersigned, hereby warrant that I am the parent or guardian of _____, a minor, and have full authority to authorize and grant the attached Consent and Release which I have read and approved. I hereby release and agree to indemnify and hold harmless (company), (agency), their successors and assigns, from and against any and all liability arising out of the use of such name, voice and likeness pursuant to the above Consent and Release.

PRINT FULL NAME _____

SIGNATURE _____

ADDRESS _____

CITY _____ STATE _____ ZIP_____

SOCIAL SECURITY # _____

Subscribed and sworn to before me this _____ day of _____

_____
(Witness)

Prize Claim Form—Sample   *Purpose:* To instruct the winner how to claim his or her prize.

PRIZE CLAIM FORM

(Date)

(Name)
(Address)
(City, State, Zip)

Dear (Name):

Congratulations again on winning the (prize description) in the (sweepstakes title) sponsored by (company).

We have received your three preapproval forms and this letter will explain how to redeem your prize.

(Describe how to claim prize—is it already being shipped UPS? Is it through a travel agent or local car dealer? Be sure to include any tracking or verification details.)

Thank you for participating and enjoy your prize!

Sincerely,

(Name)
(Title)

3

COUPONS

(Also see Chapters 4 and 5:
"Rebates/Refunds" and "Discounts")

INTRODUCTION:
CONSUMERS LOVE COUPONS

Coupons are one of the mainstays of sales promotion. For the consumer, they're a guaranteed price discount on a product purchase. For the marketer, they're one of the primary, proven ways to sell more stuff.

Coupons are a very broad topic. They can be offered in many types, styles, delivery formats, values, and the like. But the real question is: Do coupons work? Do they build product movement and help sell more stuff?

The answer is a resounding yes. Because they work, more marketers are relying on them to help boost sales with a controllable promotional tool. The beauty of coupons is that you control how many sales you want to generate by setting the value of the coupon. And you control the cost liability because you control the number of coupons you distribute and the length of time they will be valid.

Coupons work because people like to save money. Plus, having a coupon to reduce the cost of a product is a clear way to say to yourself and others that you're managing your resources wisely.

People love coupons, even to the point of going to court to keep them coming to their door. In the middle 1990s, Procter & Gamble (P&G), one of the smartest and most sophisticated marketing organizations in the world (it markets Tide, Cheer, Pampers, Jif, Pringles, and a host of other consumer products), decided coupons were becoming a problem. Based on its studies, coupon redemption rates were declining and there was considerable fraud in their product categories. With coupons, fraud generally means retailers and others were either (1) duplicating the coupons and redeeming them for cash or (2) consumers and others were misredeeming them on other products. Either way, P&G was paying out money for coupon redemption but creating no additional sales.

So P&G announced it was going to test a no-coupon policy in several markets. The plan was to discontinue coupons in those markets and instead apply the value of the coupons to promotional discounts through shelf price reduction or everyday low pricing. Other companies such as Clorox, Colgate-Palmolive, Lever Brothers, and S. C. Johnson joined the movement. Good idea? Not to consumers. Thirty-five thousand of them were so upset they signed a petition complaining about the coupon cancellation. Their widespread complaints led the attorney general in the test market state to sue P&G and the others, along with one of the supermarket chains that backed the test. The consumers won. Procter & Gamble, Lever Brothers, and their cohorts had to reinstate the use of coupons and pay a settlement to the complaining consumers as well. Proof: consumers will go to court for their coupons.

But there is other evidence that consumers love coupons. In some recent studies on what influences consumers to purchase certain products, the top-rated factor was word of mouth, a recommendation by someone who had recently used the product. The second greatest influence was—you guessed it—having a coupon for the product.

What's also important is the impact that coupons have on consumers is measurable. We can directly relate redemptions to the sale of the product. Although that's helpful in measuring how much more stuff was sold, something else helps us better understand the overall impact of coupon usage by consumers.

The four charts in Figure 3.1 show consumer purchase patterns. We've indexed typical purchase results from sales promotions. In the top chart, the volume of product purchased by consumers has been indexed at 100. The typical time between product purchases has been indexed at 100 as well. A typical consumer would buy a certain amount of our product at one point, and it would take that consumer a certain amount of time to use it up. Then the consumer would buy another amount of our product—that is, a "purchase interval." The top chart represents *a typical product purchase pattern* with product volume and product purchase intervals both indexed at 100.

The second chart shows what happens when a coupon creates consumer *purchase acceleration.* That simply means the consumer, as a result of the coupon, decided to purchase sooner than was normal. There was no change in overall purchase volume, but there *was* a change in purchase timing, so the consumer purchased outside his or her normal cycle. The coupon was an incentive to purchase earlier than usual. The third chart shows a coupon's impact on consumer *stockpiling*—that is, rather than buying one unit, the consumer might buy two or more units because of the coupon's influence. With coupon savings, consumers were willing to inventory extra product for future use—a short-term sales bump for the brand resulting from the incentive of the coupon. The fourth chart illustrates consumer *consumption increase.* The coupon encouraged the consumer to use the product more rapidly, in different ways, or whatever so the consumer bought more and used it up faster than he or she usually would.

Although this is a simple illustration, it is of great importance to promotion planners. If coupons accelerate product purchase, you sell more product over time, all things being equal. If the coupon increases consumption, you will sell more stuff in a shorter period of time. The problem with consumer stockpiling is that consumers are simply taking advantage of your coupon and not buying any more or any faster. That's bad, although it does prevent the customer from buying from your competitor (why buy more if a consumer has an ample supply). It means you're not selling more stuff—the reason for sales promotion in the first place.

Coupons are great. Consumers love them. And if you know how to use them to sell more stuff, you'll love coupons too. —Don E. Schultz

FIGURE 3.1 *Purchase Patterns*

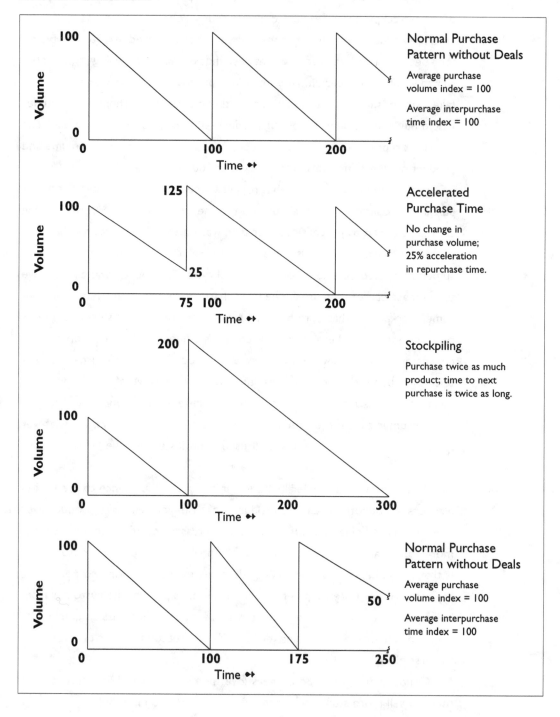

OVERVIEW

Coupons are discounts, but they achieve more specific benefits and control than does a broad-stroke price cut. They can be "wallet real estate," on-person reminders, whereas an advertised discount is easily forgotten. Coupons can provide better accounting by limiting the quantities issued and forecasting redemptions. They can zero in on specific targets through print media. They can improve product distribution by tying in the retailer. They can even merge with other promotion tactics—doubling as sweepstakes entries, offering a free sample, encouraging multiple purchases, or making the first payment of an extended "club" offer.

DEFINITION

Coupons are typically certificates entitling the bearer to an immediate discount when presented to the participating business. They differ from refunds in that they are immediate. Refunds are typically redeemed by mail (and as such offer higher discount values as a result of "slippage").

THREE CATEGORIES

1. *Manufacturer coupon*—executed, delivered, and funded fully by the manufacturer, such as the familiar coupons for soap, cereal, cleaners, and the like. Generally, a manufacturer coupon has a lower value than does the retailer/manufacturer coupon (the third category below).
2. *Retailer product coupon*—executed, delivered, and redeemed fully by the retailer, typically for the retailer's own product—a food chain's menu item, a car shop's lube job, a salon's hair treatment, and so on. It may also be a storewide discount coupon—"10% off our entire stock" or "any red tag merchandise." Again, the store product coupon allows control that an in-store discount cannot offer. It reaches people outside the store and limits redemption to one person, not every visitor. Plus, customers without a coupon purchase at full retail.
3. *Retailer/manufacturer coupon*—executed and delivered by a specific retailer; the manufacturer, however, cofunds the coupon, which is typically of a higher value than a manufacturer coupon. The manufacturer

can save clearinghouse costs in addition to negotiating better product stocking, placement, and display, even after the coupon's weeklong life. The product gets featured in the retailer's flyer. And both manufacturer and retailer are assured a better consumer value (and traffic) than that of their competitors' manufacturer's coupons.

TWO ARENAS—PACKAGED GOODS AND RETAILERS

Packaged Goods

Typical objectives:

- "Hard copy" reminder and subsequent product search
- Product purchase
- Purchase cycle—prime season, extend purchase season, increase purchases per period
- Product trial
- Product trade-up
- Multiple purchase
  - High value for multiple purchase
  - "Load" consumer prior to competitor activity
- Motivate retail activity—stocking, display, signage, shelf positioning, etc.
- Offset new price increase
- Target consumer segment through media delivery
- Participation in retail-generated coupon for additional retail stocking, display, and signage
- Controlled cost of discounting

Retail/Service

Typical objectives:

- Traffic
- Hard copy reminder and subsequent visit
- Product/service purchase

- Purchase cycle—prime season, extend purchase season, increase visits per period
- Target consumer segment through media delivery
- Trial
  - Trial visit
  - Trial purchase, such as new menu item or service
  - New service, such as "Half off the first month of service"
- Multiple purchase
  - During prepeak or peak selling season
  - "Load" consumer prior to competitor activity
- Vendor participation and support
- Offset/segue into price increase
- Controlled cost of discounting

COMMON COUPON OBJECTIVES BY TACTIC

(Also, see itemized tactics below.)

TACTIC	OBJECTIVES (Beyond Purchase)
Manufacturer discount	Seek product (hard copy reminder); retail product placement; targeted consumer distribution; trial; continued purchase behavior; off-season or prime-season purchase; multiple purchase; product trade-up; ease price increase repercussions
Manufacturer time-release discount coupon	Continuity/loyalty; extend purchase period; involve numerous products; economical group delivery
Manufacturer instant redeemable (IRC)	Impulse purchase; trial; product placement by retailer; targeted retail distribution; shelf visibility/purchase share
Manufacturer free offer	Sampling/trial (alternative to in-store sampling); product placement by retailer; targeted consumer distribution
In-store sampling manufacturer coupon	Trial/follow-up purchase; in-store location awareness; increased retail distribution; exceptional store participation
Manufacturer account-specific	Increase key retailer distribution/participation; offer high-value traffic/purchase incentive
Retailer discount certificate	Traffic; trial; targeted consumer distribution; controlled discounting

TACTIC	OBJECTIVES
Retailer/service electronic (verbal request triggers discount)	Add topspin to discount; awareness (the words consumers must say); simplicity—no coupon paperwork
Multiple purchase	Multiple sales; target large households/multiple visitors; retail product placement; liquidate overstocks; "load" consumer/retailer; increase value and redemption; targeted consumer distribution
Cross-purchase	Cross-store traffic; multiproduct economies; leverage one-stop shopping opportunity; tap into partner products and consumer base; increase value and redemption; sample and/or move new/slow product via popular product; targeted consumer distribution
Self-destruct	Reach two user profiles (diet-sugar; light-heavy user) without redemption liabilities of both combined; targeted consumer distribution; above manufacturer coupon objectives
Rub-off values	Add topspin, attention, and involvement; overlay a sweepstakes; add product attribute awareness
Sweepstakes entry	Add topspin; increase redemption; retail product placement; trial; targeted consumer distribution
Bounce-back	Repeat visit/purchase; encourage extended retail participation; build consumer routine
Time release	Establish loyal purchase behavior
Do-it-yourself values	Reach diverse user profiles with one ad; add topspin; attention to and involvement
Collector card	Consumer loyalty; increased attention and involvement
Novel format	Add topspin and attention; reinforce product attribute; achieve various objectives via tactic employed (fill shopping bag for discount = multiple purchase; trade-in = timely awareness)

ITEMIZED TACTICS

18. MANUFACTURER DISCOUNT COUPON

Definition   Certificate exchanged for discount on specified product
Manufacturer funds distribution and redemption (retailer typically paid for handling)

Advantages	• Motivates purchase
	• Can encourage trade-up
	• Combats competitive pressures—temporary lower price versus permanent new pricing structure
	• Actionable offer energizes print advertisement
	• Hard copy reminder
	• Media selection targets consumer
	• Budgeting guidelines through previous learning
	• Improves retailer stocking and placement—greases sales system
	• Eases response to price increase
Disadvantages	• Discount and costs to person who might otherwise pay full price
	• Some retail categories don't honor coupons
	• Ancillary costs—media, retailer handling, redemption house
	• May influence consumer to wait for coupon
	• Limited profile—coupon clippers
	• Redemption projections are educated guesses—open liability
	• Subject to discounting competition
	• Significant lead time
	• Potential retailer misredemption
	• Consumers often misredeem for wrong product size, past deadline, etc.

19. MANUFACTURER INSTANT REDEEMABLE COUPON (IRC)

Definition	Manufacturer coupon (above) but delivered on-pack for instant redemption at checkout
Advantages	• Motivates immediate, impulse purchase
	• Reaches consumer at the most crucial moment—point of sale (two-thirds of grocery purchases are impulse)
	• Breaks ties with adjacent competitors
	• Higher redemption rate than media-delivered coupons
	• Avoids consumer misredemption (mistakes)
	• Draws additional product attention
	• No print medium costs (and waste of nontargets)
	• Possible slippage economies

- Encourages improved stocking and placement
- Improved forecasting—maximum liability a fixed quantity

Disadvantages
- Chains not honoring coupons may refuse product
- May require suffix code system to control distribution
- Lacks mass reach and advertising benefits of print media
- Discount and costs to person who might otherwise pay full price
- Higher redemption rate and costs
- Expense, lead time, and operational concerns applying coupon to package
- May lose slippage economies from well-meaning cashiers volunteering redemption
- May be misredeemed by dishonest retailers
- Ancillary costs—retailer handling, redemption house, etc.

20. MANUFACTURER FREE OFFER

Definition
Same as manufacturer discount coupon except that product offered free

Advantages
- Sampling/trial
- Avoids live product sampling costs
- Mass, yet targeted audience through print media
- "Free" generates response
- Manufacturer coupon advantages cited above

Disadvantages
- Expensive, typically requiring full retail price reimbursement (see explanation below)
- High redemptions/costs
- Redemption projections are educated guesses—open liability
- Potential retail mistakes (cashier may have to fill in retail price blank and acknowledge coupon's maximum allowable limit)
- Other manufacturer coupon disadvantages cited above

21. IN-STORE SAMPLING MANUFACTURER COUPON

Definition
Manufacturer discount (above) but delivered in-store by contracted staff and often with product sampling

Advantages
- Reaches consumers at crucial point of sale
- In-store sampling/demo plus coupon encourages follow-up purchase
- Exceptional in-store awareness that can include other information media
- Provides possible budgeting guidelines through previous history
- Encourages improved retailer stocking, placement, and participation
- Breaks ties with competitors
- High redemption rate
- Reaches beyond traditional FSI (freestanding insert) clip-and-redeem couponer
- No print medium costs (and inevitable waste of nontarget readers)

Disadvantages
- Expensive—contracting in-store staff, supplies, signage, training, etc.
- High redemption costs
- Retailer may want full retail price reimbursement
- Requires retailer permission, participation, scheduling, space, etc.
- Limited in scope compared with media-delivered coupon and higher cost per store
- Redemption projections are educated guesses—open liability
- Requires significant lead time, presell, and coordination
- Potential for misredemption, particularly by some retailers with access to coupons

22. MANUFACTURER ACCOUNT-SPECIFIC COUPON

Definition
Manufacturer discount (above) but may be redeemed only at specified retailer chain

Advantages
- Tie with key retailer chain improves distribution and placement
- Partners may share redemption costs
- Greater accountability through single-retailer participation—custom ground rules
- Other manufacturer coupon advantages cited above

Disadvantages
- May alienate other retailers
- Requires equal account-specific offers (see Robinson-Patman in glossary)

- Less efficient media costs than national coupon drop
- Media costs wasted on those who shop other retailers
- Other manufacturer coupon disadvantages cited above

23. BUY ONE–GET ONE COUPON (BOGO)

Definition

Manufacturer or retailer coupon offers second product free (or discounted) with purchase of first

Advantages

- High value for greater redemption
- Simple for consumers and retailers
- May encourage group purchase (buy three–get one)
- Can increase usage/familiarity
- Free product may be high consumer value but low marketer cost (a restaurant fountain drink costs only pennies)
- Other advantages cited above

Disadvantages

- Generous offer lowers margin
- Lost sale for retailer
- Lost "next purchase" for manufacturer
- Vendor may pay retailer full markup reimbursement (see description below)
- Misredemptions incur greater costs
- Other manufacturer coupon disadvantages cited above

24. RETAILER PRODUCT DISCOUNT COUPON

Definition

Certificate exchanged at the issuing retailer for an offer (discount, free-with-purchase, etc.)

Distribution, redemption, and logistics funded by retailer unless vendor ties in

Advantages

- Builds traffic
- Motivates purchase
- Stimulates trial of retailer location and/or specified item (menu item, new service, etc.)

- Preempts competitor offers posted only at retail
- Controlled discount—targeted media versus everyone in store; single versus unlimited purchase
- Accountable—limited to store system
- No handling fees, clearinghouse costs, etc.
- Other coupon advantages cited above

Disadvantages
- Requires staff training
- Media expenses
- May alienate in-store shoppers without coupon
- Open to copying—competitor may offer equal/greater coupon value in same peak period
- Other manufacturer coupon disadvantages cited above

25. RETAILER/SERVICE ELECTRONIC COUPON (VERBAL REQUEST)

Definition
Discount generated through verbal request—typically a catchphrase—with no exchange of certificate (*electronic* refers to cash register keypunch system)

Advantages
- Adds topspin to traditional discount
- Builds awareness of product attribute (through required phrase)
- Builds in-store awareness as other patrons hear catchphrase
- Simplicity
- No coupon paperwork

Disadvantages
- Open-ended—no limit unlike paper coupon
- Requires consumers to remember advertising unlike paper coupon
- Consumers may feel uncomfortable publicly reciting catchphrase
- Typically requires broadcast medium expense
- Requires staff training
- Simple discount may achieve greater sales

26. MULTIPLE PURCHASE COUPON (OR CROSS-PURCHASE)

Definition
Coupon offers significant value on purchase of multiple items such as a combo meal; coffee, cream, and sugar brands, etc.

Advantages	• Greater value through combined purchase • Encourages additional purchases • By "loading" consumer (and retailer), it offsets upcoming competitor promotion • Can cross-sell or get trial of related products • Can tap into each product's consumer base • May share cost, execution, and consumer base partner • Vendor opportunity for retail display—multiple sales and cross-store shopping for retailer • Leverage usage occasion (picnic theme, family health theme, etc.) • Tie-in economies and efficiencies • Other manufacturer coupon advantages cited above
Disadvantages	• Products must share common timing, target, usage, etc. • Products must have same distribution • Multiple purchase requirement may discourage redemption • Undesirable cross-product may discourage redemption • Extensive prenegotiation and logistics • Advertising subject to too many approvals • Subject to cashier and consumer mistakes and misredemption • Redemption projections difficult with diverse variables • Other manufacturer coupon disadvantages cited above

27. CROSS-RUFF COUPON

Definition	Coupon delivered on one product package that's good for another product and possibly vice versa
Advantages	• Can offer greater value through combined purchase • Encourages additional purchase • Can tap into each product's consumer base • Implied second-party endorsement • Can leverage usage occasions, such as chips and dips during Super Bowl • Increased in-store presence, including alternate locations • Tie-in economies and efficiencies • Other manufacturer coupon advantages cited above

Disadvantages	• Dual purchase requirement may discourage redemption, especially with undesirable partner
	• Requires prenegotiation and logistics with all parties
	• Relies on exceptional scrutiny by retailer cashier plus consumer mistakes and misredemption
	• More difficult redemption projections
	• Other manufacturer coupon disadvantages cited above

28. SELF-DESTRUCT

Definition	Two coupons overlap so that clipping one destroys the other, limiting consumer to an either/or choice
Advantages	• Reaches two user profiles (diet-sugar; light-heavy user) without redemption liabilities of both combined
	• Shared media costs
	• Other manufacturer coupon advantages cited above
Disadvantages	• Additional clipping (and possible confusion) may discourage participation
	• Requires how-to clip instructions
	• Requires additional graphic space and awkward positioning
	• Other manufacturer coupon disadvantages cited above

29. RUB-OFF VALUE COUPON

Definition	Coupon value concealed by a rub-off spot (or other technique) that may reveal a prize
Advantages	• Adds topspin and interest to coupon—breaks clutter
	• Can overlay a sweepstakes with everyone getting a discount
	• Rub-off may also reveal product attribute
	• Other manufacturer coupon advantages cited above
Disadvantages	• Expensive printing and insert distribution
	• Additional consumer instructions and effort may discourage participation

- Sweepstakes overlay requires considerable cost and details
- Other manufacturer coupon disadvantages cited above

30. SWEEPSTAKES ENTRY (Also see Chapter 2)

Definition   Coupon doubles as sweepstakes entry, such as drawing entry or match and win tactic

Advantages
- Breaks through clutter
- May increase redemption
- Can reinforce brand through sweepstakes theming
- May encourage retail visit (like match and win tactic)
- Sweepstakes tactic advantages
- Can "break tie" with competitive coupon—possibly even with lower value
- Other manufacturer and retailer coupon advantages cited above

Disadvantages
- Manufacturer coupon may require months to clear grocer and clearinghouse process
- Match and win tactic requires display placement and executional details, tasks, and costs
- Additional consumer tasks (and confusion) may discourage redemption
- Sweepstakes tactic disadvantages
- Consumer may resist entering personal information
- Other coupon disadvantages cited above

31. BOUNCE-BACK

Definition   Coupon distribution requires repeat visit/purchase to redeem (in-pack, bag stuffer, receipt-delivered)

Advantages
- Promotes repeat visit and additional purchases
- Helps establish repeat behavior
- Vendor can encourage retailer participation
- May extend promotional period
- Other manufacturer coupon advantages cited above

Disadvantages
- Limited distribution alternatives
- Requires such additional operations as in-packing machinery or bag stuffing
- Other manufacturer and retailer coupon disadvantages cited above

32. TIME-RELEASE COUPONS

Definition
Coupons that must be redeemed at specified periods (often sequential such as 12 coupons, 1 per month)

Advantages
- Encourages continuity visit, purchase, usage, and loyalty
- May extend usage occasions, purchase frequency, and purchase season
- May include several different products
- Economical delivery—multiple coupons at once
- Long life may preempt competitive activities
- High-value claim for total values
- Can provide ongoing exposure and awareness, particularly with calendar, booklet, or other retained vehicle
- Other coupon advantages above

Disadvantages
- Many consumers won't retain or remember coupons over extended period
- Group coupons may suffer less redemption than more immediate solo coupons
- May establish coupon-reliant purchase behavior
- Other coupon disadvantages above

33. DO-IT-YOURSELF (DIY) COUPON

Definition
Coupon that consumer customizes via stickers, check box, or other by choosing from value levels, products selection, etc.

Advantages
- Reaches diverse targets—single/heavy users, those with different brand preferences, etc.—in single ad
- High-value claim for total values
- Adds topspin to traditional coupon, breaking through coupon clutter

- Can showcase multiple products
- Tie-in economies and efficiencies

Disadvantages
- More effective for some businesses than for others. Fast-food system can be trained to redeem while packaged or durable goods cannot train independent outlets
- Exceptional effort (or confusion) discourages consumer, particularly for lower-value offer
- Difficult to conform to manufacturer coupon requirements
- Consumer/cashier confusion and misredemption
- Cumbersome format requires additional ad space and instructions
- May require specialty printing
- Other coupon disadvantages cited above

34. COLLECTOR CARD

Definition
Combination coupon and refund
Example: Collect stickers in each pack and adhere to card that becomes a coupon when complete

Advantages
- Offers immediate reward of a coupon through the multiple purchase of a refund
- Promotes repeat visit/purchase
- Helps establish repeat behavior (without building expectation for coupons)
- Vests consumer as value builds
- Longer-term and higher ultimate value may preempt competitive activities
- Collector vehicle is ongoing reminder of promotion

Disadvantages
- Requires expense of collector cards, pieces, and distribution
- Difficult to conform to manufacturer coupon requirements
- Extended commitment and tasks discourage participation
- May discount to heavy user, otherwise purchasing at full price
- Large, awkward format requires additional space and instructions and also limited by traditional coupon requirements
- Possible cashier confusion

- Requires policy for redeemers who faithfully purchase but miss deadline

35. NOVEL FORMAT

Definition   Discount offered in unique format, such as trade-in, canned food donation = discount, or "Save 00% on everything you fit into this bag"

Advantages   • Adds topspin to traditional discount
- Can reinforce product attribute
- Achieves various objectives according to tactic employed (shopping bag full of discounts = multiple purchase; trade-in = timely awareness; canned food donation = goodwill)

Disadvantages   • Exceptional task requirement limits participation
- Requires additional executional considerations
- May accomplish the same goals as traditional coupon

COMMON COUPON COPY REQUIREMENTS

You may not need all of the following items depending on the nature of your business and offer. Where a manufacturer coupon may need a handling fee and processing information, a retailer-generated coupon can be much simpler. A retailer may want to limit the coupon to one family per one visit per day, whereas a manufacturer coupon doesn't have such restrictions. Review all the items to make sure your bases are covered.

Face value. Make the discount value of the coupon—"Save 00¢"—prominent. Assign a value in the Uniform Product Code (UPC). When the coupon is scanned, the bar code value should match the face value.

Universal Product Code. UPC bar coding allows electronic scanning. When used on manufacturer coupons, the UPC identifies the product, and a second bar code specifies the value of the coupon. Follow the Uniform Code Council's specifications, such as black ink on a white background.

Offer code. Encode the coupon with a numeric offer code—the coupon's value—along with the UPC. Follow Universal Code Council (UCC) specifications.

Consumer code. Code the coupon for consumer tracking and/or geographic market analysis. Follow Council specifications.

Redemption mailing instructions. Include directions for where to send the coupon and other retailer instructions.

Coupon processing source. Prominently identify if the coupon is a manufacturer coupon, store coupon, or other, so it's quickly identified and handled properly. A grocer's coupon will be routed to an internal system, whereas the manufacturer coupon will be routed to a clearinghouse. Coupons in a retailer's advertisement should be identified as, for example, "In-Ad Coupon" or "Acme Retailer Coupon."

Expiration date. A manufacturer coupon averages from two to four months from publication date to expiration. Short expirations should be highlighted "Hurry!"

Retailer handling fees. Manufacturer coupons should specify the fee that retailers receive for processing the coupon, such as 8¢ per coupon.

Retailer reimbursement and handling fees for free product coupons. Manufacturer coupons for free products should instruct retailers how to be reimbursed. Include a space for the retailer to fill in the *shelf price* and specify a limit.

Estimated cash value of the coupon. Reveal the coupon's estimated cash value, such as 1/20 cent or 1/100 cent. (See "Why that 1/20 of one cent copy?" on page 77.)

Consumer sales tax note. Show if consumer has to pay a sales tax, although a tax is generally not required.

Geographic restrictions. Reveal such limitations as coupons redeemable only in the United States or the Dallas metroplex area.

Fraud and policy notices. Include on each coupon a notation such as "Invoices showing purchases of sufficient stock to cover all coupons must be shown upon request" or "Submit in compliance with [company name] coupon redemption policy."

Offer restrictions. Include such limits on the offer as "Void if copied, transferred, prohibited, taxed, or restricted" or "Limit one coupon per person per visit/product/family."

Special considerations. Unique coupons may require unique instructions, such as alcoholic beverage restrictions, age restrictions, and the like.

Coupon Considerations

Show your product—shout the offer. Help shoppers identify your package with a photo on the coupon. Limit the photos to three at most, preferably one "hero" package that represents all. Make your offer message short, direct, and bold.

Why that 1/20 of one cent copy? In defining trading stamps, some states don't include the provision that excludes "any redeemable device used by the manufacturer or packer of an article in advertising or selling it." In those states, a coupon can be redeemed for its cash value, and, as a result, a low cash value (1/20 of one cent) is assigned to the coupon. That's also why the coupon's redemption value is referred to as "face value," not cash value.

Flexible versus guaranteed-position coupons. Sunday newspaper coupon inserts (freestanding inserts—FSIs) have to assure that clipping the coupon on one side doesn't destroy the other side's coupon. A flexible ad allows the ad/coupon to appear on either the top or the bottom, whichever is necessary to accommodate the opposite side's coupon. A guaranteed coupon position guarantees your choice of top or bottom but costs more.

Double couponing—the 55 cent factor. Some supermarkets (usually according to region) feature so-called double coupon offers that double a coupon's discount. The grocer picks up the additional costs, but the grocer typically limits the coupon value to 55 cents. If you want these grocers to double your coupon, limit the value to 55 cents.

Web site coupons. Consumers can visit Web sites and print their own coupons. Without special measures, this can be an open liability, allowing unlimited redemptions. If an open number of redemptions is good business (such as 10 percent off), the Internet's viral marketing capability is an excellent way for friends to give friends your coupons. However, Internet coupons are also open to counterfeiting, and many retailers refuse Web-generated coupons.

FREE PRODUCT COUPONS

Two Ways to Execute Free Product Coupons

Single free product offering. A manufacturer's free grocery product coupon should let retailers make their markup. And because such a coupon also incurs media and processing costs, it actually costs more than does the product's shelf price. The coupon should have a blank box labeled "Retailer: Fill in shelf price here. Price not to exceed $0.00." That way, the manufacturer gets the product sampled, and the retailer get its markup.

Buy one–get one free. If you're offering a free product with the purchase of a second product (or third, etc.), the grocer's scanner already registers the shelf price on the first purchase. It electronically credits the shelf price of the free product—clean, automatic, and turnkey.

Consult your couponing service for advice on which is best for your situation.

BAR CODES

The UPC (Universal Product Code) is an enabler for inventory management systems, not to mention speeding up the cashier line. A retailer's scanner reads the information in the bar code and transmits it to the store computer, which replies with the price, date, dis-

---

Insight

Face Value: $800,000! In 2003 a New Jersey resident was charged in a coupon fraud scheme that netted $800,000 from manufacturer coupons. Dozens of retailers participated, receiving cash payments for misredeeming manufacturer coupons. Hire a reputable clearinghouse to monitor warning signs of fraud.

count, or other information that is programmed in the store system. The UPC should be unique for each package configuration and/or shipping container.

The Universal Product Code is a 12-digit number coded in bar form. The 12 digits translate to the following:

- A company prefix that is assigned and managed by the Uniform Code Council and is unique to the company to which it is assigned.
- An item reference that is assigned and managed by the company.
- Specific lead-digit system numbers that are reserved by the Uniform Code Council for some industry-specific business applications. Lead-digit system characters 0, 1, 6, 7, 8, 9 are used in company prefixes for all products except the following:
  2—Assigned to random-weight products such as meat and produce
  3—Assigned for use with FDA-controlled products in the health care industry
  4—Assigned for use within a retailer's own company
  5—Assigned for coupons
- A check digit enables the scanner system to immediately verify the accurate data translation of the Universal Product Code.

Coupon bar code tips:

- Keep each coupon version in a separate file.
- Identify the publication and date in your file name. Keep the same name for each project file—just add a suffix letter(s) and/or number(s) to update them.
- Use black against a white background so scanners clearly read the code.
- Test the bar code with a scanner.
- If you're running different coupon values in different markets:
  - Track and monitor each version for each market. Have a system in place with your publication plus your graphics resource.
  - Colored coupon copy may require an expensive plate for each press change. The same applies to changing package graphics on your coupon.
- Use "For position only": Creative is presented in low resolution to save time and file size. Printers work with high resolution for quality images. Maintain two separate filing systems for each.

- Often, you cannot use an image from one project in another project. Confirm that the original file specifications are appropriate for the new project.
- Follow all Uniform Code Council guidelines. (Courtesy of Uniform Code Council, Inc.)

Note: As of this writing, a new system is being explored by some retailers to replace the bar code—RFID chips (Radio Frequency Identification). RFID tags contain an antenna that broadcasts a signal and allows constant tracking of the product throughout the entire distribution process. It carries some controversy over privacy issues.

COUPON SIZES

Manufacturer coupons must adhere to processing specifications. The most popular coupon medium is the freestanding insert. The ideal coupon size is the size of a dollar bill for easy identification and handling—$2\frac{1}{2} \times 6$ inches. A coupon can be as small as $2\frac{1}{16} \times 3$ inches. Coupons that are hard to handle may cause confusion and mistakes along the line of people who process the coupon.

PROJECTING REDEMPTIONS AND BUDGETING

Is Less Redemption More Effective or Vice Versa?

The objective of a coupon drop is not necessarily to achieve the greatest redemption numbers. Each redemption is an increased cost of sale, and it cuts into your overall marketing budget. If a high-value coupon achieves higher-than-expected redemption, you may be over budget—you manufactured 100 widgets, budgeted $1 to sell 10 of them, and spent $2 to sell 10 more, which you had planned to sell at full markup.

Factors. Even major marketers with a tremendous couponing history and database still consider projections an iffy art and science. There are simply too many factors. Protect your budget by allowing for a margin of error. Redemption factors include the following:

- *Method of distribution:* FSI, magazine, direct mail, in-store, grocery ad, on-pack, and so on. (For example, direct mail can double redemption over an FSI, whereas solo direct can double bundled direct offers.)
- *Target* (An ironic rule of thumb is that lower-income people redeem coupons less often than do higher-income people.)
- *Value* of the offer and how it compares with the regular cost
- *Length* of the coupon offer
- *Additional promotion support* (Broadcast advertising mentioning coupon, point of sale, etc.)
- *Type of coupon* (Sweepstakes entry, bounce-back, self-destruct, etc.)
- *Region*
- *Timing*
  - Demand during coupon drop
  - Weather
  - Season
  - Economic situation
  - Events and sudden trends, which can be triggered by one movie release
- *Competitive activity and counteroffers*
- *Creative execution* (Did you save money on photography at the expense of mouthwatering appeal? Was the creative director more interested in an award than in a sales message?)
- *The product itself* (Some products are more coupon responsive than are others, and some can offer larger values than can others.)

A few sample redemption figures. Again, there are no redemption guidelines that apply to all products. Use the following with caution.

Somewhere between 1 and 3 percent redemption:

Grocery packaged goods marketers typically report 1 to 3 percent coupon redemptions. Careful! Some inflate redemptions in the trade press to promote themselves or their agency's services. Research has indicated average redemption by media as follows:

- Solo direct mail—5.7 percent redemption
- Co-op direct mail—2.2 percent

- Instant redeemable (IRC)—29.4 percent
- Handouts—3.5 percent
- Consumer relations—33 percent (a coupon that is sent to a consumer in response to a written or phoned request)
- Electronic checkout—8.8 percent (coupons issued at checkout triggered by specific purchases)
- Electronic shelf—11.5 percent
- FSI—1.9 percent

Somewhere between 30 and 70 percent redemption:

One print film company made and marketed private label film for several different retailers. The film and offer were the same, though the name of the film brand varied by retailer. The norm was 30 percent redemption for an instant redeemable, on-pack coupon. However, one mass merchandiser typically redeemed at 70 percent. Lesson: Track each retailer's individual history.

Build a coupon history and test as much as you can. History repeats itself, and the best way to project redemption is to build a history. Take into account all of the above factors, possibly with a spreadsheet for each coupon drop. Supplement your historic figures with as much ongoing testing as possible.

Code coupons: Track by locations, targets, timing, and more. Have separate press runs with different coupon codes. (Simple black plate changes limit reprinting cost.) Here's a code example to isolate three factors for three different media inserts:

MN-D-TH	Minnesota—D Counties (rural)—Thursday delivery
WI-A-SU	Wisconsin—A Counties (urban)—Sunday delivery
IO-UI-F	Iowa—upper-income neighborhoods—Friday delivery

Do as much test tracking as possible before a national launch.

Redemption Process and Cost

Manufacturer coupons redeemed at grocery stores have a months-long journey. First, the consumer may take a month. The grocer gathers coupons over time, processes them for reimbursement, and finally sends them out.

Then there may be two clearinghouses. The retailer clearinghouse verifies the retailer's invoice and pays the retailer the face value and handling fees. Then the manufacturer's clearinghouse cross-references the coupon against a pre-verified master file of bona fide retailers. Each shipment is sorted by the promotion code, counted, and approved for payment. Once fully recorded, all coupons are destroyed, and payment is finally submitted. This is particularly important if your coupon is doubling as a sweepstakes drawing entry or you plan to track it closely.

Coupon redemption cost formula. Grocery packaged goods companies use the following formula to calculate coupon redemption costs:

Circulation × Coupon face value (plus clearinghouse charges, which may average 15¢ in this category) × Historical redemption percentage = Redemption dollars.

(Note: This doesn't include media costs to deliver the coupon.)

If: Circulation is 250,000
      Coupon value is 50¢
      Clearinghouse charges total 15¢/coupon
      Historical redemption is 2 percent

Then: 250,000 × (.50 + .15) × .02 = $3,250 Redemption costs

Coupon redemption budgeting and cost-per-sale scenario. The following process and average rates come from number crunchers at two different major packaged foods corporations.

Distribution costs:
   10,000,000 coupons distributed at $5 per thousand:
   10,000,000 ÷ 1,000 × $5 = $50,000
Redemption rate = 2.5%; 10,000,000 × .025 =
 250,000 redeemed coupons
Redemption cost:
   250,000 redemptions at 50¢ face value $125,000
Clearinghouse #1 to pay retailer for coupon handling costs.
   8¢ per coupon. .08 × 250,000 redemptions = $20,000

Clearinghouse #2. Manufacturer's clearinghouse for record-keeping, payments, fraud control, etc.

3¢ per coupon. .03 × 250,000 redemptions =	$7,500
Total program cost: 1 + 3 + 4 + 5	$202,500
Cost per redeemed coupon: $202,500 ÷ 250,000 =	$0.81

Actual product sold on redemption:

With 10% misredemption, 250,000 coupons × 90% valid redemptions = 225,000

Actual cost per redeemed coupon:

$202,500 total program cost ÷ 225,000 valid redemptions =	$0.90

Net-Net: A $0.50 consumer discount may actually cost the manufacturer $0.90.

A 1 percent ain't hay. A 1 percent redemption in an average metro market of 3 million people translates to 300,000 sales in that market alone. A packaged foods marketer may consider 2.5 to 3.0 percent a healthy redemption level.

The 80/20 rule. The vast majority of coupons reach a small group of frequent couponers *and* quite possibly switchers—Coke one week, Pepsi the next. Is this bad news? It could be the price you pay to stay in the game. Often, these couponers are heavy users—the 20 percent who may represent 80 percent of your sales. A coupon for one purchase could generate several. Do focus group research to learn more.

Stop crunching numbers! One reason to coupon has nothing to do with redemption. Regardless of the numbers, there is a strong perception among the trade and the salespeople that coupons generate traffic, especially cross-store traffic—shopping! So regardless of all the number crunching, when you drop a coupon, salespeople sell, retailers respond, products get stocked, signs go up, and products get sold with or without coupon redemption.

ONLINE COUPONS

Internet use of coupons is a growing field. Some coupons are delivered and redeemed strictly online. This section deals only with coupons delivered online and redeemed at retail. There are good points and not-so-good points in this practice.

The good news:

- The cost is extremely low compared with print.
- You can distribute in a single day.
- You can target coupon announcements with precision.
- "Viral" marketing can spread your coupon delivery like a chain letter.

The bad news:

- Liability can be a problem, as the quantity of coupons may be boundless.
- To avoid liability, the coupon may have to be a flat percentage discount, reducing its face value and possibly the ability to single out products.
- What little redemption history there is may be quickly outdated in this dynamic medium.
- Because the medium is susceptible to fraud, there is less retail acceptance.
- Internet coupons may require retail staff training and timing.

Unless you have redemption control measures, you can limit your liability by offering a flat percentage discount. Qualifiers can increase your effectiveness. For example, offer 10 percent off any Acme Sweater from the day after Thanksgiving until the following Sunday while supplies last. But offer a 50 percent value to anyone who purchases before 10 AM Thanksgiving Friday. That draws the early-bird-shopper traffic on the best shopping day of the year, when wallets are at their fullest.

PRESELL YOUR COUPON DROP

Depending on the trade, inform the salesforce months before the coupon drop so they can begin the sales process and the retailer can schedule for the promotion. Provide sell-in materials that might include the following:

- Publication(s) where the coupon will appear
- Page size
- Circulation

- Target market and demographics as it relates to retailer
- Impressive redemption history
- Impressive product information (share, sales, turn, desirable target market, if sale encourages other purchases (e.g., chips plus dips), favorable trends, etc.)
- Total dollar support figure (ad media, point of sale, packaging, outdoor, etc.)
- Support materials the retailer should use (signage, ad slicks, folders, etc.)
- Areas you might support retailer with (radio tags, shopping cart signs, shelf media, in-store radio, etc.)
- Plan-o-gram with the ideal product stocking quantities and placement
- "Profit calculator" to show how much the retailer can profit (See Chapter 5, "Discounts," page 144.)

GUIDELINES AND CAUTIONS

Tips:

- Make the face value (Save 00¢) prominent.
- Make the expiration date prominent.
- Allow a grace period beyond your expiration date as a goodwill gesture for late redeemers.
- Place the product on the coupon so it's easy to identify. Avoid showing more than two products.
- Focus on quick, clear advertising communication. Don't be so clever that the offer's obscured.
- Be bold and striking, but visually simple.
- Make the coupon a contrasting color with the ad to "pop." (Careful—UPC codes should be black on white so the scanner can read them.)
- Don't scream "Savings!" in the ad—the coupon does that. Create demand, and let the coupon close the sale.
- Some studies advise using people in the ad, but in the case of food, appetite appeal rules. (Don't sacrifice appetite appeal by showing the entire plate or table—a luscious close-up portion is better.)
- Use a full page if you can.
- Use a campaign approach if you run more than one FSI per year. Build familiarity and recognition.

- Reinforce the offer with broadcast advertising if possible, and offer dealer tags.
- Place the coupon in the corner, where it's easier to clip and receives higher redemption levels.
- Show dashes for clipping.
- Use a dollar bill–size coupon if possible. Smaller coupons are more difficult to handle and are easily lost.
- Avoid placing more than one coupon on one page if possible—too many on one page often reduces redemption.
- Test different coupon values to gain insights.
- Presell—and establish a timetable; retailers need sufficient notice.
- With food products, in-pack coupons require USDA- and FDA-approved inks plus special wrapping. Be sure odors can't seep into the product.
- Confirm that the trade channel you're targeting accepts coupons.
- Clearly indicate VOID on any coupon reprint, such as samples sent to the salesforce.
- Remember that coupons delivered in-store may be misredeemed by the retailer. Specify the potential for audits. You may also limit the coupon quantity per store according to the product inventory per store. You may even negotiate an off-invoice discount, leaving the coupon redemption to the retailer—a dealer discount that becomes a dealer coupon.
- Make sure publishers/distributors recover and destroy unsold issues. Prohibit overruns and bulk deliveries of coupon-day issues.
- Consider inserting your coupon only in home-delivered copies for magazines.
- Make sure the newspaper doesn't back up the coupon against another coupon. If it does, demand a refund or rerun.
- Make sure you have sufficient retail distribution in couponing markets. A rule of thumb is to have 55 to 60 percent ACV (see the Glossary) distribution in the market.
- Remember that in-pack coupons require disclosures. Either they should have no expiration date or you should allow at least six months for expiration so all inventory containing coupons is depleted before the redemption deadline. If the label or package announces that a coupon is enclosed, the label should also disclose the coupon's conditions, such as the expiration date and limitations.

See mix and match under the section "Shell Games and Funny Money" in Chapter 5 on page 141.

CONTROLLING COUPON FRAUD

Some fraudulent redeemers print their own coupons. Others "legitimately" organize clubs to collect, trade, and sell coupons, which violates a nontransferable requirement. The following guidelines are suggested by CMIS, Inc., in Winston-Salem, North Carolina, for *PROMO* magazine. Watch out for the following:

- Coupons cut uniformly in bulk on a machine rather than those cut by hand
- Sequentially numbered coupons rather than those randomly numbered
- Coupons in mint condition that appear uncirculated
- Wrinkled coupons that have matching patterns
- "Washed" coupons with a rough, bleached appearance
- Coupons with a different feel or print quality than the real thing
- Coupons outside the distribution area specified on the coupon
- Coupons redeemed for a product the submitting store doesn't carry
- Coupons redeemed after their expiration date

Source: *PROMO* magazine (http://www.promomagazine.com), a Primedia publication.

NCH Marketing Services, Inc., a retailer clearinghouse and manufacturer's redemption agent headquartered in Deerfield, Illinois, suggests the following 12 proactive steps you can take to minimize exposure to coupon fraud:

1. Establish a written, fair, and reasonable coupon redemption policy that is communicated to all your trading partners.
2. Follow industry association, legal, and agent recommendations for coupon design and efficient processing.
3. Make the coupon's intended purchase clear. State that consumers must purchase the coupon's listed item, and retailers must sell the items for the coupon to be valid. Include the redemption address and cash value of the coupon, and state that it is nontransferable. Refer to your company's available coupon redemption policy in the coupon's legal copy.
4. Alert retailers of coupon plans and anticipated response rates. Sufficient merchandise in-stock ensures a successful coupon event for the promoted product.

5. Keep purchase requirements simple. The more complex the offer, the more confusion and potential for mistakes or mishandling.

6. Audit the process. Audit coupon printers and distributors to ensure the film, plates, and coupons are secure at each step. Audit your outsourced redemption agent's controls, including its controls around any subcontracted processing.

7. Use free-product coupons with caution. These and no-purchase-required coupons mandate that the retailer write in their retail price. Print a maximum-value-allowed notice next to the write-in box, typically the item's recommended retail price. These coupons should not be distributed via the mass media or the Internet.

8. Establish a zero-tolerance policy for suspected fraudulent submissions. Your payment policies should not allow payment for suspicious or fraudulent submissions merely because they fall below a certain dollar amount.

9. Monitor redemption volume and submitters closely. Watch redemptions especially during the first few weeks—when they are the heaviest—and watch first-time submitters of coupons to your company. Compare the activity with historical patterns and your forecasts.

10. Use copy-proof paper stock or other deterrent methods when printing free-product or high-value coupons.

11. Discourage buying, selling, and trading coupons. Advise consumers and retailers of your nontransferable policy, and use all legal means to protect the rights of your property.

12. Support and fully utilize the fraud control services offered by your redemption agent, industry organizations such as the Coupon Information Center (CIC), and any third parties that have been hired to supplement internal expertise.

SIMPLIFIED CHECKLIST

Be sure to refer to the above cautions along with the following list:

_____ Salesforce is informed of coupon drop with sell-in materials in time to inform retailers (see sell-in suggestions above)

_____ Grocers/retailers informed of coupon drop in time for increased order and shipment

_____ Retailers are advised of your redemption projections so they know you're monitoring

_____ Coupon ad reprints are in sufficient quantity for salesforce presentations

_____ Sell-in materials with the coupon are marked VOID

_____ The publisher has destroyed coupon overruns, and any bulk deliveries are accounted for

_____ Universal product code matches product

_____ Bar code value matches face value

_____ Coupon size meets industry specifications

_____ Grocers/retailers copy, including handling fee and mailing instructions

_____ A consumer code to track redemption if you want it

_____ "Manufacturer Coupon" identification, if appropriate; retailer identification, if appropriate

_____ Prominent expiration date

_____ Manufacturer's free-product offer has space and instructions for retailers to specify retail price, and maximum allowable price clearly indicated

_____ Cash value of coupon, such as 1/20 cent or 1/100 cent

_____ Specific product and size clearly indicated

_____ Consumer sales tax note, if appropriate

_____ Geographic restrictions, such as United States or single state

_____ Restrictions, such as "Not to be reproduced" or "One coupon per person per visit" or "Nontransferable"

_____ Special considerations, such as:

    _____ Invoices showing purchases of sufficient stock to cover all coupons must be shown upon request

    _____ Submit in compliance with [company name] coupon redemption policy

    _____ Void where prohibited, taxed, or restricted

Coupon redemption requires experience, so lean on your vendors for help. Use this book as a guideline for your discussions with the coupon publisher, the clearinghouse, your agency, and others. They may or may not share redemption data with you, but ask. There are so many variables that you want input from the people who've seen every manner of coupon. Then start your own file and build your own expertise.

4

REBATES/REFUNDS

(Also see "Discounts," Chapter 5,
and "Coupons," Chapter 3)

INTRODUCTION:
REWARDING THE REAL PURCHASERS

The use of rebates and refunds has soared over the past few years. That huge growth has come, however, not from traditional consumer product marketers, or from retailers, or even from business-to-business promotion managers. Instead, it has come from the automotive field. Automakers have fallen in love with rebates, many of them making offers that amount to thousands of dollars. In fact, the theme today seems to be "Buy a car, get a rebate."

Why have automakers become so enamored with refunds and rebates? One obvious reason, of course, is that they work. They are inexpensive in terms of actual customer redemption when compared with the big promotional offer that can be developed around them. The second reason automakers like them is that they can be used to help the manufacturer manage his or her product inventory. Made too many four-door, red, 1.5 liter sedans? Offer a rebate and watch them move out. Through the use of refunds and rebates by the marketing organization, inventory can be managed and production flow-through improved. So from a marketer's view, refunds and rebates can be key elements in the total promotion arsenal.

The other reason promotion managers like refunds and rebates is that substantial offers can be made with the knowledge that only a limited number of redemptions will likely occur. A seemingly big promotional offer or program can be developed by the promotion manager, knowing that by limiting the offer to specific products or services and setting specific time limits for when the rebate or refund will occur and when the offer can be redeemed, plus the expected slippage that naturally occurs, the amount of promotional funds that will have to be paid out is often quite small. (*Slippage* is the product sale that occurs because the consumer bought the product with the intention of claiming the rebate or refund but never sent it in. See Steve's discussion of this term in this chapter.) The marketer generally has better control over rebates and refunds than over most other types of promotional activities.

With the exception of the auto deals, however, refunds and rebates seem to have declining interest among consumers in many product categories. Experts have suggested that's because they're a delayed form of reward. Customers have to wait until the rebate or refund is processed by the retailer and then by the manufacturer, often a period of several weeks before the consumer gets his or her due. So unlike the instant savings of a coupon or price-off, rebates and refunds don't work that well in generating immediate additional sales. Consumers want instant gratification today, and refunds and rebates really can't provide that.

From a promotion-planning standpoint, the primary reason to consider a rebate or refund is that the customer must make a purchase, often at full retail price, to qualify for the offer. You can't get an auto refund unless you buy a car. So the marketer has the money up front through a purchase before having to provide the refund or rebate. There are big advantages to managing cash flows that way.

Refunds and rebates have other advantages and disadvantages, as Steve discusses in the chapter that follows. For planning purposes, however, remember the types of customer groups we use in planning promotions. For them, refunds and rebates aren't very good at attracting new customers or new users. Even reducing consumer risk by offering a refund or rebate on all or part of the purchase price doesn't seem to have an impact on large numbers of customers who have not bought before. There are likely other reasons they haven't purchased in the past, and simply offering a refund or rebate often won't overcome those objections.

Refunds and rebates are fairly good at retaining customers. The refund or rebate is a good way to thank customers for past purchases and encourage them to continue buying the brand. You may not build new sales, but you can protect against customer loss.

Refunds and rebates can be used effectively to help grow customer usage of the brand—in other words, customers will often purchase an additional unit or units of the product if a rebate is offered in connection with the purchase of the product or service. Or refunds and rebates can often be used to get present customers to use the product in new or different ways.

And, finally, refunds and rebates are a good way to help a customer migrate through the product portfolio. If the customer is satisfied with the existing product, offering a rebate or refund on the purchase of another product in the line or for an up-sell or cross-sell often works well.

Refunds have come a long way from the days when detergent manufacturers offered a refund or rebate for proof of purchase on a certain number of boxes. And it certainly goes to show that rebates and refunds can be used and can work for most any type of promotional marketer. The secret is knowing how and when to use them. That secret is what follows in this chapter. —Don E. Schultz

OVERVIEW

Refunds fall into the category of discounts, but refunds achieve more specific benefits. In fact, one benefit is that refunds often fail to result in discounts because consumers don't follow through to redeem them. (See "How *Not* to Get Redeemed—Slippage," page 105.)

A refund tear pad on the shelf draws attention, particularly against competitors, and because it's a mail-in offer, the retailer doesn't have to do anything. Refunds also protect vendors from coupon misredemption.

Refunds generally won't generate a trial purchase because they're labor intensive and the reward is delayed. However, they *can* close a sale when someone's considering your product.

Refund or rebate? They're so similar that some say they're identical. Others maintain that a refund is a mail-in offer, whereas a rebate certificate is delivered on the spot. And still others say a rebate is for a higher-ticket item like a car, whereas a refund is for lower-priced items. This section simplifies matters by using only the term *refund.*

COMMON REFUND OBJECTIVES

- To offer a discount that isn't redeemed (See slippage.)
- To give a retailer a "sales closer" that requires no execution by the retailer
- To launch a product (typically pricey, considered-purchase item)
- To sell a "mother ship"—encouraging peripheral purchases (such as game hardware that leads to software sales)
- To liquidate old product to make room for new product, such as current year's car models
- To move slow/overstocked product, such as snow blowers in the spring
- To load product to fill stores and consumer shelves and thus cut demand for subsequent competitor offerings
- To increase purchases/usage by adding more purchase requirements than the customer's average purchase quantity
- To soften the shock of a price increase
- To encourage retail inventory in anticipation of the multiple purchases the refund requires
- To increase product visibility through a tear pad or promotional display
- To advance retail continuity and block out competitors (For example, a major print film company offered retailers one huge refund based on yearlong quotas. That year-end refund may get factored into the retailer's yearlong budget. If the quota is not achieved near year-end, the retailer orders extra product or risks missing forecasts—sorry, small competitors; bye!)

COMMON REFUND OBJECTIVES BY TACTIC AND DELIVERY

(Also see itemized tactics below plus objectives listed above.)

TACTIC	OBJECTIVES (Beyond Purchase, Slippage, and Those Cited Above)
Print delivered	• Mass delivery of offer (versus retail tear pad) • Motivate retailer participation as consumers shop for product • Soften effect of price increase • Refund form to become hard copy reminder
Internet delivered	• Economical mass delivery of offer (no printing) • Easy communication to all consumers—"Find this offer on our Web site" • Drives traffic to Web site • Softens effect of price increase • Printing refund form creates hard copy reminder • May appeal to select target—Web surfers
Point of sale delivered	• Immediate, on-site purchase incentive • Break in-store pricing tie with competitors (relying on slippage) • Draw attention to product • Soften effect of price increase • Encourage retail signage through generous offer, possibly multiple purchases
Product delivered	• Break pricing tie with competitors (relying on slippage) • Deliver on-site offer, regardless of retail signage • Avoid product's winding up on store's rebate board • Bounce-back or multiple purchase for required proofs of purchase
Partner delivered (Example: Buy Beer Nuts and receive Stanley Tool refund certificate.)	• Delivery partner receives generous consumer offer at no/minimal cost • Refunding partner receives free/inexpensive delivery medium • Partners share each other's consumer base • Access new alternative channels
Receipt delivered	• Retail tie-in, including keying program into scanner system • Retailer contribution to total refund value • Bypass problems with tear pads • Greater accountability through scanner database
Multiple purchase requirement	• Multiple sales • Increase average customer consumption • Target heavy users/families • Greater retail product placement (push) with follow-through consumer pull • Liquidate overstocks • "Load" consumers *before* a competitor promotes • Soften effect of price increase • Increase value for greater response

TACTIC	OBJECTIVES (Beyond Purchase, Slippage, and Those Cited Above)
Cross-purchase tie-in—purchase two different products for refund	• Economize, offering brand portfolio products together • One-stop shopping sales opportunity (i.e., picnic cooler and soft drinks) • Tap into partner's consumer base, outlets, and exposure • Increase usage occasions • Increase value for greater response
Continuity purchase—manufacturer offers retailer year-end refund; consumer gradually collects proofs to achieve refund	• Build long-term purchase behavior • Vest customer in program, combating competitive offers • Retain heavy users • Encourage higher purchase levels—reward for ten purchases if consumer averages eight • Business-to-business—Build higher yearlong sales while avoiding rewards for those who don't achieve quota; pressure at year-end to meet quota
Instant refund (Offered directly by the dealer upon sale transaction of typically higher-ticket items like appliances)	• Retailer participation through generous consumer offer at manufacturer's cost • Challenge "me-too" mail-in refunds through immediate value (versus lengthy mail-in procedure) • Sales-closing tool • Encourage trade-up through refund contribution • Apply refund as down payment
Sweepstakes overlay	• Add topspin • Add point-of-sale excitement • Encourage product and signage placement by retailer • Encourage redemption—rebate form is entry (negates slippage benefit)
Manufacturer/ Retailer tie-in	• Turnkey, shipping-free fulfillment • Encourage activity by key retailer chain, while the retailer enjoys an exclusive offer for a popular brand
Retailer's vendor bundle	• Retailer offers large total savings figure • Vendor receives a key retailer's involvement, while retailer also enjoys vendor funding • Cross-store shopping, multiple purchases
Collector card	• Ongoing consumer visits/purchases while preempting competitors • Build loyalty • Can have a game quality or be combined with a sweepstakes

ITEMIZED TACTICS

36. PRINT DELIVERED

Definition Refund certificate delivered through print media

Advantages
- Assures that consumers receive offer (versus POS delivered)
- Allows targeting
- Can soften price increase impact
- Greater exposure than retail delivery
- Doubles as advertising
- Certificate is hard copy reminder of product
- Opportunity to negotiate with dealer for display, flyer placement, etc. (may identify retailer in ad)

Disadvantages
- Greater redemption potential and cost
- Less redemption per impression than POS delivered
- Media costs
- May be less targeted than retail- or product-delivered refund
- Reaches more professional refunders
- Cash less economical than premiums, tie-in partner offers, and others

37. INTERNET DELIVERED

Definition Refund certificate delivered through Web site; either print hard copy or apply/redeem online

Advantages
- Less costly than print medium
- Ensures consumers receive offer (versus POS delivered)
- Can soften price increase impact
- Can link other Internet programs and advantages—online payment, point programs, download offers, and the like
- May deliver greater exposure than retail delivery (if properly advertised)
- Alternative to obscure, cluttered retailer's refund board
- Drives participants to Web site and additional brand communication
- Opportunity to capture more data than print alternative
- Printed certificate is hard copy reminder of offer

- Online redemption is easy for consumer and economical and efficient for marketer
- Opportunity to negotiate with dealer for display, flyer placement, etc. (may identify retailer in ad)
- Appeals in particular to Web-savvy targets

Disadvantages
- Greater redemption potential and cost—less slippage
- May not be delivered at actual point of purchase—retailer
- May be "invisible"; unless it's communicated outside the Web site, both retailer and consumer may be oblivious
- Less immediate and actionable than in-store offer (may give competitor an advantage)
- Quantities may be unlimited, lessening control that limited print distribution offers
- "Professional" refunders and cyberthieves may uncover vulnerabilities (Also see "Print Delivered" above)

38. POINT OF SALE DELIVERED

Definition   Offer delivered at retail through tear pad and possibly signage

Advantages
- Highly targeted at point of purchase
- Higher redemption per exposure than out-of-store redemption
- Retailer participation—can offer discount with virtually no execution or costs
- Tear pad/signage draws attention to product
- Breaks pricing tie with competitors (or offsets higher price) with slippage economies

Disadvantages
- Requires retailer participation to place/allow tear pad
- May require field service to place materials
- May require hardware or in-store media to dispense order forms
- Many retailers don't allow refunds because of clutter, lowest-price policies, or patron complaints for any mishaps
- Timing issue if refund offered beyond program deadline
- May wind up on remote, cluttered refund board or customer service drawer

- Entire tear pad may be taken by professional refunder
- Cash less economical than premiums, tie-in partner offers, and others

39. PRODUCT DELIVERED

Definition   Refund certificate delivered in or on the product package

Advantages
- Distribution control—only purchasers receive certificate
- Targeted—only where product is available and in stock
- May encourage retailer participation and support
- "Burst" on package guarantees POS exposure even without signage
- Breaks pricing tie with competitors (or offsets higher price)
- Can be an economical delivery of offer (depending on cost of package application)
- Avoids professional refunders

Disadvantages
- Requires additional packaging operations and coordination
- Requires extended deadline because of possibility of extended product shelf life
- May cannibalize sales from current unpromoted stock on shelf, further prolonging old shelf life
- Limited awareness of offer unless supported with print media and point-of-sale signage
- Cash less economical than premiums, tie-in partner offers, and others

40. PARTNER DELIVERED

Definition
- Refund certificate delivered and/or redeemed by a partner (Two examples: a mop refund offer delivered on a floor wax package, or a Stanley Tool refund offered on a Beer Nuts package)

Advantages
- Allows one partner to offer high-value reward for purchase and other partner to have free distribution of the offer (versus traditional media or POS costs)
- Allows refunding partner access to alternative channels and markets—such as a tool refund offered in supermarkets (and homes) through a soft drink carton

- Allows both partners point-of-sale awareness opportunities in each other's distribution channels or cross-store locations
- Allows two partners to target mutual consumer segments—fishing gear refund on blue-collar beer brand versus golf gear refund on imported beer

Disadvantages
- On-pack certificate requires new packaging operations, costs, and timing
- Package's shelf life may be longer than promotional period
- Exposure limited to those who purchase delivery product
- Both partners must share same timing and target market
- Partner offers should not conflict with retailer's offering
- Delivery product's offer appeal limited to those who desire refunding product
- Considerable up-front negotiations subject to management changes, new marketing plans, budget shifts, etc.
- Tie-ins traditionally time consuming and have a lot of "chiefs"

41. RECEIPT DELIVERED

Definition
- Mail-in refund form and proof of purchase are printed with store receipt; often combined with immediate in-store discount

Advantages
- Retail participation, including keying program into scanner system and flyer announcement
- Exclusive offer for retailer
- If retailer contributes immediate in-store discount, consumer receives high value and immediate gratification but still with slippage economies
- Bypasses tear pad issues—placement, depletions, professional refunders, etc.
- Consumer friendly—rebate form also proof of purchase
- Greater accountability—sale tied directly to refund authorization plus immediate scanner tracking

Disadvantages
- Limited to single partner retailer—may alienate others
- Must offer similar value program to other retailers (see Robinson-Patnum Act in the Glossary)

- May redeem higher—fewer slippage economies
- Requires retailer participation, up-front negotiations, and execution

42. MULTIPLE PURCHASE—SAME BRAND OR COMPANY PRODUCT LINE

Definition

Refund requires several same product family purchases, such as cereals, diaper boxes, or tool series; may or may not require purchase of all products—value may increase with number of products purchased

Business to Business: Flexible vendor-to-dealer (or distributor) reward system—different reward levels for different purchase levels

Advantages

- Loads consumers (and business-to-business) so competitor products lose demand
- Reaches heavy users
- Can increase consumption rate and usage
- Low price point product(s) can offer higher value
- High price point products offer an exceptional value
- Brands (and corporation) can economize on media, POS, and other costs
- Retailer can offer high-value multiple purchase offer with minimal execution
- Retailer can package vendor refunds for its own program
- Partners tap into each other's consumer base
- Cumulative value tactic (more products earn more savings)—reaches both low- and high-quantity purchasers
- Corporation can showcase product family

Disadvantages

- Appeal may be limited to more popular product in family—may dilute that brand
- Complex refund form discourages participation and leads to mistakes—same for fulfillment process
- Greater fulfillment administration, verification, and costs
- Misunderstandings may cause consumer dissatisfaction if refund request denied or returned for corrections
- Cash less economical than premiums, tie-in partner offers, and others
- Advertising doesn't allow brand building (except for corporate)

- Products must share common seasonality, target market, etc.
- Exceptional negotiation and coordination, including mutual timing
- In manufacturer-to-distributor applications, distributor may "forward buy"—purchase products and then warehouse inventory to avoid full prices later

43. CROSS-PURCHASE/TIE-IN

Definition Refund requires multiple diverse product purchases, such as bundled computer peripherals, toy family, or diverse business products; may or may not require purchase of all products—value may increase with number of products purchased

Advantages
- Compatible company/product partners can pool funds, resources, distribution, etc.
- Partners can tap into each other's consumer base
- See advantages in "Multiple Purchase—Same Brand or Company" above.

Disadvantages
- Single product may get lost in group promotion
- Products must share common distribution, seasonality, target market, etc.
- Vulnerable to partner management changes, revised marketing plans, budget shifts, etc.
- See disadvantages in "Multiple Purchase—Same Brand or Company Product Line" above

44. CONTINUITY PURCHASE

Definition Refund value accrued over time and purchases; often practiced in business-to-business and ongoing consumer applications, such as frequent buyer or credit cards (See also "Collector Card" in Chapter 3, "Coupons," page 74, and Chapter 6, "Continuity," page 155.)

Advantages
- Encourages loyalty
- Encourages higher, ongoing purchase levels
- Refund can be redeemable only for sponsor products for economies and sustained sales

- Business-to-business encourages retailer to stock and move inventory
- Business-to-business yearlong program encourages reseller to liquidate inventory at year-end (holidays)
- Database profiling improves customer relationship marketing practices

Disadvantages
- Can be expensive, particularly with direct mail and database applications
- Requires exceptional administration
- Vulnerable to discounting and other immediate reward tactics
- Cash less economical than premiums, tie-in partner offers, and others

45. INSTANT REFUND

Definition
Purchaser receives refund check immediately upon purchase, often for higher-ticket items; typically offered directly by the dealer, possibly through a co-op manufacturer program

Advantages
- Instant gratification for greater motivation versus typical mail-in refund delayed reward
- Refund check can be applied immediately to a down payment or trade-up
- Sales closer

Disadvantages
- Discourages slippage (high values redeem high anyway)
- Requires accountable system—cannot simply give salespeople blank checks (Example: Dealer shares refund's financial commitment or is refunded itself upon verification.)
- System must enable salesperson to authorize check
- Dealers/retailers may resist sharing customer, sales, and pricing information (if required by manufacturer)

46. SWEEPSTAKES OVERLAY

Definition
Refund certificate doubles as sweepstakes drawing entry when redeemed

Advantages
- Draws additional attention and excitement
- Theme can reinforce product benefit
- Encourages redemption

Disadvantages
- Additional sweepstakes expense and tasks—legal, prizes, administration, etc.
- Negates slippage benefit
- May add clutter and confusion to an already sufficient refund offer
- Timing issues—sweepstakes deadline, product shelf life, refund deadline, etc.
- "No Purchase Necessary" alternative entry requirement

47. MANUFACTURER/ACCOUNT TIE-IN—RETAIL FULFILLMENT

Definition
Manufacturer's refund requires purchase at tie-in retailer, often through a gift certificate/card

Advantages
- Retailer participation—display, flyer, stocking, etc.
- No fulfillment shipping costs
- Retailer features exclusive offer with minimal execution
- Manufacturer-assured discount passed on by retailer (*plus* slippage)
- Retailer gift card option provides turnkey, shipping-free fulfillment, and reward selection, plus economies over cash
- Manufacturer can increase distribution
- Can liquidate product
- See "Point of Sale Delivered" above

Disadvantages
- Limited reach—single retailer chain
- Account may resist sharing customer, sales, and pricing information (if required by manufacturer)
- Requires custom distribution if refund is delivered on product
- Requires retailer staff training for consumer questions—participating models, redemption timing, forms, etc.
- Some consumers may send proofs from competitive retailer
- Procedures (like audits) necessary to prevent retail misredemption
- May alienate manufacturer's other accounts
- Requires offers for other retailers (see Robinson-Patman Act in the Glossary)
- See "Point of Sale Delivered" above

48. RETAILER VENDOR COLLECTION

Definition   Different manufacturers' refunds bundled and delivered by one retailer, typically in folder

Advantages
- Retailer offers large savings figure funded by manufacturers
- Traffic builder
- Cross-store shopping
- Multiple purchases
- Manufacturer receives retailer support—flyer, POS, inventory, etc. See "Manufacturer/Account Tie-in" on page 104.

Disadvantages
- Limited reach—single retailer chain
- One offer can be lost in clutter
- Extensive coordination to orchestrate numerous refunds with different manufacturers
- Other retailers may offer the same manufacturer refunds
- Refunds and retailer must all share similar timing See "Manufacturer/Account Tie-in" on page 104.

COLLECTOR CARD

See "Coupons," Chapter 3, page 74.

REFUNDS VERSUS MERCHANDISE INCENTIVES

Cash is the most popular reward *and* one of the most uneconomical. See section on prizes in Chapter 2 ("Sweepstakes and Contests") and weigh the advantages of offering a cash refund or merchandise.

HOW *NOT* TO GET REDEEMED—SLIPPAGE

Slippage refers to a purchase made with the intent to redeem the product's refund but the consumer then fails to complete the paperwork and postage. Thanks to slippage, marketers can have higher refund discounts, knowing that a certain percentage of the refunds will not be redeemed. For example, a $5 refund for any video purchase sounds expensive, yet actual redemption numbers have come in at 1 percent. So for every 100 purchases with a $5 video offer, the brand redeems only $5. One major studio won't accept partners offering $5 refunds because the redemption is too small—the studio wants redemption (sales) but the partner wants slippage (no sales).

Some tips on avoiding redemption:

- Make the offer $5 or less toward higher-priced items.
- Make the refund for lower-priced products prohibitive with postage factored in. (Free candy bar!)
- Ask for a lot of information on the form, including personal data.
- Make the proof of purchase cumbersome, such as a bottle cap (difficult to mail) or a UPC that needs to be scissor-cut from a cardboard box.
- Use a larger package size that takes longer to use up before cutting out the purchase proof.
- Require multiple purchases (and proofs).
- Add a significant shipping and handling charge (for merchandise redemption). Shipping isn't typically marked up, but warehousing and handling are.

Careful! Don't upset customers and open the doors to competitors. Also, customers may learn to avoid future offers. Seek a balance of a good value and requirements that appear easy enough but in the end are simply a hassle.

Gambling on Slippage

If everyone redeemed the $5 video refund on a cereal box, the brand manager would be fired and the promotion would go bankrupt. A slippage-based offer is a gamble based on past performance. Some marketers hedge their bets with a higher product price that they then lower with the refund. If generic windshield washer fluid retails at $1, a premium brand can offer a two-pack box for $3 with a $1 refund, so it's "priced" the same as the generic. Yet the slippage keeps the margin high—but *only if* redemptions are low.

You can exercise some controls, such as the following:

- Curtail the number of rebate certificates you distribute. Determine your worst-case scenario, making it a percentage of total product in the universe. If a million packages are in the system and you distribute a quarter of a million certificates, the worst case is that 25 percent of your sales incur refund costs (*if* 100 percent of the certificates are redeemed).

- Distribute refund certificates to each retailer in proportion to the number of products ordered or inventoried. (If a retailer orders 100 packages per store, distribute one 25-sheet tear pad of refund certificates.)
- Deliver your offer to one retailer, one region, or one media vehicle at a time.
- Limit the period for which the offer is good.
- Require multiple purchases. (However, you may reduce redemptions by first-time or light users at the same time you discount loyal, heavy users.)
- Limit the offer to one refund per household. (Most fulfillment houses don't track this information unless you pay more, but by simply posting it, you discourage multiple redeemers.)

Rebate Shell Games—Traffic Offers versus In-Store Nonoffers

Refunds can be shuffled like peas in a shell game by a manufacturer and retailer. The two might join forces to deliver two different offers simultaneously, which in tandem achieve each party's differing objectives. For example, some retailers advertise a great refund value on an item, but they only communicate the offer in their flyer, which will boost traffic. At the store, however, there's no mention of the offer, but a display showcases the same discount on the same brand's smaller size—the old bait and switch principle, but it's legal because you can ask for the offer and receive it. Here's the breakdown:

Anatomy of a Refund Shell Game

Two Simultaneous Refund Offers	Medium	Retailer Benefit	Manufacturer Benefit
1. 100-pack blank CDs at $24.99— a mail-in refund combined with an additional discount at register	Retailer's flyer only; *no* in-store signage	• Advertised traffic generator • Minimal in-store awareness and redemption • In-store shoppers diverted to more lucrative 50-pack offer via signage	• Offer not communicated in store; only those actively following up flyer ad redeem; minimal redemption • Retailer may have contributed to cash register discount portion

Two Simultaneous Refund Offers	Medium	Retailer Benefit	Manufacturer Benefit
2. 50-pack blank CDs for $24.99—refund form printed automatically on receipt; no in-store discount	Prominent in-store signage; *no* mention in flyer that featured the same-price 100-pack offer	• Profitable, highly visible offer • Discount fully funded and redeemed by manufacturer	• Product featured in store signage • Profitable sale of 50-pack CDs versus same-cost 100-pack flyer offer (Net: Gave away fewer free disks) • Refund offer communicated near product—not on Rebate Center rack • Slippage on mail-in offer

SHIPPING AND HANDLING AND MUCH MORE

Factor in all or some of the following costs, which may or may not be allocated to the shipping and handling budget:

- Banking costs to set up the account, write checks, and so on
- The process to receive requests, verify refund requirements, and authorize the refund
- Form letters: "You neglected to include postage and handling"; "You sent the wrong retail receipt"; "You didn't include enough proofs of purchase"
- Reconciliation process for those who didn't qualify for the offer
- Training and instruction sheets for order processors
- Handling, which includes receiving the authorization to fulfill, address label generation, check "payable to" identification, check insertion (plus any literature), recording the fulfillment, applying postage, and delivering completed envelopes to the post office
- Postage

- 800 number/Web site and training and instruction sheet for questions and complaints
- Additional literature insertion—cover letter, coupon, flyer, and so on
- Data entry, storage, manipulation, and evaluation, ranging from a customer mailing list to complex customer profiling
- The refund!

Ways to handle shipping and handling costs:

- Charge for them in full as "Shipping and handling" on the order form.
- Charge a portion to offset certain program costs and at the same time easing consumer costs. (Some items, like database building, may fall into another budget.)
- Fold them into the total asking price. The order form is simpler, the offer is clean, and the consumer isn't upset by seeing additional charges.
- Mark up all the services to generate profits while you encourage slippage.

REFUND FULFILLMENT

Example of FSI Fulfillment Costs

Following is an example of how the cost *might* break down in an offer in which (1) your company receives two receipts and a refund certificate and (2) you send a $5 refund. (This is strictly an example, and costs will vary by the supplier and the job specifics.)

Item	1,000	5,000	10,000
Servicing the account	$200/month minimum	$200/month minimum	$200/month minimum
Order processing	46.50	232.50	465.00
Data entry	52.24	261.20	522.40
Capture store name (optional)	9.75	48.75	97.50
Store table creation (optional)	100.00 (one time)	100.00 (one time)	100.00 (one time)

Item	1,000	5,000	10,000
Verify one UPC five-digit code (brand) (optional)	7.95	39.75	79.50
Duplicate elimination (optional)	12.00	60.00	120.00
Computer process	27.00	135.00	270.00
FSI standard banking	25.00	125.00	250.00
Print postcard check	27.75	138.75	277.50
First class	200	1000	2000
PO Box	305	305	305
Logo digitization	200 (one time)	200 (one time)	200 (one time)
Activity report—three months	40/month $120	40/month $120	40/month $120
Setup fee	450 (one time)	450 (one time)	450 (one time)
Total w/ postage	1599.19	3295.95	6416.90
Total w/o postage	1399.99	2295.95	4416.90
Per piece w/ postage	1.60	0.66	0.64
Per piece w/o postage	1.40	0.46	0.44

THOSE WHO FAILED TO MEET REFUND REQUIREMENTS

Problems. Where there's a form, there are mistakes. Then there are professional refunders trying to beat your system. Common problems with refunds include these:

- Illegible writing
- No address
- Expiration date exceeded
- Insufficient proofs of purchase
- The wrong product proofs
- The wrong retail receipt
- The same household requesting a second refund
- Postage and handling not included

Solutions:

- Hold the request and ask the consumer to complete the requirements.
- Have a grace period beyond the expiration date. It does four things:
  1. Allows for late redeemers
  2. Provides a longer-than-published expiration period so your rejection says the applicant was 30 days late rather than 1 day
  3. Simplifies the process for people who miss the deadline by just a few days—no correspondence necessary
  4. Allows more participation
- Provide a reward for actual purchasers who didn't include enough proofs—a partial refund, a generous coupon, or a free product coupon.
- Give all rejected submissions a coupon.

Sample letter. This suggestion is a "one letter fits all." Consider a few alternative response letters for different situations.

(Date)

Dear _____:

    Thank you for your interest in Acme Widgets. We would like to fulfill your refund request; however, it did not meet the following requirement(s).

_____ Expiration date (date) was exceeded.

_____ Requires ___ more proof(s) of purchase.

_____ The wrong retail receipt was included.

_____ The wrong product proofs were included.

_____ This offer is only good for one household per offer, and our records show this is an additional request.

_____ Postage and handling were not included.

_____ We will complete your refund upon receipt of the following by (date):
        (Processor fills out requirement on this line, or checks the next box.)

_____ We are sorry we cannot give you the refund at this time, but we've included an Acme coupon in appreciation of your interest in Acme Widgets.

Sincerely,

John Smith
Customer Service Representative

REFUND REDEMPTION EXAMPLE

A national retailer would honor a $3 to $5 coupon toward a video purchase at its stores. Coupon would be a mail-back offer by a packaged food brand. ("Buy this product, send proof, and receive an instantly redeemable coupon in the mail.") Following are two redemption scenarios:

Redemption: 2% to 5% on $3 value for instant coupon
135,000 packages × 5% × $3 = $20,250 redemption cost*

Redemption: 20% to 25% on $5 value for instant coupon
135,000 packages × 25% × $5 = $168,750 redemption cost*

*Excludes certificate printing, fulfillment, etc.

Some videos redeem only at 1 percent for a $5 mail-back refund.

WHY SOME RETAILERS DON'T LIKE REFUNDS

Many retailers feature refund values in their flyers, noting in smaller type "With manufacturer's refund." Yet some retailers resist refunds for any of the following reasons:

- For many, a $5 refund redeems too low unless the partner represents tremendous volume, such as a major breakfast cereal. Even though it doesn't pay the $5, the retailer has to train its system about the promotion.
- Refunds conflict with "everyday low price" positioning. Wal-Mart might demand the discount be applied to its pricing (which undermines the refund's higher value through slippage).
- Refund tear pads and signage detract from the store décor and encourage litter.
- Refunds may represent parity with other retailers. "Why should I offer your refund when the same tear pad is at my competitor's? Give me something they don't have, or I'll take your competitor's offer."
- Consumers may think the retailer is accountable for any rebate problems, so the retailer catches the consumer's wrath.

- Many retailers feel it cheapens their image. Some retailers (and their shoppers) value their high-price policies.
- Independent, entrepreneurial contractors and durable goods stores resent manufacturers meddling in their business with refund form questionnaires asking selling price, retailer name, customer name, service questions, and more. These independents often provide their own rebates at their own expense to counter the manufacturer's interference.

Retailers: Make the Most of Vendor Refunds and Take Some Credit

By pooling all the vendor refunds into one flyer, a retailer can boast hundreds of dollars in savings throughout the store and avoid all that tear pad clutter. And even though the retailer doesn't fund the redemption, it can take credit for offering such huge savings to its customers.

Another way to trumpet savings is to showcase the price after rebate in large type and then specify "After manufacturer's rebate" in small type. If you add an in-store discount, show the math—actual price minus discount, minus rebate, and a bottom-line "only" price plus the total savings in bold.

The No-Win Refund Board

Unfortunately for all parties, too many retailers make the refund an afterthought, sticking all the tear pads on an obscure refund board. The retailer misses the opportunity to feature savings. The brand loses the sales-closer objective. The consumers typically miss the offer. Vendors should prenegotiate with refund board retailers by, for example, advertising in their flyers in exchange for promoting the refund next to the product.

Insight

It may sound like a great idea to make the refund form double as a sweepstakes entry. But do you really want to encourage redemption once the product has been purchased?

DETECTING REFUND FRAUD

Unfortunately, the high-dollar values of refunds encourage professional fraud. A "reject card" explains why a submission cannot be honored; typically, there is no resistance from fraudulent redeemers who don't want further attention.

Following are seven red flags that were culled by Marc Shafer of Accradata, Farmington, Connecticut, for *PROMO* magazine. The importance of each needs to be weighed against the potential difficulties it might cause.

1. Same-size envelopes, indicating supplies were bought in bulk
2. Same stamps—again showing bulk purchase
3. Postmark differs from return address
   "Deduping programs" may be thwarted by different addresses on the refund order forms. Refund forms should state that checks will only be sent to the return address listed on the envelope, which the deduping program can monitor.
4. Receipts without store names
   Professionals use their own cash registers or software to generate receipts. Look for bogus store names or misspellings of legitimate names.
5. Requests that go to PO boxes
   Specify you won't send checks to PO boxes.
6. Similar identification patterns
   Look for similar handwriting on multiple submissions. Good fulfillment house personnel recognize groups of misredeemers by their repetitive modus operandi. Some even nickname groups—for example, The Gold Staple Bandits (who use gold-colored staples) and The Hallmarks (who use colored Hallmark card envelopes).
7. Computer-generated labels
   Few people use preprinted mailing labels in the "To" address, so stipulate they're prohibited.

Source: *PROMO* magazine (http://www.promomagazine.com), a Primedia publication.

COMMON REFUND COPY REQUIREMENTS

The following 13 suggestions come from Mel Poretz, publisher of *The Fulfillment Fact-ery*, in an article for *PROMO* magazine.

1. State that you will reject any proofs that are not genuine.
2. Clearly reprint the mail fraud statutes so misredeemers cannot claim ignorance.
3. State refund checks will be mailed within the state the request came from to discourage cross-country accomplices.

4. Require register tapes to be dated and have a store name to discourage defrauders with their own cash registers.

5. State that order forms and envelopes must be handwritten.

6. Specify checks will be made out only to the same name as the requester to deter groups.

7. Print order forms in at least two colors with screens, tints, and other techniques that deter counterfeiting.

8. Keep expiration dates short (three months) to close the window of opportunity and networking by defrauders. You can extend the promotion later or create a second wave.

9. Stipulate prominently that proofs of purchase must be obtained by purchase of the sponsoring product. Use words like *Buy* or *Purchase* to establish violations criteria.

Source: *PROMO* magazine (http://www.promomagazine.com), a Primedia publication.

And a few extras . . .

10. State that checks will be sent only to the return address listed on the envelope, which the deduping program can monitor.

11. State that you won't send checks to PO boxes.

12. State: "This certificate has no cash value."

13. For higher-priced items, insist on the carton's UPC code, which defaces the box and discourages returned product. Try to partner with retailers to counter defaced returned packages.

Again, to avoid overly long copy on a small certificate, weigh the value of each stipulation in terms of the consequences to your offer. For example, are you simply trying to discourage misredeemers or setting legal precedent to prosecute?

I *nsight*

Expect complaints in a massive national program. Of course, the number of complaints is directly proportional to any confusing elements or other problems. Have focus groups review the program communication. Prepare a complaint line with trained reps. Show customers how to contact you. And don't let a minor percent of complainers jeopardize the vast majority of satisfied customers and a successful program.

Refund Certificate Copy Examples

EXAMPLE: SINGLE PURCHASE OFFER (Tear Pad with Account-Specific Overlay)

AJAX WIDGET MAIL-IN REBATE

From Acme Stores

1. BUY a _____ size Ajax Widget from Acme Stores
2. ENCLOSE in an envelope:
   A. The UPC bar code, and
   B. The original or a copy of the Acme Stores receipt from your Ajax Widget purchase—circle the store name, date, and price.
3. FILL OUT this certificate completely and MAIL with items A and B from above in a hand-addressed envelope, to:

   (Address)

This certificate has no cash value. This offer is good in the United States, except where prohibited, taxed, or restricted by law. Offer is good on purchase made between _____ and _____. Offer must be redeemed by _____. Offer limited to one per person per mailing address. Post office box requests will not be honored. Offer restricted to purchase of Ajax Widget from Acme Stores only. Not valid with any other offer on Ajax Widgets. Allow six to eight weeks for delivery. Neither this certificate, cash register receipt(s), or the UPC bar code symbols may be mechanically reproduced. Not responsible for lost, late, illegible, damaged, misdirected, or postage-due mail.

Offer expires _____

(Refund identification numbers)

Please print clearly

_____
Name

_____
Address

_____
City, State, Zip

_____
Daytime telephone

EXAMPLE: SINGLE PURCHASE OFFER (Tear Pad without Account-Specific Overlay—Available in any Authorized U.S. Store)

AJAX WIDGET MAIL-IN REBATE

1. BUY a __ size Ajax Widget from any authorized retailer in the United States.
2. ENCLOSE in an envelope:
   A. The UPC bar code, and
   B. The original or a copy of the store receipt from your Ajax Widget purchase—circle the store name, date, and price.
3. FILL OUT this certificate completely and MAIL with items A and B from above in a hand-addressed envelope, to:

   (Address)

This certificate has no cash value. This offer is good in the United States, except where prohibited, taxed, or restricted by law. Offer is good on purchase made between _____ and _____. Offer must be redeemed by _____. Offer limited to one per person per mailing address. Post office box requests will not be honored. Offer restricted to purchase of Ajax Widget. Not valid with any other offer on Ajax Widgets. Allow six to eight weeks for delivery. Neither this certificate, nor cash register receipt(s), nor the UPC bar code symbols may be mechanically reproduced. Not responsible for lost, late, illegible, damaged, misdirected, or postage-due mail.

Offer expires _____

(Refund identification numbers)

Please print clearly

_____
Name

_____
Address

_____
City, State, Zip

_____
Daytime telephone

EXAMPLE: MULTIPLE PURCHASE OFFER (Manufacturer's Goods Bought at Any Retail Location)

AJAX PRODUCT LINE
MAIL-IN REFUND CERTIFICATE

Save up to $00

Here's How:

1. *Bring* our refund shopping list to the store.
2. *Buy* products on the list. The more you buy, the bigger the refund.
3. *Save* the UPC symbols from the products.
4. *Circle* the item prices, store name, and date on your receipt(s).
5. *Check off* the products you bought and how many on the Refund Tally Section.
6. *Add up* the quantities and the refund you've earned, and fill in the amount on the Refund Tally Section.
7. *Fill out* the information on the Refund Tally Section—print clearly.
8. *Mail* the completed Refund Tally Section, the receipt(s), and all your UPC symbols in a hand-addressed envelope to:

    (Address)

    Must be postmarked no later than _____.

RULES:
- This certificate must accompany your request. Photocopies or other mechanical copies will not be accepted.
- Limit one refund per household or address.
- Post office box requests will not be honored.
- Allow six to eight weeks for delivery.
- Offer requests must be postmarked by _____.
- Limit one refund per household address. No group's or organization's request will be honored.
- Duplicate submissions will be rejected and proofs of purchase will not be returned.
- Your offer rights may not be assigned or transferred.
- Not responsible for lost, late, illegible, damaged, misdirected, or postage-due mail.
- Offer good only in the United States.
- Offer void where prohibited by law.

REFUND TALLY SECTION

Please indicate the products purchased and your refund:

Product	Quantity	Price	Subtotal
Abc	_____	× $0.00 =	$ _____
Def	_____	× $0.00 =	$ _____
Ghi	_____	× $0.00 =	$ _____
Jkl	_____	× $0.00 =	$ _____
Mno	_____	× $0.00 =	$ _____
TOTAL:	_____	× $0.00 =	$ _____
YOUR TOTAL REFUND			$ _____

Please print clearly

_____
Name

_____
Address

_____
City, State, Zip

_____
Daytime telephone

I *nsight*

Every year air conditioner companies employ the same tactic: refunds. It's a tie game. Trane broke the tie with an Instant Refund to use as a down payment or trade-up or to take to the bank right now—no six- to eight-week wait. But careful! How do you issue checks to dealers? How do you handle returns? The program was limited to qualified dealers and markets.

PLANNING CHECKLIST

_____ **What's your strategy:** slippage? redemption? multiple purchase? account-specific participation? How will you encourage your strategy?

_____ **What are your projections, and on what are they based?** Are there any questionable assumptions that necessitate backup projections for potential problems?

_____ **Have you figured the total cost?** See "Shipping and Handling and Much More" above.

_____ **What's your worst-case scenario?** See "Gambling on Slippage" above.

_____ **Do your retailers allow refunds?** Do they use a cluttered, obscure refund board? If so, how will you notify shoppers about your refund: advertising? the store flyer?

_____ **What are your communication options?**

_____ **Who puts up signage?** Don't count on the retailer. How will those who put it up know what to do? When will they know? How do they verify?

_____ **What are your offer dates?** Is there a grace period?

_____ **Will your rebate forms be out of circulation when the offer expires?**

_____ **Have you verified you can ship refunds in the time specified** on your order form? What if there's a delay?

_____ **Did you make the instructions simple?** For example:
Number each step: 1. Do this. 2. Do this. 3. Do this. And so on.
Or: Buy this. Save this. Send here. Receive this.

_____ **What kind of data should you capture?** Can you actually use the data you collect?

_____ **How can consumers contact you with questions?**

_____ **Are customer service people trained to handle inquiries,** unqualified refund requests, and so on? Are they coordinated with the warehouse so orders can be placed on hold or shipped? Does everyone have brief "What if and how to" sheets?

_____ **Have you created all the forms,** from thank-you notes to "Sorry" letters for nonqualifiers?

_____ **How will the fulfillment resource verify orders and payments,** and what are its internal safeguards?

_____ **Should any literature or offers go along** with your fulfillment? You're already paying for a mailing.

_____ **Is your offer susceptible to professional refunders?** See "Detecting Refund Fraud."

_____ **How will you communicate the program** to sales, distributors, and retail?

_____ **Is the timing sufficient for selling in,** orders, shipping, stocking, and so on?

_____ **Should there be an incentive program** for sales and retail?

_____ **What's the backup plan** if something in the chain goes wrong? What's the substitute program? How is damage control covered?

_____ **Do refund checks have an issue date** and a prominent "Void 60 days after issue date" announcement to aid final reconciliation?

_____ **Do you want a refund check tracking number** matched to the recipient's name?

_____ **Is your refund check protected with antiduplication printing** _and_ instructions to the bank cashing the check, such as:
"This document contains protection against alterations. Absence of these features indicates a copy." (Specify the measures.)

_____ **Have you done a dry run** of the entire process, from request receipt through mailing, documenting, and recording fulfillment? Did you include some test submissions that don't qualify for the refund?

_____ **Have you documented all your work, made profit projections, and written a summary of your hard work and successes to present to management for a raise?**

5

DISCOUNTS

INTRODUCTION: DISCOUNTING IN A RATIONAL WAY

Clearly, we live in an age of discounts, deals, weekend sales, price promotions . . . you name it. Anyone who pays full retail for almost anything these days is either incredibly wealthy or out of touch with reality. Consumers expect discounts and marketers are delivering them.

The question is: How to discount your products or services in a way that is attractive to consumers, channels, dealers, or whomever you want to sell your product to without going broke in the process. Anyone can cut the price. The question is how to do it so that it moves more products more profitably.

The first thing to understand about discounting is that *promotional discounts must be selective and directive.* That simply means the same discount on the same product doesn't have the same effect on every person in the market. Some customers are influenced and react; some don't. So if you cut the price on your product, don't expect people who have never used it before to rush in to buy. There are probably other reasons they haven't responded in the past. Simply changing the price-value relationship for a short period of time won't overcome those objections.

Remember, there are *only three things consumers can do if they respond to a price promotion:* (1) use more of the product through increasing their consumption, (2) use the product in different ways and also use more of it, or (3) stockpile or inventory it for future use. So the second thing to consider before you decide on a discount or reduced price or sale or whatever is to think through what you want customers to do and which groups you want to influence. That will help you identify the level of the discount you are willing to offer, when or where it should be offered, through what channels, and the like.

The third important issue in discounting is that *some products react better to price promotions than do others.* That is, most people have a mental group of products to which they respond when the price is reduced. And they don't respond to others. For example, retail food chains, using extensive price promotion testing programs, have discovered that only about 25 to 30 percent of the products in a store respond to a price cut. You know what they are: bread, milk, colas, ready-to-eat cereals, and the like. Things like canned tuna, charcoal briquettes, floor mops, and canned vegetables just don't generate the interest or enthusiasm that other products do. So don't think by reducing the price you're going to double or triple your business. In some categories you will, but in a large majority of the other, more mundane categories you won't.

The fourth issue is to *exercise moderation in your discounting program.* Being continuously on price discount will, at some point, convince consumers there really is no full retail price—that the discounted price is what they should always be paying. The soft drink companies have gotten themselves into that fix by continuous price promotion. Consumers have learned that if Coke is on sale this week, chances are Pepsi will be on sale the next. So just wait for the promotion. Similarly, there has been so much and such continuous discounting in the category that $4.98 per 24-can case or 99¢ per liter has become the "regular" price in the cola category. When marketers return the price to its traditional shelf price, consumers simply ignore the product and the brand.

Finally, *discounts work best if you promote them.* That seems obvious, but it's not always done. For example, price reductions on the shelf work but not

FIGURE 5.1 *Price Promotion Response Model*

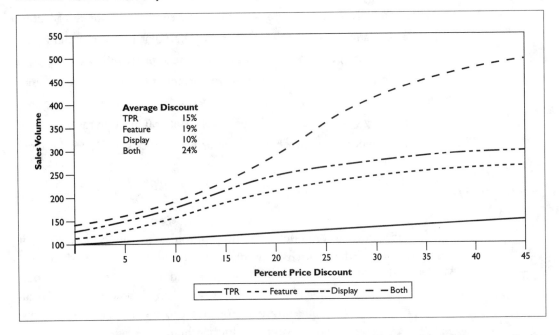

nearly so well as when the discount is promoted through a feature or a display. The chart above shows the typical response rates for four types of price promotions in retail food stores.

Figure 5.1 has been derived from a large number of price promotions in supermarkets over a long period. Although it is not specific to any one product or category, it illustrates the typical response that a price promotion achieves depending on how it is promoted and merchandised.

On the base of the figure, we show the percent discount from the regular price. On the vertical axis, we show the sales volume. Clearly, the greater the percent discount, the greater the volume increase. But the increases are not linear—that is, each of them has a bit of a curve in the response rate. Thus, certain points on the curve are more effective and efficient for the marketer—points where the greatest sales volume occurs with the lowest promotional discount.

The second important thing about Figure 5.1 is that if the price discount is promoted through a feature in the retailer's newspaper ad, circular, or whatever, the increase is greater than simply reducing the price on the shelf. An in-store display added to the price reduction performs better than do the price reduction and advertising feature. And when we combine the price reduction with a feature and a display, sales really soar. The point of the chart in Figure 5.1 is clear. You can generate different sales volume impacts with the same price reduction or discount depending on how you promote it in your store or other facility.

Discounting works and it can be profitable. But you must be rational about how you discount and reasonable about your expectations. —Don E. Schultz

OVERVIEW

Isn't discounting a self-defeating proposition? Why reduce your profit if your product's worth the price? Why encourage consumers to wait for discounts? You know the old joke: "We'll sell it below cost and make up for it in volume."

The fact is that discounting is a complex *and* profitable business. You need to factor how much to discount your products, when, how, and, perhaps most important, how to protect your brand's quality image.

Some higher-priced brands position themselves as discounts. The Men's Wearhouse isn't cheap and it isn't even a warehouse. And Wal-Mart isn't necessarily a bargain.

This chapter describes the many forms of discounts (beyond coupons and refunds in separate chapters). It even describes how to sell a car for $1 over invoice.

DEFINITION

Discounting is motivating purchase of a product or service by temporarily lowering the price to distributors, the trade, and/or consumers. (Again, this definition excludes coupons and refunds.)

Insight

The Lowest Bidder—"It is unwise to pay too much, but it is worse to pay too little. When you pay too much, you lose a little money—that is all. When you pay too little, you sometimes lose everything, because the thing you bought was incapable of doing the thing it was bought to do. The common law of business balance prohibits paying a little and getting a lot—it can't be done."

　—John Ruskin
　　1819–1900

"The more you spend, the more you save!"

　—Virgin Records point of sale

COMMON DISCOUNT OBJECTIVES BY TACTIC

(Also see itemized tactics below.)

TACTIC	OBJECTIVES (Beyond Purchase)
Bartering	Clear out merchandise; flexibility in discount amount; discount on a per customer, opportunistic basis
Trade-in	Increase consumer awareness and motivation to replace existing model
Storewide	Broad-based traffic and storewide shopping; boost slow periods; share of peak periods
Temporary price reduction (TPR)	Traffic generation on high-demand items without discounting other products
Voucher	Encourage purchase of high-ticket items
Future purchase dollars	Apply discount to future visit and purchase; amortize discount with additional purchase; possible vendor tie-in
Member card	Loyalty and frequent shopping; increased transactions per customer; promotional vehicle; database
First 200 shoppers/ First two hours	Drive early traffic to store (when wallets are full) while limiting liability
Fill this bag	Encourage volume shopping with diverse products for wide appeal while limiting liability
Value pack	Load customer—lower demand for competitor; high-dollar value at low cost of goods; increase usage
Twofers (BOGOs)	High-dollar value at low cost of goods; retailer participation with vendor
Bundling	Add discount value while sharing costs with partners; promote usage; move/ liquidate slow partner product
Financing	Encourage major purchase decision; long-term purchase (financing) requirement; overcome financial burden/depressed times; move overstocks; profit from interest
Contract prerequisite ("Club")	Trade up-front discount for extended purchase commitment at higher markups
Loss leader	Customer traffic and additional impulse purchases
Trade allowance	Additional stocking, sales, and promotion by trade, particularly during consumer promotion

ITEMIZED TACTICS

49. BARTERING

Definition   Buyer and seller offer and counteroffer price and terms often in business to business and vendor to retailer; limited in U.S. consumer applications—auto dealers, retailers clearing merchandise, Internet

Advantages
- Allows seller and buyer flexibility in sales process
- Allows creative deals, negotiating options for mutually rewarding terms
- Seller can liquidate unwanted product

Disadvantages
- Time-consuming practice
- Inefficient compared with established pricing
- May alienate buyer and seller
- Complex accounting plus contract
- May project cheap and shady image

50. TRADE-IN

Definition   Marketer offers value on a new model in exchange for old model often for creative topspin

Advantages
- Reminds consumer of deficient unit
- Helps contrast superior new unit
- Purchase incentive
- Provides means of disposing of old unit
- Trade-in units may be refurbished, provide parts, or be donated to charity (goodwill and further trade-in motivation)

Disadvantages
- Extra effort—prospect may opt for a simpler offer
- Trade-in item may have secondary usage, negating motivation to trade in—spare TV, hand-me-down, etc.
- Neglects those with no trade-in item
- Dealer must accommodate trade-in units
- Insurance liability concerns

51. STOREWIDE (DAYS OR HOURS DURATION)

Definition

Items throughout store are discounted—for example, "everything reduced 10%" or "red tag" items in every department

Advantages

- Wide appeal—all departments
- Encourages one-stop, cross-store shopping versus "cherry picking" in different stores
- Encourages impulse purchases
- Consistent percentage discount easily administered
- Retailer and vendor may tie in
- Can boost traffic in slow or peak sales periods

Disadvantages

- Cuts into margins on numerous items
- Susceptible to competitor with deeper discounts on fewer items (see "Everyday Low Price (EDLP) versus High-Low Retail Philosophy," page 140)
- Discounts items that may sell at full markup
- May discourage shopping prior to and after sale
- Consumers may limit shopping only to anticipated storewide sales
- May dilute image
- Storewide select items require repricing execution
- Sale items overlooked in scanner programming cause shopper frustration

52. TEMPORARY PRICE REDUCTION (TPR)

Definition

Short-term price reduction—one week, specific hours, etc.—may apply to one or several items throughout store; items often alter each week

Advantages

- Limited item(s) and time frame limit liability, allows deeper discount
- Short "fuse" encourages prompt response
- Retailer may take credit for vendor discounts (and maintain margins)
- Impulse purchases, possibly throughout store
- Consistent TPR offers build learned behavior for shoppers to visit and look for TPR signs
- Enhances shopping experience with surprise price reductions

- More value perception but less discount for retailer
- Can liquidate undesirable inventory prior to deep clearance discounts

Disadvantages
- Requires constant pricing changes throughout system
- Consumers may shop only the discounted brands within the category—cereals that are on sale—reducing margins and eroding branding
- "Cherry pickers" may purchase only each store's discounted items
- Possible out-of-stock, upsetting shoppers (and sales)
- Discounts limited to specific size/extension can cause confusion and checkout delays
- Competes with "everyday low price" retailer (see "Everyday Low Price (EDLP) versus High-Low Retail Philosophy" on page 140)

53. VOUCHER

Definition
Discount credit certificate toward specific product purchase; similar to a coupon but typically a much higher value and for noncouponing retailers, products, and services

Advantages
- "Free down payment" encourages purchase of high-ticket items
- Gives discount a more prestigious, exclusive inference
- Allows controls, like timing, accounting, product offering, etc.
- More immediate incentive than refund and less expensive to administer
- Numerous targeted mediums

Disadvantages
- Limited to sales avenues that accept the voucher
- Requires training and processing to handle voucher payment
- Susceptible to mistakes and misredemption
- Unlike refunds, no slippage and fewer sales avenues
- Typically requires significant discount amount

54. FUTURE PURCHASE DOLLARS

Definition
Purchase earns dollar value toward future purchase, such as a free gift card or voucher

Advantages	• Motivates immediate purchase • Discount dollars are applied to a future visit and purchase • Amortizes discount over additional purchases • Manufacturer/retailer tie-in opportunity • Clean, simple, motivating, and economical • Can introduce consumer to gift card concept—particularly during holidays
Disadvantages	• Manufacturer tie-in limited to one retailer, and similar value programs must be offered to other retailers (See "Robinson-Patman Act," page 139.) • Delayed reward, limited to retailer's selection may lose out to competitor's immediate discount • "Qualified" discount may not be as appealing as competitor's unqualified discount • Requires system to match and deliver reward according to qualifying purchase

55. MEMBER CARD

Definition	Magnetic-strip card entitles shopper to current discounts activated at checkout; may be part of relationship marketing program; "no-tech" card may simply be presented to cashier for on-sight discount
Advantages	• Rewards and motivates loyal shoppers, particularly fickle coupon users • Can tie in vendors • Easy execution for both shoppers and retailers • Collect and get extension strengthens program with additional long-term rewards (see "Continuity," Chapter 6) • Can provide valuable database benefits • See advantages of temporary price reduction (TPR) on page 129
Disadvantages	• Considerable up-front and ongoing planning, communication, education, and enrollment programs • Competitor discounts (like TPR above) invite everyone, not members only

- Enrollment hassle discourages consumers who may prefer no-strings discounts
- Electronic card requires up-front operational commitment, risk, and ongoing maintenance; consumers grow wary of so many similar programs and cards to carry
- Exit plan necessary if program fails

56. FIRST 200 SHOPPERS/TWO HOURS/200 UNITS

Definition   Discount limited to the first customers to participate for typically high-volume period, such as Thanksgiving Friday

Advantages
- Captures determined shoppers early on a peak sales occasion
- Attracts "full wallets" prior to spending at other locations
- Limits liability—accountable
- Limited number allows exceptional offer
- Opportunity for fun, in-store PR event

Disadvantages
- Limited in scope to the number of shoppers
- May upset those who don't arrive early enough; consider consolation offer
- Neglects many who cannot or will not arrive early
- Often results in long lines long before doors open, alienating many and driving them to competitors
- Subject to poor weather conditions
- "Rush" to enter could get ugly
- Cherry pickers defeat purpose

57. FILL THIS BAG

Definition   Discount on everything shopper fits into promotional shopping bag

Advantages
- Attention-getting format showcases large savings potential yet limited to bag restraints
- Cross-store selection, shopping, and appeal
- Attracts heavy purchasers

- Boosts traffic
- Can target key consumer at prime period, like Halloween or Thanksgiving

Disadvantages
- Requires system and training to register discounts
- Difficult to tie in with vendor for cofunding
- Small, high-profit items can defeat purpose—consider limitations
- Custom bags and distribution may be costly
- Limited to those with bags
- Shoppers may feel uncomfortable or hassled carrying bag, preferring competitor's discount
- May discount many popular items that sell at full markup
- Competes with "everyday low price" positioning

58. VALUE PACK

Definition
Consumer receives 00 percent more product in a bonus package size for the same price as the traditional pack

Advantages
- Offers consumers a good value at a low cost to manufacturer—the actual product cost
- Discountlike incentive without a discounting image—maintains brand integrity
- Allows the powerful word "Free!"
- Manufacturer can pass value directly to consumer without retailer or redemption issues
- Retailer offers value at full markup
- May trade up consumers' purchase behavior
- May extend usage (i.e., more recipe occasions) and family consumption

Disadvantages
- New package size has manufacturing concerns
- Doesn't move current product inventory
- May require additional shelf space and plan-o-gram
- Retailer may favor competitor's sale price with flyer advertising or coupon support (package-delivered promotions don't drive traffic)

59. TWOFERS/SERVICE EXTRA (Buy One–Get One Free = BOGO)

Definition Value on purchase of additional package(s) or services (may be a threefer, etc.)

Examples: buy two and third is free; buy one, get second at half price; clean two room carpets, get third cleaned free

Advantages
- Good, motivating value, possibly at a low cost for goods, though retailer may demand consideration
- Discountlike incentive with less of a discounting image
- Reaches heavy users
- Manufacturer can pass multipack value directly to consumer without retailer or redemption issues; retailer offers value with markup
- Can help load consumer, lowering competitor demand
- Can reduce inventories
- May be less costly than value pack's packaging
- Can be account specific with custom-banded inventory
- May extend usage (i.e., more recipe occasions)

Disadvantages
- Marketer concedes high-margin repeat purchase
- May be less efficient than similar value pack tactic
- Retailer may feel it's a lost sale and desire compensation for "free" item
- Lost "next purchase" for manufacturer
- Multipack a costly manufacturing concern that requires more shelf space
- Consumers may learn to shop only for twofer specials (common with pizza restaurants)
- Must somehow be accounted for at cashier level

60. BUNDLING

Definition Tying related products or services together into one bundled offer for consumers.

Examples: Long distance, Internet, and cell phone services; flashlight and batteries; hotel, rental car, and airline; may also be used to move/liquidate slow partner product (See tie-ins on page 102.)

61. FINANCING (0%, No Money Down, Payment Grace Period)

Definition   Purchase incentive based on financing, such as low/no interest financing, no down payment, or delayed payment requirement; typically for exceptional purchase commitment—auto, home improvement, major appliances, etc.

Advantages   • Encourages considerable purchase decision, possibly with long-term interest profits
                        • Low monthly payments make price appear more feasible
                        • Encourages purchase that may otherwise be a financial burden, particularly in poor economic climate
                        • Can be used to trade up purchase amount
                        • May allow higher price point rather than a discount
                        • Can help move overstocks
                        • May lead to aftermarket purchases

Disadvantages   • May limit profitable financing
                        • Payment delay disrupts business cash flow
                        • Susceptible to bad credit risks
                        • Price remains high, especially with principal
                        • Some buy-on-credit retailers considered exploitive

62. CONTRACT PREREQUISITE

Definition   Consumer receives considerable value up front by committing to prolonged purchase agreement
                        Examples: CD club with first few CDs for pennies; free cell phone with yearlong contract

Advantages   • Exceptional motivating offer
                        • Value built into economics of long-term sales
                        • Future sales can be full margin
                        • Long-term consumer commitment locks out competition and may build consumer affinity
                        • Database relationship marketing opportunities

- Additional sales opportunities in billing statements
- Tie-in opportunities with other marketers

Disadvantages
- Susceptible to bad credit risks, relocation problems, unexpected payment difficulties, contract jumpers, etc.
- May attract less reliable customers—mobile students, lower-income bargain hunters, etc.
- Technology increasingly makes obsolete long-term programs; CD clubs versus Internet downloading; book clubs versus amazon.com
- Consumer may feel conned once full-margin sales kick in
- Requires substantially risky up-front and long-term legal considerations, considerable paperwork, operational systems, computer tracking system, etc.
- Offers often considered exploitative

63. LOSS LEADER

Definition
Product offered below cost to draw traffic to retailer in hopes of additional profitable purchases

Examples: 10¢ bag of apples in produce section; half price introductory porcelain collectible to vest collector; $1 compilation CD hits to all shoppers

Advantages
- More motivating offer than traditional discounts and coupons—more traffic
- Offer expense may only be cost of goods (possibly cofunded by manufacturer)
- Can limit liability (e.g., first 500 shoppers)
- Sampling opportunity for discounted product

Disadvantages
- Sale actually loses revenue
- Traffic limited by item's appeal, small number of discounted choices, and brief time
- Lesser discounts on more items may drive traffic to competitor
- Cherry pickers defeat proposition
- Repeat visitors/purchases defeat proposition

64. TRADE ALLOWANCE

Definition Discount from manufacturer to retailer or distributor for orders or performance (such as price feature or POS placement); a case allowance may deliver a free case for every four purchased; an off-invoice allowance is a credit for specified up-front purchases; allowance may be applied specifically to co-op advertising, logoed premiums, fixtures, etc.

Advantages
- Motivates distributor/retailer to order and stock product
- Can motivate distributor/retailer performance—flyer ads, displays, etc. (which improve everyone's sales)
- Improves distributor/retailer margins
- Case allowance is cost of goods for manufacturer and high margins for retailer/distributor
- Can address slow or peak period objectives
- Off-invoice allowance rewards retailer/distributor for purchase *after* purchase

Disadvantages
- Distributors and retailers may "forward buy"—purchasing discounted products in one region and forwarding to affiliate in another
- Distributors and retailers may stock up during promotion, avoiding future marked-up purchases
- Discounts may not be passed on to consumers, possibly backing up inventory
- Consignment offers run risk of returns and difficult reconciliation
- Distributors/retailers may only purchase product on allowance
- Can be parity with competitor's offers, a mere cost of doing business

WHY DISCOUNT?

Discounts may lessen margins and set undesirable precedents, but following are several good reasons for a discount strategy.

- *Traffic:* Usually, customers purchase more once they're in the store. (Two-thirds of grocery sales are unplanned.)

- *Sales bump:* Sales bumps are key in prime selling seasons—for example, early winter snowblower sales, when sales volume can offset reduced margins, and share of sales is crucial.
- *Discouraging brand switching and new product launches:* Timely discounts can keep consumers from trying a new brand or can take the wind out of a competitor's grand opening. If discounts load consumers, demand falls when the competitor arrives.
- *Retailer placement and features:* A coupon drop or allowance can motivate a retailer to stock and feature a product.
- *Trial:* Motivating consumers to try a product or switch is crucial to conversion.
- *Off-season sales:* Generate sales before or after consumers would normally buy.
- *Trade-up:* Economy sizes can increase buying habits plus usage levels, and it's only cost of goods.
- *Liquidate stock:* Move out the old and make room for the new.
- *Offset price increase:* Ease the initial blow and increase sales with a coupon, refund, or "last chance" discount.
- *Simplicity:* Price reductions are simpler for consumers than are other tactics, so consumers are more likely to respond.

DISCOUNT LAW—SALES MUST BE SALES

Advertising a sale? Check with the Federal Trade Commission (FTC) as well as with your state regulations first. FTC guidelines are general and often unenforced, but they do help establish a benchmark to differentiate legitimate from fraudulent discounting practices. For example, the FTC's official guideline regarding sale prices advises:

One of the most commonly used forms of bargain advertising is to offer a reduction from the advertiser's own former price for an article. If the former price is the actual, bona fide price at which the article was offered to the public on a regular basis for a reasonably substantial period of time, it provides a legitimate basis for the advertising of a price comparison. Where the former price is genuine, the bargain being advertised is a true one. If, on the other hand, the former price being advertised is not bona fide but fictitious—for example, where an artificial, inflated price was established for the purpose of enabling the subsequent offer of a large reduction—the "bargain" being advertised is a false one; the purchaser is not receiving the unusual value he expects. In such a case, the "reduced" price is, in reality, probably just the seller's regular price.

An individual state regulation, for example, may be more specific:

- Price-offs may be utilized only by brands with an established retail price. A 30-day period must be allowed between each of the price-off offers on the brand.
- No more than 50 percent of the total volume of a brand may be generated through price-offs in any 12-month period.
- Only three price-off promotions per year are allowed on any one brand size.
- A price-off must be accompanied by communication that gives the following information clearly:
  – Brand name
  – Regular price
  – New price

Don't mislead consumers. Exercise caution if you're touting such claims as, "Retail Value $15.00, My Price $7.50"; "Half Price Sale"; "1¢ Sale"; and even the word *Free* if it requires the purchase of another product. The spirit of the law: Announce your offer, but don't mislead the consumer. Say *Free* as long as you clearly specify "with purchase of___."

Robinson-Patman Act. Don't favor one retailer over another. You must offer all same-size retailers the same discount structure or promotional value. When you offer different promotions to different retailers, they simply have to wind up being of equal value by year-end. So one grocer may get a $100,000 NFL promotion, whereas another grocer gets a series of local market promotions that total $100,000. You can tier retailer discounts or promotional funds based on order volume. You may sidestep the law short term if your program is a limited test.

EVERYDAY LOW PRICE (EDLP) VERSUS HIGH-LOW RETAIL PHILOSOPHY

EDLP retailers, like Wal-Mart, claim consistently low prices on all products. They position themselves as straightforward, value stores that don't play pricing games and are vulnerable to high-low retailers' select deeper discounts.

High-low retailers regularly rotate discounts, such as Coke this week, Pepsi the next. This may allow deeper discounts but on fewer products. These retailers are vulnerable to EDLP's greater selection of values, lowest-prices image, and cherry pickers.

Both rely heavily on manufacturer discounts.

SHELL GAMES AND FUNNY MONEY

How do you sell a car for a dollar under invoice? How do you sell cosmetics at half price when ideal margins are 40 percent? How do you offer a $5 refund on motor oil when the margin is less than $2? Here's how:

- *Manufacturer year-end rebates:* Rebates based on a retailer's yearlong sales offer a pricing loophole. An auto dealer can legitimately post a car's current invoice cost and coyly price it below that invoice, because the car will ultimately cost less with the year-end rebate.
- *Refund/rebate slippage:* People purchase for the refund, but usually never get around to the paperwork. See "How *Not* to Get Redeemed—Slippage" in Chapter 4, page 105.
- *Points and breakage:* Collector point programs are funny money by nature, in which a lot of points ultimately aren't redeemed—left behind like spare change. See "Breakage and Slippage" in Chapter 10, "Premium Programs," page 272.
- *Artificial price points:* Some marketers inflate regular prices so they can post major discounts later. (See "Discount Law" on page 138.) One way to establish a high price point is to post it in the annual product catalog. Once done, seasonal flyers announce the drastic price cut.
- *False multiple purchase requirement:* A retailer may offer "Six Acme Cereals For $12," when, in fact, each box is $2. Shoppers are misled, thinking they must purchase all six for the discount. (However, sometimes retailers really do require multiple purchases through their scanning sys-

Insight

In addition to *save*, one more powerful word that gets a response is *hurry!* Give your sale a sense of urgency.

tems, especially for BOGO—buy one–get one free—offers.)

- *Perceived price cut:* Studies show that shoppers who see a product prominently displayed believe it's on sale. Often it isn't. Manufacturers often pay retailers for that premium floor space.
- *Mix and match discount tactics:* Use different discounts to build behavior. For example: (1) Lead with a buy-one-get-one-free offer at the shelf for all shoppers—generous offer at cost of goods for trial and repeat trial; and (2) later, offer a lesser discount at the shelf on single purchase plus an in-pack coupon for the next purchase; still gets trial and a repeat purchase and builds on triers of the first tactic. It's less discounting image and doesn't establish a costly pattern.

OPTIONS TO DISCOUNTING

Consider these alternatives to cash discounts:

- *Tie-ins:* Look for a partner who needs something you've got, such as a way to deliver communications or samples, a retail presence, the same target, distribution, and so on. (See Chapter 11, "Tie-ins," page 283.)
- *Value added:* Offer additional products or services that cost you less than the amount consumers would pay. Depending on your business, offer free delivery, or free tire rotation with lube and oil change, or a free premium inside the cereal box, and the like.
- *Upsizing/value packs:* Twenty-five percent more product free. It may not cost much more to add more product, but the consumer value is high.
- *Premium packs:* Make the package itself valuable—a decorative tin, decanter, storage box, or collectible images.

HOW TO HANDLE POTENTIAL PROBLEMS

Consider potential problems before implementing a discount. Following are several:

- How will the cashier ring it up? Fast food may have a register button that triggers the discount, but how will you reply to: "Can I substitute milk for the Coke?" Anticipate situations on a tip sheet.
- With "scan-downs," the bar code generates the discount, but the programmer may miss one. Give cashiers discount sheets, including how to manually keypunch in the discount.
- Franchise networks often can't control pricing. Mike's True Value is truly Mike's store, and Mike will sell his Stanley Tools for whatever he can get. So the franchise company's "Annual Spring Cleaning Tools Blowout" advertising may say, "Great Deals Throughout the Store," even though the company qualifies specific offers with "at participating retailers." Local franchise groups may agree on specific deals for their market's advertising.
- Scan-downs cost more than the discount. A manufacturer may need to factor in up to 25 percent more to a scanned discount because of rain checks or overlapping sale days. (The retailer sales period may be Thursday through Wednesday, for example, whereas the manufacturer's is Monday through Sunday.)
- Get distributors and retailers to pass discounts on to consumers. Make the consumer offer part of the distributor's or retailer's discount package. Consider the following:
  - Offer retailers a discount in exchange for "price features" in their advertising and displays. You may have to pay extra for flyer space.
  - Offer more co-op funds when retailers provide advertising tear sheets—newspaper reprints proving they promoted your discount.
  - Advertise the promotion in consumer media with the tag "at participating locations." Do the same in trade publications so retailers hear about your deal even if the distributors don't tell them.
  - Tie retailers in with your advertising. Put a five- to ten-second tag at the end of your broadcast ad: "Available now at Acme stores."
  - Offer a complete incentive program—include the regional sales manager, salespersons, retailer, and consumers. (See Chapter 12, "Performance Programs," page 311.)

Beware forward buying. Central buyers may reroute your discount: If you earmark discounts for one region or chain, they may purchase that discounted product and forward it to another region/chain. Or they may stock up on the discounted product and warehouse it to avoid future full-margin prices. Is this really a bad thing? If so, put terms in your program that can limit quantities or specify the region or retailer.

Combo discounts yield greater profits. Fast-food combo orders save diners money and increase profits. The add-on item(s) may cost pennies but represent dollar values.

One side order	**Combo "deal" w/two side orders**
$1.29 sell price	$2.58 sell price ($1.29 × 2)
.05 cost	− .10 cost
$1.24 net	−1.00 discount (50¢ per side order)
	$1.48 net

Net Net: 24¢ incremental profit over two-item full-price order.

Combo menus and features speed up sales *and* lines. Customers need time to ponder several order choices. If you make it easy with five large feature items, they say, "Number 3, please," and the next customer can order. It speeds up the crew too. One theater chain implemented a combo signage program backed with a crew incentive, and its sales doubled—crucial in the brief window between features.

"Suggested retail." This ploy and guideline lets manufacturers and retailers offer a profitable price with a lot of wiggle room for discounting. Manufacturers can't dictate retailer prices, but they can provide their suggested retail price as a guideline, which typically represents a high margin. So if either or both want to discount, there's plenty of fat to trim and show consumers generous savings.

SELLING IN A DISCOUNT TO THE RETAILER

Arm salespeople with a sell sheet that outlines the benefits of a product and why it's good for the retailer's business. Include a profit calculator that lets the salesperson calculate the retailer's bottom-line profits. Here's an example of one from the distilled spirits business:

Acme Whiskey	Cost/ Case	Discount	Net Case Cost	Sell Price	Profit/ Case	% Sales Increase	Incremental Profit/Case
1.75 Liter							
Liter							
750 ML							
500 ML							
200 ML							

(Also see page 351.)

Consider "turns/month" for a monthly and yearly profit figure. Also include helpful specifications like case weight, case cube size, cases per pallet, and case dimensions. You're closing the sale!

GUIDELINES

Discounting factors. If you can generate sales without discounting, do it. But occasionally, you may have to combat competitors or simply grab more share in a prime sales period. Discounts may also increase usage so that loyal customers become bigger customers. Factor in how many *new customers* you can target with a sale. They may come back for more at full price. (See "Calculating volume increase requirements" below.)

"We'll make up for it in volume." A discount can substantially increase sales, but at what cost? Refer to the Price Promotion Response Model on page 125 and to the formula under "Budgeting Guidelines" (below) to calculate how large a volume increase you'll need to make up for the pricing decrease.

Make pricing a strategy, not a reaction. Discounting should be a promotional marketing tactic, not a knee-jerk solution to slow sales. Review the above tactics with a strategic perspective.

How much should you discount? It's all relative. Some say discounts must be a minimum of 15 to 20 percent off the regular price to have much effect. Retail-generated discounts are frequently 10 percent, often storewide, or for a large family of products. High-margin products like jewelry and apparel may discount 80 percent! Commodities, like sugar, use very low-value coupons. Lower-selling brands probably need larger reductions than do sales leaders. Balance your objectives: Larger discounts tend to attract new triers, whereas smaller discounts help maintain current users. If the vendor and retailer partner, they can offer a larger discount than their respective competitors acting alone. If you need to get rid of old inventory, breaking even may save money on overhead.

Confirm stocks and timing. If you're having a sale, stock more, and make sure your supply chain is stocked and can deliver on time. Use historical data for projections. Also, there's often a residual effect after the sale. Have a backup plan, such as similar merchandise ("of equal or greater value") or rain checks.

Selling out is safe, but be prepared. Many marketers prefer to sell out of a product than to be overstocked, but consumers may complain it's a bait and switch. Have a rain check system, making it clear when the new stock is expected. Train the staff for rain checks and delegate authority to the store manager for tough customers. For substitute products, specify "equal or greater value" product substitutions.

Are your discounts reaching consumers? The 2003 Cannondale Associates Trade Promotion Spending & Merchandising Study reveals that 63 percent of retailers claim they are passing money directly through to consumers, but only 55 percent of manufacturers agree. Try to verify, or at least encourage, performance by hiring a scanning verification or other auditing service, requesting feature advertising tear sheets, or demanding other proofs of performance.
Source: Cannondale Associates Trade Promotion Spending & Merchandising Study.

"While Supplies Last." This disclaimer does two things: It alerts consumers there are no guarantees, alleviating potential complaints. Second, it gives a sense of urgency to hurry up and buy. Still, have a backup plan so you don't upset consumers.

A discount posted on your package has a long journey. You'll need to do a lot of coordination if you plan to advertise a package-delivered offer that coincides with the package arriving on the shelf. Consult manufacturing first about packaging lead times. Then review the distribution process to determine when the product actually reaches the shelf.

A discount costs more than a discount. Factor in advertising, signage, sales materials, package labels, allowances, misredemptions, and so on. See "Calculating volume increase requirements" below.

Don't be shy about discounts. Your ad agency may object to a prominent "Sale!" announcement, but if oblivious shoppers fail to see the offer, you've lost the sale.

Leave a blank price spot on retail signs. Vendors should allow retailers room to boldly write in their special price on the display sign. Leave a prominent blank price circle or square on the sign (without varnish). Try making it 20 to 30 percent of the sign's size.

Don't discount your image. Discounting too much may give a perception of poor quality. Many fast-food operations have actually lowered volume through discounting, while simultaneously lowering their margins—"If it costs that little, I'm afraid to eat it." What's more, consumers may anticipate and wait for discounts, so you reduce your ongoing higher margin sales— Coke this week, Pepsi the next. Consider giving a reason for your discount "event," even if it's as pedestrian as a President's Day Sale. Some retailers make the discount appear rare: "This sale only comes once a year!" doesn't mean you don't have other sales. You can make the discount require a higher transaction size—second item is half price. Direct mail or the Internet can announce something like "Exclusive pre-Thanksgiving offers only for our Special Customers." It's hoped those special customers e-mail the coupons to their friends.

BUDGETING GUIDELINES

Calculating a markup percentage. Markups are usually expressed as a percentage. If you know the dollar increase you want, use this calculation to reveal a percentage:

Dollar markup amount ÷ sell = Markup percentage
Example: Markup = 42¢. Cost = 99¢. (Therefore, sell = $1.41)
$0.42 ÷ $1.41 = 30% markup
Proof: $1.41 × 30% = $0.42 markup

Calculating a markup dollar figure. If you want to mark up a cost by a percentage, use this calculation to determine the marked-up sell price:

Cost ÷ [1.00 − Markup %] = Marked-up sell price
Example: Cost = $0.99. Markup = 30%
$0.99 ÷ .7 (i.e., 1.00 − .3) = $1.41 sell price
Proof: 30% × $1.41 = $0.42 $1.41 − $0.42 = $0.99

Calculating volume increase requirements. Budgeting a discount program requires a balance of the costs of media, point-of-sale materials, and other communication; any sales incentives; the margins lost in discounting; and incremental profits gained through greater sales volume.

Before you discount, calculate how much volume you need to make up for the margin loss. A simple formula reveals your breakeven volume requirement:

1. Current volume/period × current margin = x
2. Increased volume (v) = x ÷ new margin
   Example: You've decided to lower your margin from 40 percent to 35 percent, and your current volume is 90 units a month. (*v* stands for the volume you need to achieve a breakeven at the lower margin.)
   1. 90 units/month × 40% = 36 (*x* in above formula)
   2. v = 36 ÷ .35 (new margin)
      v = 103
      You have to sell 103 units at a 35 percent margin to break even with selling 90 units at a 40 percent margin.
      Proof: 90 × 40% = 36
      103 × 35% = 36
   (The above numbers are rounded.)

However, you'll incur additional promotion and communication costs. Consider the following:

- Project all the costs for advertising creative, media, point of sale, training, rain checks (redeemed during unpromoted period), sales incentives, and so on.
- Divide that number by the dollar profit margin per discounted sale to determine the volume necessary to cover those costs.
- Add this communication and promotion volume requirement to the previous calculation for volume increase/margin loss.

Example:
Total program cost:　$100,000
Discount margin:　　$2 (profit per discounted sale)
100,000 ÷ $2 = 50,000 unit sales to break even with program cost
Proof: $2 × 50,000 = $100,000

Adding the two volume numbers from the formulas above reveals the total volume your discount must generate to break even. However, consider such other factors as the impact of loading the consumer with product and a subsequent sales decline.

Use sales history for projections and consider these variables:

- Advertising mediums
- Advertising reach and frequency
- Advertising creative effectiveness
- Selling season
- Seasonality (which varies regionally if you're selling clothes, air conditioners, ice cream, lawn and garden items, etc.)
- Regionality—right down to neighborhoods and demand
- Retail traffic (during promotion period subject to many variables)
- Retailer participation, such as flyers and product placement
- Promotional point of sale (a huge factor)
- Discounting tactic—card program versus storewide versus contract versus value pack versus rebate, and so on
- Amount of discount
- Competitive activities
- Weather
- And a lot more

Insight

Discounting may sound like a low-profit proposition, but the largest retailer in the nation, Wal-Mart, built a brand on "Always low prices."

TRACK RESULTS!—BUILD A LEARNING CURVE

Create a spreadsheet for all the above variables every time you run a discount. You'll gradually build a database that will make your projections better and better.

TRADE DEALS—PROMOTIONAL ALLOWANCES

The bartering system is alive and well when it comes to wheeling and dealing with manufacturers' sales reps and retailers. (See "Trade Programs," Chapter 13.)

CONTINUITY

(Also see "Performance Programs," Chapter 12)

INTRODUCTION:
THE DATA MAY BE WORTH MORE THAN THE SALE

Over the past few years, continuity, or loyalty programs, as they are sometimes called, have been one of the fastest growing forms of sales promotion. Yes, the number of coupons has exploded. The number of price discounts continues to expand. The volume of point of purchase seems to grow exponentially, but continuity programs are really the hottest ticket today. Whether you're talking about airline programs or supermarket customer cards or frequent "stayers" or "visitors," or whatever, continuity programs are the thing most every marketer believes he or she needs to do.

Much of the interest has come from a number of books and articles written by such "loyalty" gurus as Frederick Reicheld, Earl Sasser, Frederick Newell, and others. In his work *The Loyalty Effect* (Harvard Business Press, 1996), Reicheld demonstrates convincingly that loyal customers are more profitable customers. Therefore, every marketer is chasing customer loyalty, and continuity programs are one way to build, or at least encourage, that loyalty.

The only problem is that continuity and loyalty programs often carry a hefty price tag (e.g., getting sign-ups, maintaining the records, funding the reward programs, etc.). And as most marketers have learned to their chagrin, once you start a continuity program—at least one where customers expect to generate rewards over time—it's really difficult to stop or withdraw from the scheme. Customers who are halfway to a trip to Hawaii fight like tigers to keep the program going until they can redeem their trip.

The advantages and disadvantages of continuity programs follow in the chapter so we cover that later. It is important to know, however, that a continuity program should not be evaluated simply on the continuing sales it generates or even the increased loyalty it can engender with ongoing customers. Sure, there are returns, but the real value of a continuity program is the customer data that come along with it. A continuity program may provide more value in helping marketers understand their customers (i.e., what they buy, when they buy, what products they buy individually and together, and a whole host of other information about customer behavior) than do the increased sales it might initially generate. It's the data that count in continuity as much as the sales increases.

Much customer marketplace understanding comes from the ongoing capture, storage, and analysis of purchase data that come from customers' continuous use of the loyalty or continuity card. The card is the basis for the demonstrable data that commonly show that a relatively small number of customers account for a disproportionate amount of a marketer's or a brand's business. The 80/20 rule some call it. Indeed, it is more important to know who the most valuable customers are than it is to know market share, sales volume, or a host of other traditional measures.

The key ingredient in continuity programs is the willingness of the customer to use the card or identification number or whatever is used to connect the customer to his or her purchases. That means there must be some reward for the customer—more than just "happy faces" at the till—for customers to agree to let the marketing organization capture information. The key question from the customer is always: "What am I going to get in return?" Thus, continuity programs require meticulous planning if they are to succeed.

Many marketers don't know very much about their customers. Oh, they can make guesses or estimates about them, such as that they are generally between the ages of 18 and 34 or they live in upscale suburbs or they seem to be better educated than is the general population. But beyond that, unless they have some way to capture data or information through something like a frequent shopper card or a continuity program, marketers are generally guessing or, worse, assuming that customers are the types of people they want to serve. So the data from continuity programs become invaluable. They can be used to sort out which customers are most valuable, whether in terms of sales or of profits; which ones respond to promotions and to which promotions; which ones are "promotion-only" buyers and which are full-price purchasers. In other words, the data that flow from a continuity program, if properly managed, can be a gold mine of information that can make the organization a better marketer and you a more successful promotion manager.

But many argue they can't develop a continuity program. Customers pay cash, or they won't carry a card, or we can't keep the necessary records, and on and on. All of those are fine excuses, but they are just that—excuses. Any marketer can build a successful continuity program if he or she wants to, and it can often be done fairly inexpensively. Just look at what Starbucks has done with its Starbucks Card. Why would a company like Starbucks, one of the most successful retailers and brands in recent history, launch a continuity program? It already has a very loyal core of customers for most of its stores. The reason: to learn who their customers are, where they live, how often they visit the store, their migration patterns, and all the other things that make a good marketer a *great* marketer. Sure, Starbucks expects to sell more cups of latte or cappuccino or bags of coffee beans. And it likely expects that having a frequent-shopper card helps build more brand loyalty among the customers who carry it, assuming those customers will not be as likely to stray into other, competing coffee emporiums. But the real value to Starbucks is in knowing who its customers are, how often they visit, how much they spend, and all the other data that come along with card usage. That's probably worth more than the customer loyalty that the continuity program may build.

Clearly, one of the key things successful marketers know better than do their competitors is their customers. And continuity programs are a great way to learn about customers on an ongoing basis. Indeed, the data may be worth more than are the results of the promotion. —Don E. Schultz

OVERVIEW

If there's anything better than a customer, it's a repeat customer. A rule of thumb: *It costs five times more to get a new customer than it costs to retain a current one.* A good continuity program generates more sales from each customer. And loyal customers spend more. One supermarket study revealed that a loyalty card based on customers' transaction size was about four times that of noncardholders' transactions. There's also the 80/20 rule of thumb: 80 percent of a company's business is generated by 20 percent of its customers.

Shorter-term programs, like a collector card, can establish a usage pattern. Convenience stores cite that it takes three to five visits to establish a visiting pattern.

Sophisticated programs can build customer relationships by utilizing data on personal preferences, birth dates, purchase patterns, and the like, and then customizing programs to a customer's profile.

Some continuity programs are profit centers; for example, airlines sell miles to tie in partners for additional continuity programs. In business-to-business applications, retailers, distributors, office supply managers, and others may earn rewards or rebates for ongoing orders.

This chapter helps you evaluate and implement various programs to retain customers as well as to increase their purchases.

COMMON CONTINUITY OBJECTIVES BY TACTIC

TACTIC	OBJECTIVES (Beyond purchase and those cited above)
Collect and get	Shorter-term, immediate motivation to repurchase Build sustained or increased usage behavior Lock in a key sales period Combat new competitor or competitor's activities
Loyalty	Establish long-term customers Discourage switching Build customer relationship through database profiling Foundation for short-burst, opportunistic promotions (like double points) Value perception for premium-priced product

TACTIC	OBJECTIVES (Beyond purchase and those cited above)
Relationship (database)	Establish long-term affinity and sales with customer Build knowledge of individual customer profile and promote specifically to that profile Increase purchase frequency Leverage profiling asset for tie-ins Provide easy, electronic-point accumulation for customer Value perception for premium-priced product
Club/contract	Establish immediate loyalty commitment Exceptional number of full markup purchases over extended period May collect up-front membership fees
Collector series	Engage consumer with collectible mystique Suspend, then continue, program opportunistically Reinforce icon or logo (holiday ornaments, steins, etc.) Enhance image and value perception Performance reward for sales and distribution
Collect and win	Economical motivation for continued purchases Increase excitement and awareness Motivate retail participation through sweepstakes excitement and sales Communicate product attribute through creative theme
Business to business	Motivate sales performance and customer purchase with incremental goal Establish long-term commitment, such as year-end refund; become part of customer's budgeting in the process Sales training, buyer education vehicle

ITEMIZED TACTICS

65. COLLECT AND GET—REFUND

Definition   Shorter-term program rewards series of purchases with refund; a tiered structure increases the value per purchase with increased purchases (Business applications may be long term.)

Advantages
- Encourages series of purchases with short-term, easily achievable reward goal
- Slippage—customers purchase for reward but never do paperwork (see "Rebates/Refunds," Chapter 4, page 106)
- Establishes usage pattern

- Can lock in sales during key period
- Can combat competitive offers once consumers are vested in collecting
- Can increase average purchase rate
- Easier to administer than merchandise
- Accountable
- Business-to-business incentive for prolonged, increased purchases and simultaneously discouraging returns

Disadvantages
- Proliferation of card/collect programs
- Delayed reward lowers participation—vulnerable to competitor's instant gratification program
- Considerable costs and executional details—collector vehicles, verifications, consumer and staff instructions, fulfillment, etc.
- Cash less economical than merchandise (see "Sweepstakes," Chapter 2, "Prizes," page 34)
- Too many requirements, such as save, circle prices, fill out data request, etc., discourage participation
- May upset customers if deadline expires
- Misredemption—wrong product proofs, insufficient proofs, erroneous calculations, etc.
- In business-to-business applications, returns (consignment) may negate benefits while adding reconciliation difficulties

66. COLLECT AND GET—MERCHANDISE/SERVICE

Definition
Shorter-term program rewards series of purchases with merchandise; reward value per purchase may increase with increase of purchases

Advantages
(See "Collect and Get—Refund" above)
- Merchandise/services can cost less than their retail value versus cash refund
- Partners can offer economies
- Can be a fun, involving, game format (and sweepstakes overlay)
- Merchandise rewards are far more memorable than cash-sustained gratitude.

Disadvantages	(See "Collect and Get—Refund" above)

- Merchandise more difficult to administer than is a refund—shipping, stocking, warehousing, etc.
- Merchandise is subject to quality flaws, missed deadlines, etc.
- Merchandise offering may not have universal appeal
- Relies on high-premium demand to succeed
- Additional retail staff tasks—may require incentive
- Retail execution can be sloppy with unaccountable collector pieces
- Possibility of underordering or overordering merchandise

67. COLLECT AND GET—FREE/DISCOUNTED PRODUCT

Definition	Program rewards series of purchases with free or discounted products

Advantages	(See "Collect and Get—Refund" above)

- Economical rewards—cost of goods
- Desirable reward—more of what shopper already purchases
- Reward easy and economical to administer
- In business to business, provides incentive for prolonged, increased purchases—no costs until products are purchased

Disadvantages	(See "Collect and Get—Refund" above)

- May cannibalize sales by consumers who would have purchased free product
- May exclude less-frequent-purchasing consumers
- Consumers may prefer competitor's more exciting reward alternative, such as a movie ticket instead of a widget

68. COLLECT AND GET—ESCALATED PLAN

Definition	Collect and get reward escalates with more purchases at a greater proportionate rate (Buy three, get $3, buy four, get $5, etc.)

Advantages	

- Escalating value encourages more purchases
- Can increase incremental purchase levels per consumer

(See "Collect and Get—Refund" and "Merchandise" above)

Disadvantages
- Escalating value also reduces margins
- More complex and difficult accounting and redemption process
- Complexity may discourage participation and cause mistakes
(See "Collect and Get—Refund" and "Merchandise" above)

69. LOYALTY—FREQUENT BUYER

Definition
Reward values accumulated over prolonged period/usage and redeemable on an ongoing basis (Frequent Flyer or Frequent e-tailer Buyer programs); often tied to database relationship program

Advantages
- Builds long-term loyalty
- Increases purchases
- Discourages switching
- Can build relationship with customer
- Foundation for short-burst, opportunistic promotions (like double points)
- Value perception for premium-priced product, such as high-interest credit cards or premium-priced e-tailer
- Potential profit center, selling points (like airline miles) to partners
- Convenient for customers—electronic point accrual
- Breakage economies—leftover, unredeemed points
- Once in place, administration can be economical with electronic and database efficiencies

Disadvantages
- Limited to applications with dedicated, sophisticated billing systems and to frequently purchased products with high transaction sizes
- Costly setup with new database, administrative and fulfillment systems, and communication programs for both consumers and personnel
- Major up-front commitment regardless of future success; requires exit plan
- Future program operations may rely on original system's integrity and flexibility
- May be less effective than immediate reward programs
- Competitors may have more flexible and opportunistic options

- Consumer perception of inflated pricing
- Difficult to implement in independently owned franchises
- Requires trained question and complaint call-in center
- May be a parity program with competitor
- Requires broad appeal reward selection
- Corporations may require lower-priced alternative suppliers
- Unforeseen market and technology shifts can jeopardize long-term goals and investment

70. LOYALTY—ELECTRONIC CARD

Definition   Frequent buyer program in which an electronic card is used as the point collection or instant savings device

Advantages

- Basically the same as "Loyalty—Frequent Buyer" above, with a card, allowing more flexibility in purchases, visits, offers, and customization
- May cost less to set up than "Loyalty—Frequent Buyer"
- Easy for consumer

Disadvantages

- Limited to applications with frequent purchases (more appropriate for retailer than for a single manufacturer)
- May require advanced system capable of capturing and manipulating transaction data
- Proliferation of card programs
- Requires major up-front commitment, regardless of future success; have an exit plan
- Future operations and flexibility may rely on the original system's integrity
- May require extensive communication materials for consumers and staff
- Magnetic cards have limited data storage capabilities
- Consumer may forget or lose card—backup required
- May give competitors more flexible and opportunistic options
- Difficult to implement with independent franchise operators

71. LOYALTY—PREMIUM CATALOG PROGRAM

Definition

Consumers choose reward from a catalog selection for achieving purchase (or performance) goals; sustained but not a permanent program—often low-tech or with Web site alternative

Advantages

- Allows sustained loyalty program without the extreme frequent buyer program costs
- Flexible for promotion extensions, double points, and reward specials
- Diverse reward appeal
- Merchandise has economies over cash and is memorable for sustained gratitude
- Tiered reward values allow heavy and moderate users to participate
- Builds product usage pattern
- Vested participants may ignore competitor offers
- Unlimited reward potential can increase purchases and performance
- Accountable
- Breakage economies—leftover points
- No overordered or underordered reward concerns
- Reward costs not incurred until products are purchased
- Catalog vendors provide proven tracking, ordering, and fulfillment services

Disadvantages

- Requires sufficient margins and sales frequency to motivate and pay out
- Prone to human error, both with consumer forms and administration personnel—requires policies
- Competitors may have more flexible and opportunistic alternative programs
- Materials cost—catalogs, stamps, how-to communication, etc., for both staff and consumers
- Rewards *may* need to be purchased up front and incur warehousing expenses and liability
- Merchandise subject to quality flaws, missed deadlines, etc.
- May upset customers if deadline runs out
- In business-to-business applications, returns (consignment) may negate benefits while adding reconciliation difficulties
- Corporations may not allow buyer incentive programs (See "Performance Programs," Chapter 12)

72. RELATIONSHIP (DATABASE)

Definition   Frequent-buyer program that also tracks and profiles consumer behavior and then markets according to each consumer's personal profile

Advantages
- Builds more effective marketing programs, addressing individual profiles, purchase cycles, reward preferences, aspirations, etc.
- Shows appreciation for continued patronage
- Can build lifelong consumer relationship recognizing changes in consumer's lifestyle and behavior over time
- More effective motivation through individualized rewards and timing
- Discourages switching
- Platform for additional promotions, like double points
- Tie-in programs (leverage profiling for partner contributions)
- Value perception for premium-priced product
- Convenient for customers—automatic point accrual
- Breakage economies—leftover, unredeemed points

Disadvantages
- Limited to applications with sophisticated billing systems and to frequently purchased products with high transaction sizes
- Extremely costly setup with sophisticated, custom hardware and software, ongoing programming, continuous analysis and updating, and administrative and fulfillment systems, as well as communication programs for both consumers and personnel
- Major up-front commitment regardless of future success; requires exit plan
- Future program operations may rely on original system's integrity
- May be less effective than immediate reward programs
- Competitors may have more flexible and opportunistic options
- Consumer perception of inflated pricing
- Requires trained question and complaint call-in center with hardware and custom software investment
- Requires broad appeal reward selection
- Unforeseen market and technology shifts can jeopardize long-term goals and investment

73. CLUB/CONTRACT

Definition	Reward given up front in exchange for long-term commitment for continued purchases (book clubs, bank account, magazine subscription reward, free cell phone with service, etc.)

Advantages

- Immediate generous reward lures consumers
- Commitment to purchase products for extended period, possibly at full markup
- May lock out competition
- Economical cost per sale
- Appeals to most profitable frequent users
- Promotes higher-volume purchase levels
- Accountable
- Simple administration *after* initial setup
- Can build ongoing customer relationship

Disadvantages

- May suffer exploitative image
- Long commitment to unspecified pricing discourages prospects
- Eventually susceptible to price competition
- Many consumers default, requiring remedial actions and jeopardizing profits
- Consumers may jump to next offer at earliest possibility
- Expensive direct and telemarketing setup and maintenance
- May require advertising and media
- Unforeseen market shifts can jeopardize expensive commitment (CDs to mp3s)
- Major initial commitment and expense

74. COLLECTOR SERIES

Definition

Free or value-priced series of premiums offered with ongoing visits/purchases—fast-food–licensed toy characters, in-pack baseball cards, holiday ornaments, etc.

Advantages

- Immediate *and* sustained purchase incentive
- Premiums cost less than cash value

- Can be self-liquidated
- Builds excitement and awareness, especially with popular property
- Can target specific profile
- Can become a yearly equity event with a following
- Can establish or refresh an icon for the brand
- Collector aspect enhances value perception
- Provides performance reward for sales and distribution

Disadvantages
- Financial risk in producing, warehousing, shipping items that may not prove popular
- Extensive cost and lead time to manufacture exclusive items, especially imports, which also require a reliable on-site monitor
- Merchandise consumes valuable retail space
- Redemption can hold up customer lines
- Licensed properties are costly and can be risky (may not prove popular)
- Limited offering may have limited appeal
- Requires staff and customer communication
- Near-pack items frequently stolen (see "Near-pack" section in Chapter 10, "Premium Programs," page 279.)
- Occasional users less motivated—can't collect all items
- May be vulnerable to competitive price promotions

COLLECT AND WIN

See description in Chapter 2, "Sweepstakes and Contests," page 25.

BUSINESS-TO-BUSINESS APPLICATIONS

Although the above descriptions apply primarily to consumers, they can also be applied to salespeople, retailers, or distributors. However, many companies don't allow employees to participate in vendor reward programs. In these cases, consider rewards for the business itself—free product, training, equipment, or even a donation to its favorite charity. Some chains may authorize a promotion at headquarters and then leave it up to each store manager whether to participate.

It may be difficult finding out whom you really want to motivate—the corporate purchasing agent or the end user. The computer personnel may use your media products, but the corporate buyer actually places the order. You may need to advertise to the end user and promote to the buyer. Take advantage of your target's trade magazines.

(See also "Performance Programs," Chapter 12.)

BUDGETING

Designing a program and budgeting for it go hand in hand. Determine how much you can spend to increase your sales, say 3 to 10 percent, and then divvy up that money between reward cost, communication, fulfillment, and administration. After that, start calculating point values that ultimately fund both. (See below.)

Materials Checklist

Check off what you need to budget for from the list below (your company's various departments may already have cost histories for some):

_____ Advertising media
_____ Advertising creative
_____ Advertising production
_____ Point-of-sale signage, flyers, instructions, etc.
_____ Collector pieces (stamps, game pieces, etc.)
_____ Collection devices (like point tally boards)
_____ Point statements (for direct billing applications)
_____ Rewards
_____ Reward catalogs, folders, flyers
_____ Submitting and reporting redemptions for accounting
_____ Warehousing—rewards, point of sale, collateral, etc.
_____ Fulfillment costs for mail-in programs—processing, pick and pack, packages, cartons, postage, etc.
_____ Rain checks or other kinds of deferral forms for out-of-stocks
_____ Ongoing communication to sustain momentum:
　　　_____ New reward offers
　　　_____ Newsletter

_____ Regular flyers

_____ Letterhead (including design and several applications)

_____ Program instructions—for consumers, field managers, store managers, employees, etc.

_____ Motivational programs for managers, staff, etc., if needed—including rewards, communication, break room posters, etc.

_____ Promotional novelties—caps, buttons, etc.

_____ Program administration—order taking, processing, etc.

_____ Handling, verifying, fulfilling, and filing redemptions

_____ Customer service for questions and problems—for consumers, regional managers, retailers, etc.—800 numbers, mail-back replies, retailer hot lines, etc.

_____ Database, including what you want to capture—how it's reported, how it's retrieved, and how often

_____ Program tracking and overall monitoring

_____ Program reporting—from field to warehouse shipping to database

_____ Contingency fund—consider 10 percent for the unforeseen

(See "Shipping and Handling and Much More" in Chapter 4, page 108.)

Some Budgeting Criteria

Answering the following questions can be a guide to budgeting:

- How much of your current discounting can this program replace?
- Will your rewards cost less than discounts through tie-in partners or wholesale versus retail value?
- What and how much are all the communication and operation costs?
- Who are the target customers and what are they worth? You may gain big with a few heavy users and lose with lots of lesser users as a result of processing costs.
- Less frequent users may prefer the competitor's simple discounts; is that a bad thing?
- How will a loyalty program impact your discount practices? Good riddance to cherry pickers. Will couponers switch without coupons? Will you lose margins rewarding heavy users or increase purchase levels?
- How will your new Sunday newspaper ad compare with that of your couponing competitor's ad? For example, if your competitor boasts

"Up to $10 in savings this week," can you advertise "Up to $780 in savings this year—$15 a week!"? Because enrollment makes or breaks some continuity programs, consider launching yours with a generous offer.

- How much does it cost to offer and redeem a 55¢ coupon compared with 55¢ worth of points—communication materials, fulfillment costs, and so on? (See topic of redemption costs in Chapter 3, "Coupons," page 82.)

Budgeting Benchmarks

You may want to first divide your budget into three areas: (1) rewards; (2) communication; and (3) administration.

Rule of thumb: Consider 50 percent of your budget for rewards; 25 percent for communication; and 25 percent for administration.

Another rule of thumb: Loyalty marketing agencies often allocate 5 percent of their total budget for developing the plan.

Gross reward budget formula. Amount you can spend per purchase × projected purchases *by participating consumers* (heavy and moderate users) minus cost of communication minus cost of implementation equals reward budget. However, this assumes 100 percent redemption.

Collect and get reward formula. This is for the short term, such as asking consumers to purchase a few items and receive a premium in the mail. Following is the formula:

Number of purchases per person you desire* × Amount you can spend for those per-person purchases = Reward budget per person

Reward budget per person (above) × Projected number of people who will qualify with that purchase amount × Projected percentage of actual redeemers** = Total projected reward budget

(Use this number to negotiate your bulk reward purchase. Purchase quantity: Projected number of people who will qualify for reward × Projected percentage of actual redeemers.*)

*Base projected purchases on incremental sales gains—not average sales. Otherwise, you're paying for a flat performance. If average sales per person are five, go for six.

**What percentage of customers will actually save wrappers, fill out forms, address and stamp an envelope? Base your slippage on previous similar offers. (See Chapter 4, "Rebates and Refunds," page 106 for example. Also see "Coupons," page 83.)

Incremental sales! Retaining current customers is crucial, but if you don't increase sales and profits, you're treading water. Your total budget may come solely from a percentage of incremental profits.

Incremental volume requirements. See "Discounts," "Budgeting Guidelines," page 146.

Motivation threshold. If the reward doesn't motivate meeting the purchase requirement, forget it. Refer to past promotion history, interview focus groups, and study similar programs by other companies. If you can't afford a merchandise reward, consider a free product, a discount offer, a tie-in partner offer, or a refund (with potential slippage).

Calculating a Point

The value of a point is up to you. First, structure your reward system so that rewards are desirable and attainable for consumers. Giving high quantities of points adds perceived value to your program, such as 1,000 points for every dollar purchase. It also provides flexibility, so you can offer double-point promotions on occasion (e.g., preseason items or overstocks). High-point-per-dollar numbers can also establish milestones for consumers to strive for (by purchasing more). Your reward plateaus can be 50,000, 100,000, 200,000, and so on. Consider all factors that influence the overall margins and bottom line, for example, promotional discounts to distributors and retailers.

Note: See discussion of budgeting in Chapter 12 ("Performance Programs," page 331) for an example of how to calculate a point to pay for a performance program. Use the same math for purchases-to-earn rewards.

Close-Ended or Open-Ended

In an open-ended program, there's no limit to potential redemptions. Project worst-case redemption levels and make sure the sales can pay for the

Insight

Don't just talk paradigm shifts; look out for them! Some loyalty program providers were caught off guard when mobile phone services began competing on price instead of with premiums. Bye-bye frequent caller programs!

redemptions. Otherwise, you can suffer major losses. Base your projections on past promotions or run a few tests. Or run your promotion one market at a time to limit risk.

A close-ended program sets a limit on liability. If you know you can afford $2 for every required purchase, you aren't at risk no matter how many redeem. Downside: Your no-risk offer is a lower value and less motivating as you aren't factoring in nonredeeming purchasers. You can also stipulate "Offer limited to first 0,000 respondents," "One reward per household," or limit the collection vehicles you distribute.

REWARDS

Rewards versus awards: A *reward* is merchandise, service, cash, and the like. An *award* is a plaque, trophy, certificate, or other token of achievement.

Make rewards desirable *and* attainable. Participation in a reward program hinges on the consumer's desire to earn and the ability to attain the reward. Target heavier users to gauge your purchase requirement, and raise their average purchase level to qualify. Different reward levels encourage more consumers to participate.

Focus on "aspirational" rewards. Rewards are more appealing when they're items we would really like to own but wouldn't splurge on self-indulgently. What's more, if the reward is too popular or utilitarian, chances are your target already owns one.

Premiums or cash. Premiums deliver more bang for the buck. (See this topic under "Prizes" in Chapter 2, page 34.)

Stretch reward dollars. Consider tying in with a manufacturer, retailer, direct mailer, or e-tailer partner for rewards. Swap out what each of you has to offer. (See the discussion of tie-ins in Chapter 11 for extensive information.)

How will you redeem your partner rewards? You'll need to devise a system that does the following:

- Delivers a valid redemption vehicle to your customer (like a certificate)
- Provides a redemption vehicle your partner's staff recognizes and responds appropriately to
- Has security systems—that vehicle is like money!
- Has efficient accounting procedures
- Reconciles both partners in a timely, accurate manner

You may save by offering your own product as a reward, though you may be giving away a sale and delaying the next purchase. Consider your own product reward (or a discount) for lower-level purchasers, which may even increase their usage rate and loyalty. If you have several different products, consider one that isn't moving well at the time or needs trial.

Consider a single, major name partner with a variety of value levels and product types, such as an electronics manufacturer/retailer or a recreational products company.

Soft rewards. Make program members feel privileged—for example, with sneak product previews, members-only offers, extra services, a special fast lane, newsletters, and the like.

Merchandise. (See Chapter 10, "Premium Programs.") Merchandise delivers greater economies than does cash and fond memories. You may also negotiate price and fulfillment in exchange for the big order and exposure. (See "Tie-ins," Chapter 11.)

Most major brands already have systems in place for other companies' reward programs, whether it's a retail cataloger or a sporting goods manufacturer. However, you can probably beat their discount with your own research and negotiation efforts. Try bypassing the corporate reward department and go directly to the sales department, which may be more motivated and resourceful. (See Chapter 10 for details.)

DON'T USE THE *FREE* WORD TOO FREELY

Your lawyers may not allow you to print the word *free* because you may be requiring extended purchases.

What's more, research reveals consumers don't like the word *free* because they know it isn't. Consumers respond more favorably to the word *earn* and the fact that they're entitled to the rewards.

LOYALTY, CONTINUITY, RELATIONSHIP, ONE-TO-ONE, PERMISSION—WHICH?

These terms overlap. Generally, *loyalty* is longer term than is a *continuity* program, even lifelong. A loyalty program may also be a *relationship* marketing program, using extensive data capture and profiling analysis to identify and predict each consumer's individual purchasing behavior. These programs attempt to build a long relationship with the consumer, even through lifestyle changes.

One-to-one marketing, permission marketing, and other trendy terms basically mean the same things as relationship marketing, motivation, and other established practices.

RELATIONSHIP MARKETING

Four Relationship Program Phases

The first phase of a relationship program is the most crucial: *enrollment.* It requires extensive communication, motivation, and simple enrollment procedures. No enrollment—no program, so give prospects a reason to enroll.

The next phase is *gathering and processing the data* to begin profiling consumers. These data come from enrollment forms and surveys (which should reward participation). Organize profiles into various "buckets"—light users, heavy users, sports lovers, travel lovers, birthdays, business members, purchase dates, average point redemption levels, and so on.

The third phase is *communication.* Make this a two-way process to learn what your target really wants and responds to. Build the relationship and sales insights in the process.

The final phase never ends: *evaluation and improvement.* Relationship programs are a constant learning curve, dropping ineffective practices and building on successful ones.

What Data to Track

Data gathering can be as simple as a sweepstakes entry or a warranty form questionnaire. Or it can be a sophisticated relationship marketing system. The sophisticated database approach has four major considerations:

1. Hardware requirements
2. Software requirements
3. Data transmission (how data are gathered and transferred to your host computer—and in some cases relayed back to the consumer)
4. Profiling (the preprogrammed, computer-processed interpretation of the data—output based on your input)

What data to track boils down to four basic questions:

1. What information can you actually use?
2. Exactly how will you use it?
3. How will you organize the data you need to create manageable data buckets?
4. How much will your budget allow?

Profiling and Modeling

Profiling assembles various lifestyle and behavioral attributes of each customer. For example, your data (from surveys, purchases, redemptions, address changes, etc.) may indicate Seymore Sample likes sports and music, is middle income, just upgraded to a $200,000 suburban home, has elementary age kids, redeems points monthly at a 1,500 point total, and so on.

Modeling uses the cumulative data for all customers combined to analyze and then *predict* behavior, such as future purchase occasions, family graduations, upgrade timing, and the like.

Following are suggested profiling data for extended relationship programs:

- Value of the customer (seasonal, yearly, and lifelong)
- Tenure of the customer
- Volume the customer represents
- Customer's profession

- Likelihood to purchase competitor's product
- Response to various incentives and levels
- Demographics and psychographics
- Personal insights—kids, ages, college, and the like
- Interests—cooking, sports, fashion, travel, etc.
- Lifestyle—hobbies, family activities, vacations, clubs, etc.
- "Touchpoints"—favorite TV programs, periodicals, Web sites, affiliations
- Business insights—profession, company, product, role, title (and promotions), business travel, airline preference, hotel preference, even trade magazines
- Services/products used
- Purchase cycles
- Income
- Usage behavior
- Reward preferences
- Retailer preferences
- Key dates: purchase anniversaries, program enrollment anniversary, birthday, point plateau achievement, major redemption dates, etc.
- Points accumulated (a lot of points means a customer may be ready to redeem *and* defect so a reward to continue may be in order)
- Contract-ending dates (and alerts)
- And much more

Key: Your system shouldn't just collect data—it needs to *act* on the data. It must be programmed to detect and flag behavioral changes and opportunities. For example, someone who's just redeemed all of his or her points is at risk of defecting, so vest him or her again with bonus points.

The trunk of the tree. In the initial design, it's crucial to determine what data you want to access and how you want to manipulate the data, because once the software foundation is laid, it may become difficult to alter. Purchase behavior may be valuable but may also require significant up-front programming to capture and analyze an individual's purchasing cycles, spending levels by cycle, product preference, and so on, *plus* changes and trends. Imagine yourself once a quarter saying, "I would like to send a mailing to a group of customers who _____. I would also like to contact people who haven't purchased in the past _____. And my heavy users should receive a letter from me, saying ____." And so on. Start hanging out with programmers.

Data warehouses—"data schmata." Major companies have huge data warehouses detailing endless sales, customers, seasonality, regionality, retailers, and other information. Most of those data can't be applied to relationship programs because they're too general, and the system isn't configured to manipulate the data properly. Consider an outside agency or supplier system.

Direct Survey

Direct, a direct marketing trade publication, published the following results of a 2000 survey:

Maintain your own database

83%	Yes
18%	No
1%	Don't know

Functions for which database is used

Total

Cross-selling	55%
Customized mail offer	63%
Modeling	39%
Profiling	39%
Provide information to direct sales staff	48%
Provide information to telephone sales staff	32%
Promotion	76%
Regression analysis	22%
Revenue through sale of names	28%
Upselling	48%
Other	3%

Business to business

Customized mail offers	52%
Modeling	15%
Profiling	70%
Providing information to direct sales staff	58%
Regression analysis	4%

Consumer

Customized mail offers	58%
Modeling	63%

Profiling	75%
Provide information to direct sales staff	38%
Regression analysis	31%

Type of information maintained in database
  Total

Individual dollar amount of purchase	75%
Number of annual purchases	77%
Dollar value of annual purchases	74%
Recency	61%
Frequency	68%
Age/date of birth	34%
Length of time has been customer	73%
Source of original lead/contact	63%
Competitive products used	32%
Sociodemographic information by overlay	33%
Standard industrial classification code	41%
Promotional history	48%
Company information by overlay	33%
Company information by survey	34%
Track nonrespondents	35%
Names of prospects	74%

  Business to business

Individual dollar amount of purchase	67%
Number of annual purchases	67%
Dollar value of annual purchases	67%
Frequency	52%
Length of time has been a customer	63%

  Consumer

Individual dollar amount of purchase	81%
Number of annual purchases	88%
Dollar value of annual purchases	75%
Frequency	81%
Length of time has been a customer	81%

What happens to warranty forms? Valuable warranty information often gets filed forever. Track it down and ask the IT (information technology) department how you can turn it into an actionable database.

Lists. Database companies evaluate lists by how current they are, how many consumers are on it, and how much marketable information your list includes—from birthdays to purchase behavior. List companies may have a starting price of $75 per thousand, moving higher the more data the list contains. The homework's easy. Look up direct marketing in your local listings and invite a sales rep.

Relationship Program Cost and Execution Considerations

Before you contemplate your "one to one future," consider the expense and effort you're about to take on and how much it will really move the sales needle. Here's a shopping list:

- Program plan
- Program database—design, hardware, software, and the like, ongoing plus major setup cost
  - Load and update billing data
  - Track point earnings
  - Point statements
  - Identify and track all new enrollments plus new member correspondence and rewards
  - Generate monthly reports
  - Complete reward fulfillment processing
  - Accept, process, store, and manipulate data
  - Custom software and information technology department requirements
- Service center materials and operations—phone system, computer tracking system, Web extension, 800 number, automated voice response system
- Service center staff, training, and materials
  - Program eligibility status
  - Inquiries—point balance, reward details, program rules, promotional program, the program itself
  - Handling special requests
  - Receiving, verifying, and processing reward requests: normal requests and rush rewards
- Sales education materials and training
- Predictive model to benchmark current behavior and establish program goals and parameters

- Enrollment materials
  - Including incentive to enroll
  - Including processing and responses
  - Including point(s) of introductory consumer contact
- Consumer communications—ongoing
- Point-of-sale materials—ongoing
- Point statements—ongoing processing and mailings
- Rewards—ongoing
  - Fulfillment materials, shipping, processing, etc.
  - Rewards program administration
- Postage—ongoing
- Program administration and management—ongoing
- Tracking and monthly reports
  - Membership counts
  - Volumes
  - Mail count and response rates
  - Communication materials inventory
  - Reward information and inventory (including any partner status)
  - Survey response information
  - Ongoing evaluation, profiling, recommendations, etc.
  - Budget and payout

CONTINUITY GUIDELINES AND CAUTIONS

Three Hallmarks

Insight

Don't forget two of the most valuable customer contact resources: product registration forms and customer service centers. In fact, take the customer service people out to a long lunch or even bowling—and sit, listen, and learn.

Successful continuity programs are built on three foundations:

1. Rewards: Desirable and achievable for all target customers
2. Communication: Frequently, clearly, and prominently communicate the rewards, simple requirements, and easy participation. Where applicable, keep participants informed of their point progress
3. Participation: A must. Make it easy, even rewarding to sign up

Turn and Profit per Target Customer—Cost

The bottom line is how much you can spend per customer per sale, and how much motivation that figure adds up to once you subtract all the program costs.

Participation: How Many or Who?

Again, the 80/20 rule. If you have 20 percent participation, and it's the heavy user 20 percent, you've probably hit gold! The February/March 2000 issue of *Your Money* reported that heavy users can use as much as ten times the amount of product as average users. It also reported that 8 percent of the population consumes 85 percent of Diet Coke. So it's not necessarily *how many* participate in your program, but *who*!

Advertising Campaigns Don't Have Continuity

Don't tie a long-term continuity program's name to the advertising slogan. Chances are your continuity theme will outlive the advertising slogan. Consider Coca-Cola: "Coke is it," "It's the real thing," "Always Coca-Cola," "Give the world a Coke," and many more.

Do It Yourself versus Outsourcing

Continuity programs range from investments in paper and postage (refunds) to massive systems and equipment. Vendors range from refund clearinghouses to huge loyalty marketing firms. If your ambitions are simple, use this chapter as a how-to helper. For a major undertaking, use this chapter as a foundation to review and direct vendors.

Program Duration—Increased Consumption

A key criterion for program duration is how long it takes your target to reach your purchase goal. You may consider purchase volume instead of program duration. If your target's average purchase is eight in a given season, go for ten. Another approach is peak selling periods—summer, Thanksgiving through New Year, and football season. Remember any newcomers halfway through your program—consider a low-level reward.

Get Personal

Give your correspondence a personal quality, such as your member's name. Include his or her current personal point balance, and romance the rewards the member can attain. Make special mailings for birthdays and include a reward or discount.

Overstocked/Understocked

Be prepared for overwarehoused or underwarehoused product. Can you return it to the manufacturer, liquidate the stock, use it for employee incentives, give it to trade managers, use it in field promotions, and so on? If consumers overrespond, can you restock quickly or substitute a product? (Provide a second backup gift choice on the form.) Have communication materials in place for out-of-stocks. Use the policy and the wording "equal or greater value."

Questions and Complaints

Have a call-in question and complaint service available and post the number clearly. There will definitely be mistakes, misunderstandings, misdirected mailings, and more. Use the Web, but always allow for personal contact (you can economically hire a service).

Have a Return Policy

Perhaps your vendors' policy will cover you. Consider broken product, customer dissatisfaction, exchange requests, and the like.

Have a system to track and verify reward shipments, including who signed for the package.

Budget up front for misredemption, damaged goods, and dissatisfied customers who need "make-good" rewards.

Insight

Just cashed out! When a club member suddenly "cashes in all his chips," he may be defecting to a competitor's program. Lure him back *immediately* with some free bonus points.

Encourage Participation While Reducing Reward and Fulfillment Costs

Review the information in this book about slippage, partners, your own product rewards, and more. In some cases, you might even charge for membership.

Review Vendors' Advantages and Disadvantages

Review the advantages and disadvantages listed in the above tactic description matrixes. Discuss them with the vendors to evaluate their policies and capabilities.

And review "Performance Programs" (Chapter 12) and "Premium Programs" (Chapter 10), where you'll find more budgeting and execution details.

EXIT PLANS

What if your program isn't panning out, and you've enrolled many valuable customers expecting rewards? Before you enter a loyalty program, have an exit plan. Determine how to close the system while still offering some consolation to those who participated. Determine how to communicate the exit plan, and make it easy for your faithful consumers. Consider the following:

- Have customers redeem all their points at once when closing out their accounts.
- Have a closeout special that may offer even higher value rewards to appease participants, while it gets you out of the plan fast.
- Consider giving discounts or free product (cost of goods) to replace the original items you may have offered.
- Consider having a retailer partner accept the points, driving traffic to his or her business and building goodwill for both of you.
- Give sufficient warning, make the program's end date very clear, and allow a grace period even after the program's end date.

7

POINT OF SALE

(Also see Chapter 13, "Trade Programs,"
page 341.)

INTRODUCTION:
PROMOTING TO THE WELL-TRAINED CONSUMER

While we sales promotion "experts" believe we can influence consumers with our promotional skills, increasingly we must understand that consumers are almost as expert in the area as we are. After all, by the time they reach 30, they've been exposed to all types of sales promotion activities for at least a quarter of a century. That's more than most promotion managers have been developing promotional programs.

So in most product categories, we're dealing with a well-informed and well-trained consumer of promotion. Most consumers know that if Coke is featured in the food store this week, most likely Pepsi will be promoted next week. And if Charmin is on sale this week, Northern or Scott will soon follow. So even though we think we are creating incremental sales, generally, we're simply shifting volume from our competitors when we promote. Then they promote and shift the customers back. It's almost like renting customers during the promotional period.

Given this educated-consumer scenario, can any type of sales promotion program really generate profitable sales for the marketing organization? The answer, of course, is yes. But it takes consumer insights and understanding to make promotions pay off or pay out today.

One of the most important sales promotion tactics is in-store promotion or point of sale. Estimates in some product categories place impulse sales at two-thirds or more of total volume. Therefore, what goes on in the retail store is critical for most marketers. Yet in too many cases, point-of-sale (POS) or point-of-purchase (POP) materials are the last to be planned and developed. And it's often done in a rush so that the POS is simply a rip-off of the media advertising program. Although we agree that in-store materials must support and enhance the messages that are being delivered through the media, reproducing the television commercial or the newspaper advertisement in-store is generally not a good idea. The reason? Product shopping is not the same as media watching, no matter what the advertising people might say. The consumer's mental state is different and the conditions for exposure and involvement are radically different.

The primary difference between media exposure and POS materials is the attention the consumer gives to the task. In media situations, when and where advertising appears is an interruption of the consumer's mental processing. People watch television to see the programming, not the commercials. On the other hand, consumers look for and respond to in-store or point-of-purchase materials. It helps them save time, effort, and, in many cases, money. So where there is generally a lack of interest in seeing another television commercial, there often is a sincere interest in finding an informative sign, poster, or display in the retail store.

The fact that consumers seek out and respond to point-of-purchase materials doesn't mean they read and absorb all the information the marketer is trying to communicate. Most consumers don't even read the material; they simply respond to what they have been trained to respond to (e.g., displays, end-aisle features, shelf talkers, and flashing red arrows). All of those displays say to the consumer "Special Offer," and that generally means a price discount, a special savings, or some other worthwhile value, whether it really is or not. Research conducted by two professors found that about 50 percent of the consumers, immediately after they had placed a product in their shopping trolley in a food store, didn't know how much they were supposedly saving or even what the shelf price of the product was. They were responding instinctively to in-store signage that seemed to indicate to them that the product with the sign was a special value. Whether the product was really a special value was immaterial. The consumers thought it was. So even though we are dealing with a very sophisticated consumer, we're also dealing with a time-rushed and harried shopper.

Other research shows the marketer can signal a promotion with in-store point-of-purchase materials and at the same time maintain the same price points. Other studies have shown that many middle-aged women take off their eyeglasses when they go into retail stores. They apparently want to appear younger to other shoppers. As a result, they tend to buy by colors and package shapes and yes, you guessed it, by the presence of signs, arrows, displays, and other elements they perceive as signals of special promotions, events, or products. Simply knowing how consumers respond to POS/POP can suggest a number of in-store promotional techniques that could be quite successful if your target market is middle-aged women.

It's true 21st-century shoppers are quite savvy. But they are well trained in responding to promotional activities. Like Pavlov's dogs, when Pavlov rang the bell, they salivated. When the sales promotion manager manages to get some type of display or merchandising feature set up in the store, consumers will generally respond. The promotional training of the consumer works both ways. That's a key element in developing successful point-of-purchase materials. —Don E. Schultz

OVERVIEW

First, is it point of sale or point of purchase? POS or POP? A sale is also a purchase. For no apparent reason, this book uses point of sale.

Of course, a point of sale could be the Internet, telemarketing channels, direct marketing, or telesales. However, point of sale traditionally refers to a physical territory where goods and services are bought on the spot—primarily retail.

In the words of Point of Purchase Advertising International in Washington, D.C., a leading point-of-purchase association, "It's the last three feet of any integrated product campaign and the only one where buyer, product, and the required purchase dollars merge." With the average American bombarded by over 3,000 messages each day, the best time to reach buyers is at the point of sale. Up to two-thirds of grocery purchase decisions are made on impulse. Studies vary, but they all point out that having a product displayed off the shelf can increase sales from 50 to 700 percent. Point of sale is where the action is.

DEFINITION

A point-of-sale program is a display tactic, permanent or temporary, that a manufacturer creates for placement at a retail location to gain product attention and often to deliver a promotional event. Inherent in the program are concepts to motivate the retailer to place the display. (Retailers may execute POS programs with the same intentions.)

Some terms have a dual meaning. Here are some definitions used in this book for clarification:

- **Feature**—the featured product and price in the flyer and on the floor stacking
- **Display**—the stacking of product, possibly with promotional signage
- **Signage or display signage (or display program)**—the short-term signage that showcases the product, typically with a promotional event
- **Merchandising fixtures**—permanent shelving the manufacturer (or chain retailer) provides to present and stock its product
- **Merchandisers**—a permanent or semipermanent construction designed to showcase a product's function or unique benefit

COMMON POINT-OF-SALE OBJECTIVES BY TACTIC

(Also see itemized tactics below.)

TACTIC	OBJECTIVES (Beyond Purchase)
Promotional POS program	• Store display placement through promotional offer (though other factors are often involved) • Command shopper attention • Purchase through offer and placement • Reinforce product image, benefit, sponsorship, etc.
Loader	• Display placement through a promotional premium for the store manager • Shopper attention and purchase (sometimes multiple) through premium offer • Reinforce product image or benefit
Near-pack	• Highly visible display placement and sales through an immediate offer for shoppers • Encourage retailer advertising of brand's promotion • Reinforce product image, benefit, usage • Add value without discounting image • Tie-in economies with premium partner
Self-shipper	• Secure visible floor or counter location while showcasing product with all-in-one shipper, product bin, and header card
Cross-merchandising	• Display placement through cross-store traffic and multiple sales opportunity for retailer • Secondary signage placement • Encourage retailer advertising feature • Economize by sharing cost with partner • Tap into partner's market, possibly through new usage occasion • Reinforce product image, benefit, usage
Account specific	• Secure display authorization • Commit retailer to additional stocking, better placement, and flyer inclusion • Support new product launch • Comarketing—tie in with retail partner's marketing • Strengthen retail relationship
Spectacular (and contest)	• Create attention-commanding display extravaganza • Stock multiple brands/products together • Reinforce product image, benefit, sponsorship, etc. • Leverage major selling season • Motivate manager participation (display contest)

TACTIC	OBJECTIVES (Beyond Purchase)
Merchandising fixture	• Secure permanent, prominent in-store product placement • More efficient and profitable stocking, dispensing, and shopping unit than is traditional shelving • Stand out with a glitzy permanent fixture • Showcase product in the most favorable backdrop • Provide additional product communication • Facilitate shopping with ergonomic design • Consumer interaction through unit's mirror, usage guides, etc. • Increase restocking efficiency • Reinforce product image or benefit • Routinely update unit, retrofitting new signage
Merchandiser	• Display placement and attention through exciting, fun product presentation • Dramatically demonstrate unique product usage and benefits • Stand out from competition's shelf position or corrugated display
Special effects	• Display placement through unique, exciting, fun display vehicle • Break through clutter—command attention • Dramatically demonstrate unique product usage and benefits
Specialized services	• Guarantee retail exposure through a preestablished in-store service • Utilize specific service for specific objective—in-store couponing, shopping cart signage, in-store media advertising, etc.

TACTICS ITEMIZED

75. PROMOTIONAL POS PROGRAMS

Definition   A display program that carries a prominent promotional offer such as a sweepstakes, mail-in offer, tie-in offer, etc.

Advantages

• Excitement and offer encourage display placement
• Promotion draws shoppers, especially with "borrowed interest" of sweepstakes prize, movie tie-in, etc.
• Offer motivates purchases
• Promotion can reinforce image and benefit
• Opportunity for loader benefits (see below)
• Media support ("Look for special display") encourages placement and increases response

Disadvantages
- Expensive—promotional offer, any loader or licensed property, carton fabrication and packing, shipping, service to assemble display at store, dealer allowance, etc.
- Short term—often one to two weeks
- Difficult to project placement and quantities
- Route salesperson earning commission on stores stocked may not be motivated to assemble display—may require merchandising service
- Depleted tear pads may not be replaced
- Any entry boxes require maintenance, collection, and considerable space
- National program may lose out to a competitor's account specific tie-in (see below), because all of that retailer's competition have the same national program, so the account specific tie-in actually breaks the tie.

76. LOADER

Definition
Retailer receives premium as motivation to participate in the promotion; may simply be handed over or mounted on the display for visual impact and then given on program completion

Note: Loader doubles as a self-liquidator mail-in offer for shoppers

Advantages
- Premium and optional promotion encourages display placement
- Premium on display commands attention
- Offer can require multiple purchase
- Premium's value perception can be greater than cash alternative and have greater impact
- Loader can become permanent signage—wall clock, mirror, etc.
- Premium can reinforce brand attribute
- Tie-in premium partner can share cost and execution (See "Tie-ins," Chapter 11)

Note: Most loader programs are not evaluated by premium sales, but rather, by the number of displays placed because the retailer wants the loader.

Disadvantages
- Loader adds expense to program
- Requires custom display costs to mount premium—subject to shoddy assembly, unbalanced construction

- Many chains don't allow loaders for store managers
- Distilled spirits industry is highly regulated (see "Premium Programs," Chapter 10, page 270)
- No guarantee the retailer will follow through once he or she receives the loader

(See "Promotional POS Programs" above)

77. NEAR-PACK (Also see Chapter 10, "Premium Programs," page 279.)

Definition

Display offers value on premiums that are stocked *near* the display

Example: Purchase house paint off shelf, receive free disposable brush (in near-pack bin)

Often offered for sale without tie-in purchase so that (1) retailer can justify valuable retail space with a 100 percent markup and (2) discourages pilferage by employees who may justify pilferage by thinking, "It's free anyway"

Advantages

- Shopper offer encourages placement
- Instant-gratification-purchase incentive
- Adds value without discounting perception
- Premium can reinforce product benefit, usage
- Exceptional product visibility
- Stands out from competitor
- Can encourage trial
- Can establish usage behavior—such as free Jello mold
- Can economize, distributing partner's sample

Disadvantages

- Additional cost for bin, premium, packing, shipping
- Custom premiums require time and expense
- Cumbersome to execute
- May suffer employee pilferage because perceived as a free item
- Premium may compete with retailer product
- Requires valuable space (and allowance)
- May require cashier training and a new stock-keeping unit (SKU)

78. SELF-SHIPPER (AND SET-SELLS)

Definition Shipping container doubles as display unit—both product bin and header card; counter units (for candies, mints, etc.) often termed *set-sells*

Advantages
- Efficient all-in-one package—shipper, bin, sign
- Places product in a high-visibility location—the aisle floor or counter
- Can carry a promotional offer
- Easy accounting—the product quantity, shipper, and shipping costs

Disadvantages
- Additional custom display and packing costs
- Requires assembly—may require merchandising service
- Competes for valuable space
- Short-term duration with limited volume capabilities

79. CROSS-MERCHANDISING

Definition Display offer ties in with other store item(s), often in a separate location
Examples: Save on purchase of ice cream brand and wafer brand; buy perfume and receive eyeliner value

Advantages
- Dual purchase and cross-store traffic encourage display placement
- Encourages product purchase
- Secondary display placement and additional exposure through partner
- Economies of tie-in program
- May extend and promote usage through partnership

Disadvantages
- Exceptional up-front negotiating, sell-in efforts, and executional co-ordination with partner and retailer
- Partners must match distribution
- Additional retail considerations, such as cashier training and scanner system
- Possible misredemption—ringing up the wrong combinations, sizes, etc.
- Dilutes branding
- Creative execution may be compromised

80. ACCOUNT SPECIFIC

Definition   Vendor program ties in with a retailer, such as retailer identification on signage and retailer-specific consumer offer

Advantages   • Assured display placement
                      • Increased retailer commitment—stocking, placement, flyer feature, etc.
                      • Accurate budgeting
                      • Retailer enjoys exclusive program versus national program all other retailers run
                      • Opportunity to tie in both parties' marketing objectives
                      • Builds retailer relationship

Disadvantages   • More expensive on a per-store basis than is a national program
                      • Significant up-front planning and operational details
                      • Can compromise branding
                      • Less impact than national program because of economies of scale and compromised creative

81. SPECTACULAR (AND CONTEST)

Definition   Point-of-sale program of grand proportions; massive stacking, sometimes with a few brands, creative displays, even shopper involvement, such as coloring contest submissions; often tied to holiday, sponsorship, etc., and often supported by a display contest with salesperson and store manager joining forces

Advantages   • Dominates shopper attention
                      • Diminishes competitor's presence
                      • Mass product stackings and sales
                      • Exceptional retailer participation
                      • Maximizes key selling opportunities, like holidays

Disadvantages   • Expensive, complex, and labor intensive
                      • Sales rep must devote exceptional time and effort from tough sell-in through execution

- Some retailers may feel the display contest is unwinnable
- Scope of program may be difficult to sell in—requires exceptional sales projections and retailer allowances
- Requires a brand with clout
- There may be more efficient tactics

82. MERCHANDISING FIXTURE

Definition Permanent/semipermanent fixture designed to stock and showcase products

Examples: mirrored cosmetics fixtures, branded battery merchandisers, grocery snack centers, wristwatch merchandisers

Advantages
- Encourages prime placement by offering retailer an attractive store addition that efficiently stocks and sells product—typically higher-turn, higher-margin products
- Showcases product in ideal, controlled setting
- Locks in valuable real estate long term, locks out competitors
- Efficient stocking, restocking, and shopping system—ergonomic
- Can dispense and position product, such as gravity-feed beverage trays or spring-loaded package slides
- Units can offer additional information and consumer interaction—mirrors, audio, guides
- Can be retrofitted with updated signage or promotional offers

Disadvantages
- Expensive, including prolonged prototyping, retailer testing, approval process, hardware, hand labor, delivery, and installation
- Complex "nuts and bolts" requiring diverse disciplines
- Requires up-front negotiations with retailers to assure placement
- Ongoing maintenance, such as replacing faded colors, repairs, cleaning, etc.
- Retailers resist AC cords
- May not allow for new style trends, etc.
- Payout is dependent on how long it's placed

83. MERCHANDISER

Definition

Display unit, often permanent, showcases or demonstrates product attribute.

Examples: Dimensional cutaway models of automotive systems; videogame demonstrator; Swiss Army Knife motion display

Advantages

- Commands attention, upstaging competitors
- Dramatically showcases product attribute(s)
- Can continuously demonstrate product—no reliance on retail staff
- Offers retailer an exciting store addition and "salesperson"
- Can lock in sustained prime retail location

Disadvantages

- Expensive, including prolonged design phase, custom manufacturing, and installation
- May require up-front retailer involvement to assure placement
- May require consumer communication tests
- May require ongoing maintenance, such as battery, lights, parts, literature, etc.
- Retailers resist power cords
- Product updates may make unit obsolete
- Ultimate payout dependent on how long it stays on display

84. SPECIAL EFFECTS

Definition

Display incorporates dramatic and unique device to command attention; may or may not demonstrate product attribute; motion displays, crawling text, fiber optics, 3D, "dissolve-action," audio, etc.

Advantages

- Commands attention
- Offers retailer an entertaining store addition that encourages sales
- Studies show motion displays dramatically increase sales
- May dramatically showcase product attribute(s)
- Can dramatically reinforce image
- Can accomplish specific objectives—product location, extended copy message, benefit, etc.

Disadvantages	• Expensive, possibly complex
	• Less functionality than merchandising display
	• May suffer short in-store life—poor payout
	• May require ongoing maintenance, such as battery or lights
	• Retailers resist power cords
	• Most lighting options quickly drain batteries and store lighting dims them
	• Requires delivery and assembly

85. SPECIALIZED SERVICES

| *Definition* | Point-of-sale tactic delivered by a service with preestablished retail capabilities. |
| | Examples: Grocery cart signage, automatic coupon dispensers, in-store demo services, in-store audio/visual media |

Advantages	• Services guarantee access to retail location and shoppers
	• Historical data often available to help evaluate and plan the program
	• Can plan far in advance and integrate other activities
	• Locks in peak selling period
	• Prenegotiate with retailer, who knows product is being supported in store

Disadvantages	• Limited choices with limited capabilities
	• Additional media costs beyond traditional signage
	• Parity if simply swapping media periods with competitor
	• Limited to the service's capabilities
	• May lack drama and attention if shoppers have tuned out media

THE SHEER SELLING POWER OF POINT-OF-SALE DISPLAYS

- Studies suggest that a display can increase sales fivefold to sevenfold versus shelved product.

- The same studies indicate that 70 percent of supermarket brand purchase decisions are made in store on impulse, 74 percent at mass merchandisers.
- A 2001 study by A.C. Nielsen/Pete's Wicked Ale showed that the sales lift for specialty beers on display ranged from 52.52 percent to 176.92 percent. It also suggests the creative influences results—Pete's Wicked Ale was three times higher than the higher-profile Sam Adams. (A.C. Nielsen data provided by Pete's Wicked Ale.)
- Studies show shoppers spend 12 percent more than intended in supermarkets, 5 percent more in mass merchandisers.
- Moving from the bottom shelf to waist level *increases* sales 43 percent. Moving from top to bottom *reduces* sales 80 percent. (Reprinted with permission of *Progressive Grocer*. This 1969 study was for one product category so others may vary.)

POINT-OF-SALE SIGNAGE STRATEGIES

What's your point? It's an honor to have a shopper's attention, but you'll only have it for two or three seconds. Prioritize your message and assume only one message will actually register with shoppers. Some communication objectives to consider include these:

- The promotional offer
- The primary product benefit
- Package graphics, so shoppers know what to look for
- Visual appeal—appetite appeal, a diamond's brilliance, a car's drama
- Retail imprint on the display
- How easily the product benefits the consumer—end results
- New (and improved) and the benefit
- Where to find it

Vendor and retailer strategies. Vendors want consumer awareness and product sales. Retailers want traffic to the store, cross-store shopping, multiple sales, trade-ups, in-store excitement, and credit as the place for values. Retailers know vendors need signage, so many sell the space or create their own signage programs they sell to vendors.

I *nsight*

In the rush to the Internet, are you driving traffic to the Web site instead of the store shelf? Displays are king at closing sales, so drive them there.

Fast-food chains use point of sale as a cumulative traffic and trade-up vehicle. (See "Retail Zone Strategies" below.) The faster the line moves, the more sales per minute. So a menu board's prominent combo selection isn't just about bigger orders, it's about quick decisions— "I want a Number 3."

Some retailers prohibit vendor point of sale, or allow nothing over five feet high or, at best, allow vendor signs designed by the retailer. Prestigious department stores consider their store decor part of their pricey image. To get signage in these stores, you need to work at the headquarters level, understand their philosophy, and introduce a unique concept that will meet their objectives as well as yours.

Some retail categories value vendor signage. They may need organized merchandising systems or promotional excitement. Some, such as bars and restaurants, opt for decorative signage. It helps if they're functional—like clocks, beer tap handles, lamps, napkin holders, change trays, and the like.

How should your product be displayed? As the owner of a national merchandising agency remarked, "Just walk through the store and look for problems and opportunities. They're all over the place."

Also see "Tricks of the Trade," page 353.

RETAIL ZONE STRATEGIES AND ATTENTION SPANS

Many retailers map their stores into zones and assign different signage objectives for each zone. For example, fast-food retailers try to trade visitors up as they move from the street to the cash register.

Zone	Consumer Mind-Set	Objective	Tactic
Street or parking lot	Should I choose this restaurant?	Motivate visit	Large banners and window signs with exceptional value ($1 Biggie Burger!)

Zone	Consumer Mind-Set	Objective	Tactic
Store entry	What to eat? I saw a Biggie Burger special.	Trade up to featured item	Door decal and entry signs for featured item (such as "Our Biggie Rib Sandwich for only $1.99")
Order lane	What to order? That Biggie Rib sounds good.	Trade up to value meal	Menu board and counter card featuring combos* (like Combo #3— Biggie Rib with Coke & Fries only $2.99)
Cash register #1	I'll have that combo #3.	Add another item to the sale	Counter and cash register sign with dessert or take-home offer
Cash register #2	Oh, what will my kid want. (Kid: a toy!)	Have kid request high-margin Kid Meal	Counter display and large translite feature of Kid Meal and toy

*Combo meals have large names or numbers for fast, easy decisions and ordering, so lines move quickly.

I n s i g h t

The most efficient merchandising display configuration also suffers the most heinous name, "swastika." Viewed from above, the construction resembles this pattern. It utilizes virtually 100 percent of its space for stocking products and 360-degree access.

TIME NOT ON YOUR SIDE

Harvard psychologist Dr. George A. Fuller once calculated that people cannot deal with more than seven units at one time. The average FSI reader spends just three seconds reviewing each ad. Many look at the coupon first, the ad second. Fast-food zone strategies suggest communication parameters.

Location	Attention Span	Number of Messages
Outside restaurant	4 seconds or less	Up to two
Counter area	3.5 minutes, but only 30 seconds viewing merchandise	4 seconds per sign—may view menu board for 22 seconds total, 8 to 10 of which are at the counter. Most viewed: Menu board's combo meal section, translite, register topper, and counter mats/displays
Dining area	Leisurely, but limited signs mean limited viewing time	View and comprehend up to seven messages
Drive-through	2 to 3 seconds, but up to 18 to 22 seconds on the menu board	Two—focus is on menu board

GUIDELINES AND CAUTIONS

- **Stores are cluttered, purchases impulsive.** Vendors, don't be too subtle or clever. Retailers, display the timeliest need in each section.
- **AC cautions.** Retailers need their AC outlets and don't want cord clutter or potential hazards.
- **Light cautions.** Lights deplete batteries. Explore LEDs, light thieves, reflective materials, and new technologies. Besides, lights don't shine in a well-lit store.
- **Your sound may be someone else's noise.** Retail workers quickly tire of noisy displays and may pull the plug.

- **Get retail compliance.** Secure retail authorization long before you produce displays. Provide layouts, support plans, and business benefits.
- **Pay or barter with retailers.** Valuable floor space often is bought and sold. Vendors can also barter with case allowances, advertising support, profitable tactics, and even a loader.
- **Check each retailer's point-of-sale policies.** Hold off creative or planning until you have the retailer's guidelines.
- **Break a tie.** Retailers are sensitive to vendors offering the same program to their competitors. One way out is spin-offs: For a Super Bowl sponsorship, give one retailer a football offer, another a sweepstakes ticket offer, another a player tie-in, and so on.
- **Plan a plan-o-gram for sales and retailers.** A plan-o-gram depicts how products should ideally be placed on the shelf. A simple illustration presents how many facings, sizes, varieties, and the like should be placed and where, such as lead sellers at eye level, poor sellers at the bottom.
- **Integrate the timing** of point of sale with your other marketing efforts—advertising campaign, publicity events, sales incentives, and so on. Inform retailers how it's all coming together for them.
- **Place key products at eye level:** Out of sight—out of mind. Remember, women are smaller than men, and kids smaller than women.
- **Signs compete with signs.** A 2001 grocery store study found there are 150 signs per store per week. Break out!
- **Show the product!** Studies reveal that prominently showing the product in store signage increases sales significantly.
- **Can someone clean it, dust it, and mop around it?** Don't just worry about your display's base—even a gondola banner is at the mercy of a nightshift forklift.
- **How do consumers "shop it"?** Are all products easily seen? Can every size person see and read it?
- **How easily can it be restocked?** The freshest products go to the back, which hampers front-end loading. Can quota-obsessed route people stock it quickly?
- **Safety concerns?** Will people trip over the base? What havoc can kids wreak? Can heavy products fall on heads? What if it's bumped?
- **Dog ears?** Die-cuts, like human cutouts, look great—unless they're bent in shipping and handling. Caution in the packing process.

- **Make assembly fast and easy.** Yours isn't the only display a sales clerk or route person needs to put up. If yours takes too long, too bad. Consider a merchandising service.
- **Reinforce the advertising, but close the sale.** Studies reveal that reinforcing advertising at point of sale increases results. However, the POS objective is more promotional than pure advertising. The offer is the primary message.

Ten tips from an insider. The following comes from Mike Lauber, CEO of Tusco Display, Gnadenhutten, Ohio, in *PROMO* magazine, 10/96 (http://www.promomagazine.com), a Primedia publication. These abbreviated comments are meant primarily for permanent and semipermanent fixtures.

1. **Respect the three- to five-second window.** POS displays are like outdoor billboards with fast-moving traffic. The display must communicate its message in three to five seconds (or less).
2. **Work with the retailer for high-traffic locations.** No matter how good your display is, it won't do the job unless it's seen. Collaborate with the retailer for end-aisle or checkout areas.
3. **The medium is part of the message.** If parts break or wear easily, if the display is subject to dents and scratches, or if materials don't last, the display's appearance will decline—and so will your brand image.
4. **Play the numbers game.** The more times consumers receive your POS message, the more likely they will be influenced by it.
5. **Headlines must be benefits.** Send a simple, key benefit statement, using personal pronouns like *you* and *your.*
6. **Anticipate the changes.** Build flexibility into your display design with adjustable shelving and movable peg hooks.

I *nsight*

Will it fit in the car trunk? Consider the route salesperson's physical limitations when it comes to delivering point of sale.

7. **Be certain the setup is simple.** Supply clear and accurate instruction sheets.
8. **Make the display experience an active encounter.** It does not have to be expensive electronic inter-activity: A tear-off coupon, a recipe, a sweepstakes entry, a free catalog—all influence behavior toward the display and the brand.
9. **Trial ship the package.** This detail can create enormous headaches if overlooked.
10. **Follow up for future success.** Monitor the display's performance with your retailers and route salespeople. Get their input on possible improvements and upgrades.

SPECIAL EFFECTS

Motion

Motion displays increase sales, but you need to weigh the added cost, assembling the display, and its longevity. (Plus, who replaces expensive batteries?)

Motion can do more than grab attention. It can display a product's benefit or demonstrate befores and afters, withs and withouts, and so on.

Sales gains—motion versus nonmotion. The following study (Point of Purchase Advertising International, Washington, D.C., February 1997) is based on three sets of stores in three display groups: control with no display; display with motion; identical display with no motion. Store types: supermarkets, grocery, package, drug, stationery, camera.

- Displays without motion averaged 39 percent sales gain above normal shelf sales. (Range: plus 7 percent to 170 percent)
- Displays with motion averaged 83 percent gain above no display. (Range: plus 20 percent to 317 percent)
- Displays with motion averaged 44 percent more sales than the same displays without motion. (Range: plus 5 percent to 147 percent)

I *nsight*

Sometimes retailer security systems are set off by motion displays. Research the retailer's system.

Nine case histories:

Category	With Display	Display with Motion
Liquor	Summer graphics: Plus 50%	With rotating top: Plus 77%
Liquor	Hand with glass by bottle: Plus 26%	Hand moves: Plus 34%
Juices	Can close up: Plus 26%	Can moves: Plus 39%
Pens	Static pen: Plus 31%	Convertible pen moves hand to hand: Plus 114%
Cameras	Hand holds film: Plus 170%	Hand loads/unloads film: Plus 317%
Personal Care	Hand holds purse case: Plus 20%	Hand and case move side to side: Plus 53%
Beer	Message on price rail: Plus 9%	Message rotates: Plus 64%
Beer	Model photo: Plus 7%	Model and product rock and revolve: Plus 32%
Cigarettes	Cigarette filter focus: Plus 15%	Filter opens and closes: Plus 20%

Retailer Attitudes:

"Which type of display—with motion or without—do you think attracts more consumer attention?"

Favor motion	Favor nonmotion	No opinion
73%	11%	16%

"Which type of display—with motion or without—do you think brings more sales?"

Favor motion	Favor nonmotion	No opinion
67%	12%	21%

"Given a choice between a display with motion—or the same display without motion—which would you prefer?"

Favor motion	Favor nonmotion	No opinion
70%	23%	7%

A 1996 study, again with Point of Purchase Advertising International, with 16,000 consumer interviews in 458 different stores revealed the following:

- When displays and advertising were both used, the increase in purchase rate for snacks was 639 percent; for paper product, 919 percent; for beer, 995 percent; for soft drinks, 1111 percent; and for coffee, 1242 percent. Other categories, such as candy, gum, shaving items, and pet food, also showed significant sales gains.

Sound

Sound is a popular display effect with manufacturers but not necessarily popular with retail personnel, who often disable it after so much annoying repetition, so use it in more controlled environments. Motion-activated sound helps because the display literally addresses the passing shopper and is less repetitious for the retail staff.

Another factor is extraneous sounds—price checks, piped-in music, audio-video demos, closed circuit TV, and the like. Ask your vendor to recommend preset volume levels. Provide guidelines to people placing the display for volume and placement. Because retailers frown on AC, consider batteries.

Pretest sound's results. Place nonsound displays in similar environments and monitor the results of both. If sales increase with sound, do they justify the additional cost? What's the retailer's reaction? Finally, have random store audits to confirm the sound display is active and batteries are fresh.

Lights

First, will anyone notice lights in a well-lit store? Second, how do you power them if AC is not allowed? Most lights drain batteries. If you have permission for AC, is it in a decent store location? Will the cleaning crew unplug it? Consider creative uses of fiber optics, LEDs, even mirrors. (See "light thieves" in "Glossary of POS Formats" below.)

Lenticular

You've played with lenticular graphics—move the frame back and forth and the picture moves. Lenticular displays add a dramatic motion effect (or 3D) and can make high-impact messages, like before and after. However, these displays are very expensive and should be for long-term placement. And even with long-term placement, if they only reach repeat regular customers, they will lose their luster and effectiveness.

3D

The simplest 3D display isn't really 3D. Use two planes, placing one layer in back—perhaps a beach scene—with your product photo mounted separately in front. You can also "bow" a paper element so it sticks out from the display. Dollhouse constructions are toylike, fully dimensional paper-stock replicas of a house, car, computer, and so on. You can use 3D glasses to convert a processed image into a 3D effect. But asking shoppers to wear glasses is a lot, though it may work at trade shows or for kid programs. There are truly dramatic 3D imaging formats that arrest attention, but they also arrest budgets. Again, make them permanent (a merchandiser) or for expensive, high-margin, high-turn products (fashion).

Others

- Holograms
- Back-lit transparencies (translites)
- Floor graphics
- Motion—breeze activated
- Audio—sensing movement to activate
- Slate (popular with restaurants for specials)
- Dissolve scenes
- Functional—mirrors, clocks, department signs, pricing, place mats, temperature, change mats
- Mobiles
- Inflatables

(See the "Glossary of POS Formats" descriptions in this chapter.)

In s i g h t

Don't use the term *loader* in the
liquor business, because loaders are
illegal in that business. Say *display enhancement*. And make sure the item
supports the theme of the display.

DISPLAY LOADER TIPS

- If the premium is mounted on the display, back it
  with a photograph in case the premium is removed.
- Always make test prototypes to be sure the display holds the weight and can handle an occasional bump.
- Use diagrams in assembly instructions.
- Distilled spirits should not require purchase for
  consumers to order a premium.
- There may be legal or corporate rules covering the value of your loader,
  so check with state laws and retail headquarter policies.

ADVERTISING VALUE OF POINT-OF-SALE SIGNS

Several studies show dramatic sales increases from point-of-sale displays.
But how much of that sales action does the sign itself generate? If you stack a
hill of beans on the grocery store floor, sales will rise dramatically even without a sign. Likewise, if the retailer writes in a price by hand on cardboard,
sales will rise—even if it's a full markup. What is the *advertising* value of point
of sale when you strip it of any promotional message?

POPAI (Point of Purchase Advertising International, Washington, D.C.)
attempted to evaluate how effective point of sale is strictly as an advertising
medium by factoring out all extraneous purchase influencers, such as sale
price, offers, seasonality, product stackings, and so forth. Following are some
of POPAI's findings.

Grocery category results: At this writing, more retail categories were being
researched. Compared with advertising's "cost-per-thousand impressions" criteria, POP (point of purchase) was comparable to radio and was approxi-
mately half the cost of television. The average grocery store weekly reach
ranged from 2,300 to 8,000 impressions depending on store size and volume.

Sales increases ranged dramatically from 2 to 65 percent, depending on
the brand, type of vehicle, combination of pieces, and the message itself. Shelf
merchandisers *alone* generated sales increases of 17 percent, whereas POP displays generated a 12 percent sales lift.

Again, this was strictly on an advertising basis competing with other purely advertising media (except that POP is in-store, where sales happen). Other research shows sales increases from 200 to 700 percent for products displayed off the shelf and typically with a consumer offer beyond the ad message.

Combining signs. The study also indicates sales increase as the number of materials increase. Again, the following figures are based strictly on the advertising value of POS, without promotions, product stackings, pricing, and the like.

- A sign communicating a brand message increased sales 2 to 6 percent.
- Addition of base or case wrap increased total sales to +12 percent.
- Adding a standee increased total sales to +27 percent.
- An inflatable or a mobile increased sales to +40 percent.
- Adding a sign that communicated the brand's thematic tie-in with a sport, movie, or charity increased results to +65 percent.

Note: The last item suggests a promotional spin.

Remember that in the competition for display placement by the retailer, it's usually the promotional offer and excitement that wins the day. Don't rely on reproducing your print advertisement to motivate the retailer to choose your display.

ASSIGNING POINT-OF-SALE VALUES FOR TIE-IN PROSPECTS (AND FOR YOU)

Print media prices are often based on cost-per-thousand people reached (CPM); point-of-sale measurements, on the other hand, are less easy to define. You need to know each retailer's different traffic count by period and display location, even by weather. What's more, a POS impression is more valuable because it occurs in the store, not in the living room.

Display value. A display's value can be judged in several areas that can be used to negotiate with tie-in partners:

- Exposures to *in-store* shoppers, particularly in high-traffic areas like entries and end-aisles

- Trade class and the market it reaches—from automotive to fashion to tweens to diapers
- Store section location; for example, a hardware store's paint section reaches a highly targeted market
- A message delivered right where products are purchased
- The cost of the display itself
- The amount invested and the system in place to authorize and place the display
- The size and impact of the display
- Any promotional topspin—a licensed property or celebrity graphic (and the fees)
- Any display functions—sample delivery, product demonstrations, literature dispensing, and so on. (For example, compare the cost and effectiveness of distributing a partner's literature on your display with direct mail—list, envelopes, postage, assembly, less targeting, and delivery at home instead of in-store.)
- Any direct-to-store execution capabilities you have
- Your brand's breadth of appeal compared with a partner—Coke's appeal versus STP
- Most important, the fact that the communication is occurring in the store, not about to be zapped by the remote

Exposures. Use this formula to calculate the number of exposures a display delivers:

Quantity of displays × weekly store traffic × week's duration

However, this assumes a 100 percent exposure location, such as a store entry or prominent gondola-end. Research or take your best guess at what percentage of total store traffic visits your display's section.

Remember to never simply compare a display with print media exposures. A display's exposure accomplishes much more. (See above.)

Media weights. You can also barter tie-ins with the value of any broadcast or print media supporting your promotion. Many marketers assign a 10 percent media value to a display with advertising support, so a $2.5 million advertising campaign translates to an additional $250,000 display value.

SELLING IN YOUR DISPLAY TO RETAILERS*

Actually, you probably have to "buy in" a display from a retailer—pay for the space *if* the retailer even picks you over the competition. (See "Trade Programs," Chapter 13.)

You have to convince the retailer your display is more valuable than the next guy's. Arm the salespeople with a simple sell-in sheet that lets them tell the story in just one precious minute. And remember, even if headquarters authorizes a display, the store manager may not. Consider these points for your sell-in literature:

- Profit per square foot: This display holds X product in only X square feet, and the product will turn at X rate at $X margin, giving you $X per square foot per day.
- In the past, displays like this have generated X results.
- This is our peak selling season, so if shoppers see it, they'll buy.
- This display will generate impulse purchases, *incremental* profits for you.
- This display will enhance your store décor with colorful graphics designed by a leading agency specializing in retail excitement.
- The celebrity/property/sponsorship is hot! We paid a zillion dollars for the rights, and you get to showcase it in your store free.
- This sweepstakes and its prizes will catch everyone's attention for impulse sales. And the in-pack instant win tactic generates additional sales. It's exciting! Someone in your store may win!
- Shoppers will respond to this promotional offer with incremental purchases. If they don't see the offer, you'll miss out.
- Displays on average generate two to seven times more sales. (Careful, the retailer will know the store display's track record. Don't talk down to the retailer's experience.)
- We've imprinted your store's name on this display/ad/literature/price sign, so shoppers will identify you with the offer.
- Your competitor doesn't allow vendor displays, which gives you a competitive advantage.
- We're supporting this program with advertising that will drive traffic to the display.

*See "Performance Programs," Chapter 12, page 311, for sales incentives like display contests.

- This display offers recipes, and that makes people shop for ingredients. (Same for other "how to" applications.)
- After the display period, you keep the loader.
- This display could win a prize in our display number drawing—*if* it's up.

GLOSSARY OF POS FORMATS

banner Sign suspended across window, wall, ceiling, and outdoor fixtures.

base wrap Repeat pattern signage comes in rolls to wrap around the base of a mass display.

bin A display's container to stock merchandise or premiums; can be a self-shipper, a near-pack display, a dump bin, etc.

bottle topper A small cardboard tag that hangs from, or wraps around, a bottleneck; typically attached by hand, often at the point of sale (to avoid manufacturing interference).

buying break A space in a display stacking made by removing one or two packages for easier consumer access and also for giving the impression that others are buying the product.

case card Cardboard sign with slits at the base to slide into the product's case and stand upright (slits often called "lollipops").

channel strips See *shelf strip*.

corrugated Cardboard with two stiff cardboard laminates reinforced by a rippled inner layer; as the common cardboard appliance box, it's exceptionally strong, versatile, and lightweight.

counter card Sign with an easel back for countertop placement. (Some include double-sided tape for wall applications and a string hole for mobiles.)

counter unit Permanent or semipermanent unit that stocks and showcases the product on the counter.

cross-merchandising Placing product(s) in two different, but complementary, category locations, such as soft drinks in the salty-snack section.

cut case A shipping carton that's cut into an open tray to stock and showcase product; "stadium cuts" are diagonal cuts along two sides for product visibility and access like bleacher sides.

dangler A plastic sign that connects to a store shelf price rail through its neck and tab, dangling beyond the shelf with the product message.

display To some store managers and salespersons, a prominent stacking of product with a feature price; to some marketers, the promotional program's in-store signage; for many, any in-store signage that showcases the product.

dump bin A container for merchandise that is simply dumped inside, as opposed to a neatly stacked self-shipper or gravity feed bin.

end cap A product stacking at the end of the store aisle or gondola.

entryway trip wires Opening doors pull a wire, which raises, then lowers, a sign; popular Halloween tactic makes goblins rise and fall.

extrusion molding Think of licorice; molten plastic is forced through a preformed mold (toothpaste style) that creates a long, preshaped piece that's chopped into the desired sizes; used for permanent fixture side and corner trims, fiber optics, channel strips, etc.

floor case Glass-sided fixture for pricey products, sometimes locked.

floor graphics Temporary product signage adhered to the store's floor.

gondola Shelving unit, open on two sides, typically placed in rows that in turn create the shopping aisles.

gondola end (cap) A featured product stacking/display at the end of an aisle gondola.

gondola topper Two-sided sign on top of the aisle-end gondola and visible from both aisles coming and going.

gravity-feed Dispensers in which stacked product drops down to replace shopped product. (Examples: slanted milk trays; J-shaped cola can stacks, gumball machine principle.)

hangtags Small signs that hang from the product by string or slot and typically attached by hand.

header card A sign placed above the case, bin, self-shipper, etc.; a pole header (or pole topper) sits on a floor pole; a case header sits on a product case; a self-shipper header sits on the bin. (Also *riser card* or *case card*.)

injection molding Molten plastic is injected into a mold to create a solid three-dimensional figure—for example, toothbrushes, plastic squirt guns, plastic model airplanes. Used for permanent, full-dimensional fixtures like contoured lipstick fixtures, floor stands, or even brand characters, such as M&M figures.

in-store media In-store communication media available through the retailer or media services, such as audio advertising, shopping cart signs, and coupon dispenser signs.

island Retail floor display section with a 360 percent shopping area.

light thieves Translucent fixtures placed beneath a ceiling light to capture its light for illumination.

mass display An exceptionally large display and product stacking.

merchandiser A unit that showcases and stocks product or highlights product features, benefits, price, etc.; often permanent shelving units, such as cosmetic units, battery display cases, or hardwood floor brand units.

mobiles Ceiling-suspended signs that capture additional attention through natural air-generated motion.

off-shelf display A display that places the product in a location other than its traditional shelf position.

Peg-Board (hook/merchandiser) A wall or gondola panel with industry-standard holes to accommodate pegs that hold the product. (See *slat wall.*)

plan-o-gram (See Glossary at back of book.)

pole signs Cardboard signs placed on top of temporary pole fixtures; poles are typically cardboard tubes with reusable (or disposable) metal feet. Also called *pole toppers.*

pole toppers See *pole signs.*

prepack display See *self-shipper.*

price circle A blank area on a display sign where the retailer can fill in the product's price.

product spotters Small shelf signs, pointers, or arrows that call attention to a product.

rack A floor stand with shelves, pockets, or hooked arms; often solid wire, to hold, for example, salty snacks.

rail strips See *shelf strip.*

riser The part of a display that projects above the product or rises above the top shelf for high visibility. (See *header card* and *case card.*)

section overlap The tendency of products from one section to drift or carry over into another product section.

self-selector A merchandising display that organizes product so shoppers can readily select color, size, style, etc.

self shipper A self-contained combination shipping container, display sign, product inventory, and stocking bin. Also called a *prepack.*

set-sell A self-shipper for countertops and small spaces; often at the cash register for high-turn, impulse items like mint tins, lip ice, etc.

shelf extender A small tray affixed to a shelf that extends the shelf's space.

shelf strip A strip of tag stock or plastic, pressure-fit into the price railing under a product to gain added attention. (Also *rail strip* or *channel strip*.)

shelf talkers Printed card sign for stacked or shelved product; may use double-sided tape but is often folded with one edge tucked under the product to hold it in place.

sign A more specific term than *display,* referring to the printed graphic presentation.

slat wall A wall or gondola panel with industry-standard horizontal grooves to accommodate slats for product merchandisers, shelves, etc. (See *Peg-Board.*)

spectacular A major island-product stacking, typically flanked by other signage elements—pole signs, banners, base wrap, etc.; common with themed seasonal events like Halloween, Thanksgiving, Super Bowl, etc.; often involves a sales/retail display contest and often used for multiple products—cola, chips, and dips.

stadium cut (See *cut case.*)

stacker card A card sign often on top of a pole, gondola fixture, or product cases and designed to showcase stacked product.

static clings Plastic cling signs that adhere like plastic wrap to coolers and door windows.

tag stock A paper stock named for the thickness of price tags.

tear pads Notepad style pads on displays and shelves for shoppers to tear off—for sweepstakes entries, refund forms, etc.

trim kits Kits containing several elements to build a mass store display (spectacular), such as base wrap, mobiles, header cards, decals, multiple shelf talkers, and price signs.

vacuum-forming Refers to flat plastic sheet placed over a dimensional mold and heated waffle iron–style to form a dimensional sheet. (Examples: Halloween masks and colorful, dimensional signs.)

wire (rack) Product stocking units that use solid wires with baskets for CDs, books, salty snacks, etc.; may accommodate "slip-in" signs.

BUDGETING CONSIDERATIONS

You may want to base your POS budget on incremental sales projections—tapping only into incremental profits to fund the program. Consider allocating 10 to 20 percent of your increased revenues to the point-of-sale program.

If the program is a long-term fixture lasting a year or more, ongoing product prominence may justify tapping into the total budget. Use this checklist to determine items to budget for:

- Each display item's cost: creative development, art, photography, production. Include everything—header, tear pad, pole, legs, price signs, etc.
- Warehousing
- Shipping cartons, including dividers and padding
- Packing and addressing cartons
- Label generation—from data to labels
- Shipping
- Delivery from warehouse to retailer
- Instructions for sales, store managers, display assemblers
- Merchandising services to assemble and place displays
- Retailer allowances for display space
- The program itself, such as refund costs, licensing fees, sweepstakes execution, and prizes
- Materials and efforts to sell the program to distributors and the trade
- Whatever it takes to monitor and facilitate execution, from confirming deliveries to replacing damaged goods

EXECUTION CHECKLIST

_____ What will the retailer allow—height, width, sound, counter, floor, motion, etc.?

_____ Should you offer variations of the same display construction to accommodate different retailers' requirements?

_____ What store section will the display be in—what limitations and possibilities? How wide are the aisles?

_____ Should you offer to imprint the retailer's name on the display or literature?

_____ Have you factored in display packing and shipping costs, including custom cartons?

_____ How will your display arrive at the retailer's, and who's going to assemble and place it? Vendors: Do not rely on the retailer.

_____ Have you received authorization from the chain's headquarters? How is this communicated to each store? Alert salespeople. Remember, authorization doesn't mean each store will agree to the display.

_____ Have you allowed time in the sell-in process? How far in advance do you need to book a display with each retailer, when should it ship, when should product ship and arrive—where?

_____ Have you included *simple* assembly instructions?

_____ Will your fancy die-cuts become dog-eared in shipping? A simple layout revision right now may save money and headaches.

_____ Will your signage be destroyed by:

    _____ Floor mopping?

    _____ Shopper collisions?

    _____ The warehouse store's forklifts loading pallets at night?

    _____ Children?

_____ Have you run tests for stability, product weight, assembly, and actual consumer interface—both shopping from and bumping into the display?

_____ Can route people quickly and easily restock the merchandise from the back to move older product first?

_____ Are there any ergonomical considerations—shopper's height, visibility, easy access, easy flavor selection, and the like?

_____ Will the last products be visible and accessible?

_____ How long will your battery last, and who will change it? How will the chosen person be reminded? Will the retailer allow AC cords? Is there an outlet near your display? Does it limit where your display will be placed?

_____ Is there a big blank price spot for the retailer (20 to 30 percent of display's size)? Is it varnished so markers won't work?

_____ With sound, what if the staff finds it annoying and removes the batteries? Will the display still communicate?

_____ Will the display still communicate if the loader is removed?

_____ Is it simple?

_____ Can you retrofit a permanent display fixture with new messages?

_____ Will your display's coupon get misredeemed? It's a small version of a blank check. (See "Coupons," Chapter 3.)

Go shopping. Once the display program is in the field, give field people a checklist of authorized stores plus a questionnaire, including where the display is placed, how it is stocked, competitor activity, and so on. If it hasn't been placed, try to get store manager comments. Have the form faxed or e-mailed *immediately* to allow quick reaction to any problems.

Record everything. Because there are so many variables at work, make a list of every factor: the display type, location, retailer, region, promotion type, pricing, allowances, timing, and even the weather. Get feedback from retailers, salespeople, distributors, and even consumers. Start a grid or spreadsheet to compare programs. Every program can be the foundation for future programs and greater results.

8

SAMPLING

INTRODUCTION: TRY IT, YOU'LL LIKE IT

Ever since the corner grocer pulled a pickle out of the barrel for the customer to try, sampling has been one of the primary sales promotional tools. There is no better proof of product value than a free trial, whether a test-drive in an automobile, a sachet of coffee, or a trial run with a new computer game. If the product has visible or recognizable differences, value, or quality, one of the best ways to generate a sale can be through a sample. Marketers recognize this and have been increasing their use of this tried and proven tool over the past few years, according to the April 2004 *PROMO* Industry Trends Report.

Almost anything can be sampled, from Neutrogena soap in an upscale hotel bath to Crest and Colgate toothpaste and Oral-B toothbrushes in dentist offices to perhaps the most successful sampling plan ever: the serving of Starbucks coffee on United Airlines. The coffee company had only regional distribution when the United program started, but it catapulted Starbucks to industry favorite quickly and, one would assume, inexpensively.

Although sampling has been increasing, much of that increase has been due to the new methods developed to distribute samples. Where door-hangers and through-the-mail once were the way samples were distributed, today there is a wide variety of new methods, many of which rely on the media. Although in-store or at-location is still the most common approach to sampling—accounting for 65 percent of all samples—home distribution, commonly through media forms such as newspapers or magazines, now accounts for 20 percent of all samples, with special events making up the other 15 percent.

The key elements in developing a sampling strategy are: (1) determining whether product sampling can be an effective promotional tool and (2) selecting the right audience to receive the sample.

Product sampling works best under the following conditions:

- The product is new or improved. In most cases, this means a discernible quality that can be determined by the customer or prospect based on a trial. If the product doesn't perform better in trial than does its competitors' products, sampling is not generally recommended.

- The product really needs several uses to establish an identifiable difference. Even though a food product can be sampled with one taste, such products as shampoos, skin cleansers, ointments, lotions, and the like may need multiple uses to establish the clear difference. Multiuse samples are more difficult for marketers to use in terms of sampling effectiveness since they require several uses for the consumer to see, understand, or experience the product difference, but they can often achieve greater results.

- The audience for the product is unknown. For example, a few years ago, the company producing Cheer detergent discovered that some people were allergic to the perfumes and dyes used in detergents. The company therefore developed a version of Cheer for those people. The problem, however, was the absence of a way to identify skin-sensitive consumers, so the company used a sampling program. It offered a sample of the new "no additive" product via media advertising. In other words, it let consumers determine whether the product was right for them. Through sampling based on consumer self-identification, Cheer's maker built a viable business quickly and efficiently with its free-sample approach.

- The product has suffered from bad publicity, product problems, or over-shadowing by competition. In some instances, the best way to dispel rumors of product problems or questions about quality is through a sampling program. Proof that the product has been improved or that previous problems have been resolved can often be achieved through product sampling. For example, one of the key elements in resolving the Tylenol product-tainting problem that occurred a number of years ago was a broadscale sampling program to show the public the safety measures that maker Johnson & Johnson had taken to ensure it didn't happen again.

The key element in sampling is the same as that in other forms of sales promotion—that is, identification of the proper customer audience for the sample. Generally, we might classify the objectives of sampling as follows:

- Sampling to reward existing users
- Sampling to generate new users
- Sampling to draw customers from competitive products
- Sampling to illustrate new uses or expanded product value
- Sampling to "migrate" customers through a product portfolio

Got a great product that people need to experience? Sample it! —Don E. Schultz

OVERVIEW

Sampling is the top brand influencer, followed by word of mouth, coupons, and advertising. Sampling can be costly and labor intensive, but the return on investment in the form of more customers is your ultimate goal.

This chapter may seem less strategic than other chapters, but its objective is simple—get the product and consumer together.

DEFINITION

Sampling simply means getting a prospect to experience your product, typically at no charge to the prospect. Whether it's a test-drive or a free cereal minibox, sampling creates trial and, it's hoped, customers by giving prospects a firsthand experience.

COMMON SAMPLING OBJECTIVES BY TACTIC AND DELIVERY

(Also see itemized tactics below plus objectives listed above.)

TACTIC	OBJECTIVES (Beyond Trial and Purchase)
In-store (or lot)—free product handout	• Ensure product reaches consumer • Reach consumer at point of sale • Spot and sample target profile—by age, lifestyle, image, etc. • Prepare product (serve hot/cold) • Retailer support
In-pack/on-pack/near-pack delivered	• Economical distribution of product (no booth or handout costs), possibly riding on sister-brand distribution • Targeted distribution through partner—free Internet provider disk with software; free Dairy Queen coupon in cereal box • Increase product visibility
Coupon delivered	• Economical, broad reach • Encourage retailer product stocking • Combine advertising message
Service delivered (free fries, free inspection)	• Ensure consumer experiences product • Introduce new offering • Relaunch previously unaccepted product • Traffic-building offer at low cost of product • Create opportunity for house call
Direct mail delivered	Note: May be free product coupon or the sample itself delivered in newspaper wrap, CD mailer, its own box, etc. • Ensure product reaches consumer—possibly at lower cost than for in-store distribution • Target demographic • Leverage neighborhood mailing to secure local retailer stocking • Tie in retailer
Alternative media delivery (newspaper overwrap, magazine tip-in, Internet downloads, etc.)	• Ensure product reaches consumer—possibly at lower cost than for in-store distribution • Tie into popularity of vehicle—Web site, magazine, etc. • Target demographic • Leverage neighborhood delivery to secure local retailer stocking • Tie in retailer

TACTIC	OBJECTIVES (Beyond Trial and Purchase)
Door delivered	• Ensure product reaches consumer • Reach entire household, including kids • Highly targeted neighborhood demographic • Leverage neighborhood reach to secure local retailer stocking • Tie in retailer • Neighborhood word of mouth
Free short-term trial offer—subscriptions; test-drives; first 100 minutes; one-week vacuum trial; software demo version	• Offer "no-risk" trial of an otherwise considerable purchase commitment • Give salesperson (and advertising) a compelling "closer" • Demonstrate product that requires exceptional hands-on experience
Demonstrations (live and videotape)	• Present complex product usage and results • Encourage retailer participation and product stocking • Interface with consumers • Simultaneously demonstrate to retailer sales staff • Controlled distribution of literature, coupons, rebates, etc.
Referrals	• Product demonstration and recommendation by a trusted personal contact • Economical
Intercepts (plus guerrilla)	• Ensure product reaches consumer • Target strategic locations • Reach trendsetting areas • Increase visibility beyond store • Trained sampling team communicates message • Command attention • Encourage retailer participation
Venues (health clubs, delivery wards, airlines, etc.)	• Utilize venue's established, turnkey sampling service • Reach highly targeted audience in relevant location (power bars at health club) • Economical cost-per-target profile • Reach a captive audience (airline) • Deliver both product and extensive information
Events—bar nights, fairs, open houses	• Command attention through themed vehicle—traveling stage, radio remotes • Establish community presence • Establish an operational base stocked with literature, product, order forms, sales table, etc. • Draw greater attention through door prizes, novelties, exhibits, etc. • Economize with high-traffic site, possibly over several days • Product registration through flags, balloons, T-shirts, bags, etc. • Ability to interface with prospects (and key accounts)

ITEMIZED TACTICS

86. IN-STORE (OR LOT)—FREE PRODUCT HANDOUT

Definition	Sample delivered in-store; often includes coupon for follow-through purchase
Advantages	Proven effective
	Assures shopper will actually sample product
	Delivered at point of purchase for follow-through sale, particularly with coupon
	Sampler may target profile by age, moms with kids, etc.
	Increases in-store presence and inventory
	Event adds excitement to brand
	Sampling services lend expertise and performance
	Scanning allows analysis by store
	Also acquaints store personnel with product
Disadvantages	Limited reach
	Sampling day and daypart misses other shopper occasions
	May require expense of on-site preparation
	Reliance on samplers to properly prepare and present product
	Requires extensive planning
	Expensive on a cost-per-sample basis

IN-PACK/ON-PACK/NEAR-PACK DELIVERED

See descriptions in "Point of Sale," Chapter 7, page 188, and "Premium Programs," Chapter 10, page 265.

87. COUPON DELIVERED

Definition	Coupon for free product or service
Advantages	• Clean and simple
	• Allows additional advertising communication

- Encourages retail stocking
- Package photo on coupon teaches consumer what to look for
- Hard copy reminder
- Allows tracking and accountability
- Mass media allow broad reach

Disadvantages
- Packaged goods often redeem at full retail markup (Retailer writes marked-up price on coupon—see "Coupons," Chapter 3)
- Incurs media cost
- Chance for misredemption if someone accesses multiple coupons (see "Coupons," Chapter 3)
- Less targeted than other tactics

88. SERVICE-DELIVERED OFFER

Definition
Service offers a free sample of its product, such as free fries with visit, first salon visit free, free first consultation, etc.

Advantages
- Encourages trial that might otherwise be too big a hassle, such as a trip or consultation
- Filters out nontargets who won't make the effort
- On-site sample may generate immediate follow-up sale—free water analysis closes bottled water sale
- Follow-up offer (coupon) encourages follow-up purchase
- Free sample often results in additional purchases
- Economical—cost of goods
- Second chance for new, improved product
- Implies assurance of quality
- Vendor may participate in cost
- May expose other products in portfolio
- Controlled execution—the service's personnel

Disadvantages
- May be expensive cost per sample
- May cannibalize sales—giving away product you'd normally sell—and margins
- May be a freebie for those with no intention of purchasing
- May require procedures for one-sample-per-prospect delivery

- May require system communication, timing, and training
- Follow-up purchase may be outflanked by competitive action such as discount offer—you set the table, they eat the dinner

89. DIRECT MAIL DELIVERED (Solo, Co-op, Special Target Services)

Definition   Sample or coupon for free sample delivered through mail

Advantages
- Reaches consumer at home
- Targets select households
- Can include sales communication materials
- Can customize communication by target profile
- Reaches niche target at time of need—new homeowners; new parents; back to school, etc.
- Tracks and tests results to perfect program
- Can economize through co-op mailings
- Vendor can leverage neighborhood reach for retail participation and vice versa

Disadvantages
- Expensive medium
- Postal regulations can be limiting
- Co-op mailings suffer clutter
- Sampling in home versus point of sale
- Free sample coupon often incurs full retail markup
- Requires accurate and current mailing list

90. ALTERNATIVE MEDIA-DELIVERED SAMPLES

Definition   Deliver samples through unique, but pervasive, media, such as newspaper overwrap bags, magazine tip-ins, video inserts, Internet downloads, or interactive demo CDs

Advantages
- Depending on medium, delivery can be interactive, entertaining, intriguing, and the like
- May be relatively economical way to deliver sample to mass audience
- Commands attention and personal interaction

- Exceptional targeting through niche medium
- May allow insertion of literature, coupons, etc.
- Vendor can leverage neighborhood reach for retail participation and vice versa
- Internet provides cost-efficient sampling

Disadvantages
- Custom media are more expensive than mass media
- May still suffer mass media waste
- May require expensive custom packaging and sample size costs
- May have limited reach
- Limited to postal regulations and particular medium's production capabilities
- Delivered in-home versus point of sale
- Internet sampling limited to specific products and subject to clutter
- Internet downloads require awareness of offer

91. DOOR DELIVERED

Definition
Sample hand delivered to doorstep, typically in bag on doorknob

Advantages
- Excellent targeting of neighborhoods and households—entire family
- Commands attention and interaction with sample
- Product size and weight more flexible than other media
- Can include literature, coupons, etc.
- Vendor can leverage neighborhood reach for retail participation and vice versa

Disadvantages
- More costly than other media or store handouts
- May be impractical in apartment houses, condominiums, etc.
- Subject to pilferage
- Reliance on unsupervised, low-pay person who may even dump samples

92. FREE SHORT-TERM TRIAL OFFER

Definition
Target retains and samples product for short period
Examples: Trial subscriptions, mail-order vacuum cleaner, Internet service, time-limited software, etc.

Advantages
- Familiarizes target with complex product
- Allows sampling of "price-issue" product
- Only prime prospects may bother to apply
- Propensity to purchase products in hand rather than to return

Disadvantages
- Exceptional executional considerations
- High per person trial cost, especially factoring nonpurchasers
- Requires advertising, possibly with sophisticated response mechanism, such as an 800 number service
- Requires exceptional effort for consumer to respond
- Risks—need system in place to prevent fraud
- Returned product may have to be refurbished or replaced
- May require liability clearance

93. DEMONSTRATIONS

Definition
Supervised trial or demonstration of product at retail, during event, on cable TV, Web site, etc.; may be live, videotaped, or interactive demonstration

Advantages
- Familiarizes target with complex product
- Allows sampling of "price-issue" product
- Reduces fear of inability to use product
- Clearly demonstrates benefits
- Controlled demonstration should be problem free
- Knowledgeable presenter with sales skills
- May allow interactivity—questions, instructions
- Encourages retailer to stock and display
- Also trains retailer's salespeople

Disadvantages
- High cost per person—demonstrators, training, booth, materials, etc.
- Limited reach
- Requires extended time, effort, and logistics, including permissions, security, equipment, safety, and cleanup
- May require liability clearance

94. REFERRALS

Definition
Product recommended by an acquaintance, communicating product experience; referring party may be rewarded for successful referral

Advantages
- Creditability of a trusted acquaintance
- Pleasant product experience described in detail
- Highly targeted with similar, like-minded profiles
- Saves cost of salesperson
- Referral incentive and purchase incentive motivate referring party (and purchaser)
- Familiarizes target with complex product
- Allows familiarity with "price-issue" product
- Reduces fear of inability to use product

Disadvantages
- Reach limited to those who own product
- People may feel uncomfortable "selling" to friends, particularly for a reward
- Incentive reward may diminish referral's credibility
- Rewards add to cost per sale
- No guarantee of follow-through—lack of control
- Requires system and personnel to verify and reward referrals
- Product may be returned after referral reward

95. INTERCEPTS (PLUS GUERRILLA)

Definition
Sampling person intercepts passersby with product and communication materials; delivered at strategic locations, such as commuter trains, retailer entrances, malls, beach, etc.
Guerrilla marketing (see page 228) goes further with a public relations topspin and trained crews at select locations: headache tablet at tax day lineup, trend product at inner-city midnight basketball, trendsetters drinking product at bar

Advantages
- Product delivered directly to consumer
- Targets key locations—near retailer, usage occasion (sunscreen on beach), active high-visibility area (commuter train), competitor's location

- Spurs word of mouth
- May have a professional interacting with consumer versus handout service
- May command attention through themed sampling vehicle or proactive sampling team
- Can reach lifestyle locations—where target works, shops, relaxes, etc.
- Guerrilla extends public relations topspin and can link to consumer's lifestyle in dress, behavior, enthusiasm, etc.
- Guerrilla's influence in trend areas also influences broader areas— inner city, sandlot sports, bars, fashion, etc.
- May encourage retailer participation

Disadvantages
- Considerable up-front research and planning
- Samples may not be delivered near sales outlet
- Expense of trained, higher-priced professionals
- Possibly unsecured sampling areas
- Higher cost per target
- Remote location may require considerations to provide sufficient stock, crew, food and restroom facilities, parking, loading, even security
- Susceptible to weather, traffic, overcrowding, and other unforeseen problems—backup plans essential
- Potential to annoy and alienate consumers
- May require city/community/business permission
- May be open to mishaps and liability claims

96. VENUES

Definition
Samples are distributed at established targeted locations, such as health clubs, hospitals, doctors' offices, airlines, schools, music venues, etc.

Advantages
- Venue provides definitive target profile
- May deliver the right sample to the right person right at the time of need
- Venue may participate as a service to customers
- Implies third-party endorsement (diapers from the hospital)
- Can be ongoing, efficient program
- Staff-delivered samples reduce cost

Disadvantages	• Time and resources to establish partnership, logistics, etc. • Reach limited to venue and its demographics • Possible field services' expense • Some venues less targeted, like airlines • Samples may be distributed by unprofessional or apathetic individuals, jeopardizing effectiveness • Venue's fees, which competitor may also bid for • Site may not sell product • May be open to mishaps and liability claims

97. EVENTS

Definition	Samples delivered at special events, created by either product company or an existing event—bar nights, fairs, festivals, open houses
Advantages	• Piggybacks on popular consumer activities and attractions • Event draws target demographic in a receptive mood; may economically reach large numbers • Publicity opportunities • Implies event endorsement • Brand-created event can provide ongoing recognition and become a profit center—namesake music festivals, cook-offs, etc., plus VIP extensions
Disadvantages	• Sampling experience may be overshadowed by event's distractions • May suffer clutter among other handouts • Weather concerns • Exceptional logistics—stocking, restocking, crew breaks, parking, electricity, security procedures, liability measures, etc. • Brand-created event requires major commitment and runs many risks—popularity, liability, talent problems, etc.

PACKAGED GOODS: INCLUDE RETAILERS

In the end, retailers sell products, and your sampling program ultimately has to sell products. Brands have doubled retail sales short term with sampling. If consumers try it and like it, you've got long-term results plus a head start with the retailer.

Demonstrate lifestyle, set the trend. Some guerrilla sampling services specialize in trendsetting areas and tactics. Professionals blend in and interact with select demographics—music bars, fashionable lounges, midnight urban basketball, art events, and so on. These advocates demonstrate how your product with a lifestyle spin (sometimes surreptitiously) and their targets in turn influence more prospects. It may not result in immediate sales, but it can eventually mushroom and make yours the first-call name.

Wet and dry and hot and cold. These terms quickly communicate the sampling format and requirements. Kool-Aid can do a *wet* sampling in a cup for immediate consumption or a *dry* sampling with a free sample pack to take home; a tea brand may offer a *hot* sample or a *cold,* iced sample.

GUIDELINES AND CAUTIONS

There's no such thing as a free candy bar. A company's candy bar may cost only cents to manufacture (cost of goods), but it costs a lot more to sample, especially through a retailer. Retailers want to make money, and giving your product away is a lost sale. Consider the following alternatives:

- See "Free Product Coupons" in Chapter 3, page 78 and "Near-Packs" (under "Guidelines and Cautions") in Chapter 10, page 279.
- You can deliver free samples with a partner's near-pack promotion. See "Near-Packs" (under "Guidelines and Cautions") in Chapter 10, page 279.
- Use minisize sample packs so the retailer doesn't lose a sale and may gain one on the full size. Many sample sizes are sold in stores as trip or convenience items—toothpaste, shampoo, soap. If you don't want your sample sold, print "Not for retail sale" on the package.
- Hire a demo service with a staff to serve or demonstrate products in the store—from fresh baked frozen pizza samples to painting demonstrations. Retailers often welcome demos and may also support your product. (However, some retailers require you to purchase your own samples from them.)

- Video monitors can demonstrate product how-tos even better than salespeople. You'll need to sell the concept to the retailer as it's taking valuable retail space, making noise, using AC, and requires maintenance.

How and how often will you need to restock? What good is an expensive sampling program if there isn't enough product to sell? Make sure the restocking system's in place and then monitor it. Also, keep the product stocked in the days and weeks *after* the sampling for a consumer's next shopping trip—make it part of the contract with the retailer. It's good business for both parties.

Projecting reach and quantities. How many prospects do you want to reach in an event and will you have inventories, supplies, and people power to achieve that objective? (Rule of thumb: Number of prospects to be reached up to 300 per day per store in supermarkets or a third of attendees at an event. Factor in: Is the sample cooked, prepared on location, or simply handed out prepacked? Preparation slows up sampling.)

Days and daypart. Consider the day of the week and the part of the day, particularly for in-store sampling. When is the sampling most likely to match your target's shopping habits? Malls vary greatly. Also, research the stores' busiest shopping days, times, and locations.

Who's conducting the sampling in which retail category? Does the service have an arrangement or affiliation with the chain(s) you desire so the learning curve and system are in place? Many chains offer their own sampling service—ask the independent service why it's better than the chain's own service.

Training and backup plans. What will you need? A script? A video? Rehearsals? A policy sheet on special situations like kids, spills, electrical outlets, missing materials, rain, and the like.

Has every store been booked and confirmed in advance? Don't assume your preferred date six months from now is available. Don't even assume the store will remember you booked it—call and confirm two weeks before your event.

Is the sampling service setting its own schedule? It may have its own system that may not sync up with your advertising campaign. Communicate your plans far up front.

If your product isn't prepared and presented properly, run! Your demo staff better not scald tongues with a pizza slice or neglect to have the sample paint stirred. Have the sampling company provide details on training procedures and employees, such as average age, tenure, sampling experience with products like yours, reserve replacements, references, and so on.

Verification. Ask your vendor what its quality controls are, how it verifies performance, what reports are generated, if retailers are spot-checked during the sampling, and so on. Get a Dun & Bradstreet to check references—including where the vendor has previously sampled. Let the vendor know you'll be spot-checking yourself.

The right sampling service. Too much is at stake to go for the lowest bidder. Some topics to question and evaluate:

- Track record
- References
- Why this service fits *your* situation. Every service says it does everything, but in reality each has strong and weak areas. Which area does it have the most and best examples of?
- It's perfectly legitimate to ask how the service makes money. It deserves its markups, and you deserve to know what you're paying for. It can help both of you maximize the relationship.
- Security—what is its *written* policy for both theft prevention and reparation?
- Disaster coverage—fire, water, etc. Is it bonded and insured? Get it in writing.
- Trade and professional organizations and activities—beyond the PR value, does it truly and actively pursue its professional organization's objectives for quality standards?
- How will the service coordinate getting equipment and supplies to the sites?
- What are its performance verification methods?

- Can the service also do audits for you, monitoring the number of samples, coupons, or folders distributed; sales; competitive pricing information; competitive activity; consumer response; etc.?
- Can it recruit enthusiasts for your particular product—hobbyists, semi-pros, etc.?
- Can it produce a training video? How does it conduct training across the country?
- How will samplers handle requests for additional free samples?
- What's the notification and backup plan if the sample fails to show up?
- What is the policy for samplers handing out coupons? They cannot be entrusted to the retailer or staff. How do you verify coupons were handed out and not just dumped?
- How will the service document its expenses? What's the pricing policy and how is it verified?
- What's the price and procedure for a test in three markets?

How many trials for conversion? Some retailers think it takes six trips to convert a customer. Others say it takes three, so he or she knows the route to the store. Consider an introductory high-value offer to drive the first visit and lesser-value bounce-back offers to bring those first visitors back. (See "Bounce-Back Coupons" in Chapter 3, page 72, and also see "Continuity," Chapter 6.)

A power tool may only take one try to convince the consumer it's superior. Bose Wave Radios and Oreck Vacuums allow an extended trial period by mail. One food sample may not do the trick—an "acquired taste." The best way to learn is to conduct actual test scenarios and consumer interviews.

Ventilation, noise, traffic flow. Does your product have a distinctive smell, like paint or perfume, that may be unpleasant (or pleasant)? Check the air vent locations. Are you or your location too noisy—near a PA speaker or video monitor? Is your display obstructing traffic?

What about kids? Is your demo station kid-proof and are demonstrators trained to handle the unpredictable situations kids can cause? Remember, kids *must* be smiled at, adored, and enjoyed, no matter what havoc they wreak.

Litter? Don't settle for a trash receptacle—how often will it be emptied and replaced by whom?

Generate traffic to your demo. If you're demonstrating a product, consider traffic generators like snacks, novelties, prize drawing, announcements, and the like.

Get names and give cards and literature. With a prize drawing, you can collect prospects' names and information. If someone seems interested in your widget but hesitant, get a phone number, address, or e-mail address for a "comfortable" next step. Give the person literature and your personal business card. It's sales-closer time, so you might offer a coupon or discount offer, possibly with a short-fuse expiration.

While you're educating shoppers, educate the staff. Allocate time to staff members to train them as well. Offer them a nice premium, a deal on your product, or even a "spiff" for extra sales they help generate. If you can, let them have your product and enjoy the experience.

Other stuff to worry about:

- Prepared for bad weather?
- Need a photographer?
- Are demonstrators briefed on your product, ready for consumer questions (including how you compare with the competition)?
- Is there enough product in stock for both sampling and sales?
- Is everything available, from waste bins to your product literature?
- Can you rotate meal and bathroom breaks?
- Are there towels or any cleaning materials for accidents?
- Where will you park the truck?
- Where will you store everything?
- Need a cart?
- Is the union involved, prepped, and ready? It may not even let you plug in an AC cord.
- Do you need a power source? How many?
- What are the event hours? Does everyone know them?
- When should staff arrive before the event?
- When does the facility open and close?
- Does your staff need passes?
- Want to make your own worry list?

Insight

Smile at precious little monsters! Kids can wreak havoc with a demonstration. But showing anger can make it worse.

ABBREVIATED SAMPLE TO-DO LIST

- Compile store/location list.
- Research and determine timing for various sites.
- Coordinate execution dates with sales, services, retailers/locations.
- Coordinate with field force.
- Prepare training materials (for each role).
- Create Who-What-Why-Where-How-When report for all parties.
- Secure demo agencies and personnel.
- Assemble demo kits.
- Distribute demo kits to agencies.
- Do dry runs.
- Create and deliver in-store sales script.
- Verify each store's awareness and preparedness one or two weeks prior.
- Make a "We Need" list for the event.
- Distribute literature, samples, coupons, and the like to consumers.
- Verify execution for each store each demo day.
- Report store-by-store results within 45 to 60 business days.
- Perform continuous communication with client point person.

BOOTHS

If you plan to sample often, plan on a booth. Contact an "exhibit house" and see what it has in stock—predesigned booths that accommodate your signage. If you prefer a custom booth, give three competitive companies a request for proposal (RFP) with all the input they need, including a budget range. They can even make suggestions for the form. Consider the following:

- Space requirements:
  - People
  - Storage—product, literature, and tools or preparation equipment, coats, personal items, etc.
  - Cleaning materials (be prepared!)
  - Trash
  - Food, water
  - Samples
  - Space for competitive literature you plan to collect at the event

- Security measures
- Electrical equipment
- Ease and time to set up, take down, store, and ship
- Weight and transportation from truck to site
- The site's requirements, particularly with union workers
- How to clean after beverage spills, etc.
- Retrofitting for changes and future needs, including expansion
- Flagging your location

Other booth considerations include the following:

- Sanitation
- Finding you—increase your presence in the event's program with a drawing to draw entrants, free novelties, a big balloon, and the like
- Remembering you—business cards, literature
- A follow-up vehicle—a coupon, a retailer's location, an 800 number, Web site, etc.; a sweepstakes gathers names on entries
- How's your location? Near a competitor? Near food and/or restrooms? (Fantastic!) An obscure corner? Near noisy neighbors? Near low-traffic neighbors?
- Keep reminding your crew to smile, smile, smile.

BUDGETING

An expensive proposition? Sampling is expensive, but some say it's comparable on a cost per new-conversion basis to couponing. The objective isn't immediate profits but, rather, a customer. You may lose the sales per expenditure battle but win the marketing war.

Insight

Is your 30-day guarantee a sampling device? Some companies, like Oreck, position it as a 30-day free trial program and may also offer a free gift just for trying.

Budgeting definitions (See examples).

Simplified sampling cost: This formula is a simplification to demonstrate the subsequent budgeting steps. Refer to the "Cost Variables" below to determine your actual sampling cost.

Cost of good + Distribution cost + Shipping cost
× Distribution quantity

Profit per user per year: Average number of annual product uses × profit per unit.

Breakeven conversions: Sampling cost ÷ profit per user per year

Conversion rate: The percentage of people sampled who convert and become customers

How do you project conversion rates and uses per year? It's educated guesswork. Use historical data. Conduct research, such as product sampling intercepts, focus groups, in-store demos with posttrial interviews.

Calculation Example 1:

To determine the return on your sampling investment, calculate the breakeven conversion rate: Divide the distribution cost (and cost of manufacturing the samples, if applicable) by the profit per user.

Example: If your total costs amount to 75¢ per sample and you distribute 1 million samples, your investment is $750,000. Next, calculate the profit per user by multiplying the annual number of uses of the product by its profit margin. If six is the average number of annual uses, and the profit is $1 per unit, you get $6 profit per user per year.

For the breakeven conversion rate, divide the investment ($750,000) by the profit per user ($6). In this scenario, you need 125,000 conversions—a 12.5 percent rate (125,000 ÷ 1 million)—to break even after one year. Successful sampling programs often exceed breakeven with gains in the 12 to 15 percent range.

Calculation Example 2:

Here's another, more comprehensive description for determining your sampling cost effectiveness:

If . . .   You plan to distribute 200,000 samples
The per unit cost to make them is 25¢
The per unit cost to distribute them is 15¢
The shipping costs are estimated to be $10,000
The average number of product uses is ten per year
The profit per unit is 75¢

Then . . .   Total sampling cost is $90,000 [200,000 × ($.25 + $.15) + $10,000]

Profit per user per year is $7.50 ($10 \times \$.75$)

Breakeven conversions are 12,000 units ($\$90,000 \div \$7.50$)

Breakeven conversion rate is 6 percent ($12,000 \div 200,000$)

Payout . . . If your actual conversion rate is twice the breakeven (12% vs. 6%), you had 24,000 converters contributing $180,000 in profits ($24,000 \times \$7.50$)—a net payout of $90,000 ($180,000 profits – $90,000 cost).

Cost Variables:

- *Sampling service*
- *Sampling site fee*
- *Samples*—quantity × cost. However, some retailers require samples be purchased from their stores. (It may cut delivery costs at the same time it motivates the retailer. Negotiate the retailer's margin.)
- *Support communication*—advertising, literature, novelties, etc.
- *Shipping, warehousing, delivery*—including any sampling equipment, sampler wardrobe, tablecloths, signs, etc.
- *Weight and dimensions for direct mail or hand delivery*—create a prototype for the shipping department to evaluate. If samples are awkward to warehouse, handle, deliver, or carry, costs rise. You'll need cartons and padding, possibly customized, plus packing. (See "Cartons and pick-and-pack cost!," Chapter 10, page 280.)
- *Coupon handouts*—to encourage a follow-through purchase. Explore placing a coupon on the sample to avoid service costs. Factor in redemption costs—and sales.
- *Cost of goods versus lost sales*—see "Free Product Coupons" in Chapter 3, page 78.
- *Co-op versus solo*—it costs more to mail your sample alone, but the results may double. A co-op mailing with other product offers saves cost *and* you can request category exclusivity—no competitors allowed.
- *CPM versus conversion rates*—lower cost per thousand (CPM) samples doesn't equate to better return on investment if you're sampling the wrong target. Your delivery vehicle must be highly targeted, which costs more per thousand but with less waste.
- *Training*—from an instruction sheet to a script to producing a video.
- *Booth or media*—from a table with a sign to a kiosk, a Sunday newspaper tip-in to solo direct mail.

- *Demo "fer instances"*
  - A standard demonstrator (versus a specialist) may be $125 per day (or $200)

    . . . plus training.
  - One demonstrator may handle six stores in a week ($750 to $1,200 per week).
  - A grocery program may distribute 300 samples per store per day, depending on if samples are prepared or packaged.
  - The retailer may charge $15 to $50 to cover additional labor, or more to conduct the sampling, plus the samples themselves—"would-be" sales.
  - "Kitting" the store package may run $7.50 or more for packaged goods.
  - National shipping may run $6.20 (up to ten pounds); local delivery may run $7.20 to $30 (up to ten pounds)

    . . . plus the table or booth

    . . . plus materials for unforeseen accidents—towels, cleaning supplies, etc.
  - A sampling service may charge $10,000 for production and then $2 per copy, for a 15- to 30-minute training video. (Consider incorporating advertising and infomercial excerpts to save production costs.)

EVALUATION

What are your evaluation criteria and measures?

Consider these factors:

I *n s i g h t*

How do you do a "Pepsi Challenge"–type event and win the challenge? Act local, think global. There are geographical pockets where even underdog products are the favorites. Some marketers test in select markets but broadcast the results nationwide.

- See the above calculation examples
- Samples delivered compared with incremental sales—how much did the quantity of samples compare with incremental sales?
- Precontrol, postcontrol, and test-control sales comparisons
- Coupon redemption (code and track sampling coupons)
- Display activity
- Retailer reorders
- Regional sales gains

- Cost per sale (realizing there are longer-term benefits)
- Weather, competitive activity, and other unforeseen factors
- The product itself—is it as good as research indicated?
- All the above budgeting considerations

Do a test. Test in 20 to 30 stores in a few markets, including the home office market so associates can be involved. The retailer may be able to provide data that show immediate results. Direct mail tests can isolate several variables. Also, there are services that will interview and videotape consumers at the site.

Other test procedures. Code coupons to get a quick read on results. Track overall scanner data for sales without redemption and compare.

Check postprogram sales one and two weeks later, and get more retailer data on any bounce-back coupon redemption or repeat purchase activity.

Consider consumer evaluation forms about the sampling experience. Motivate participation by offering another value. Consider a postprogram telemarketing interview. Find out why people did or did not respond and their reaction to the sample.

Save the data! Use them to compare one sampling with another and to ultimately build the learning curve for future programs. Categorize everything on a spreadsheet.

After the sampling, follow through. Offer a demonstration discount, a coupon, a rebate, or even a referral coupon that earns a reward when redeemed. Attach a bounce-back coupon for a repeat visit and sale (which your retailer may stock up for).

Plan for postprogram sales in the initial sales call. Make sure there's inventory, a replenishment process, and a tracking system to implement at least one month after the sampling.

Fun, creative approach to traffic-driving value and tie-in offer.

"Self-destruct" coupon reaches
more users and limits liability.

Creative collect and get refund
accommodates different purchase levels.

Contest (skill) may require purchase.
Can also reinforce brand.

"Red reveal" drives traffic to display decoder.
2nd chance drawing entry for unclaimed prizes.

Match and win tactic drives traffic to product's/display's
match-up symbol and can reinforce brand.

Coupon + Entry – Two reasons to redeem.

Value packs offer excellent consumer value at low cost of goods and ensure offer will pass through to customer.

Newspaper-delivered sample coupon vehicle.

©The Procter & Gamble Company.
Used by permission.

Value and premium packs deliver great value without discount perception.

Free premium instead of refund reinforces image and may cost less.

Advertisement reprinted with the permission of the Quaker Oats Company.

Partner-delivered refund benefits both parties – free media to targeted market, strong purchase incentive for low-cost item.

Used with permission.

Giving dealers an arsenal of promotional tactics lets each use the best for each market: Referral Door Hanger, 3-Month Intro Offer, Preferred Service Card, Inspection Offer, and more.

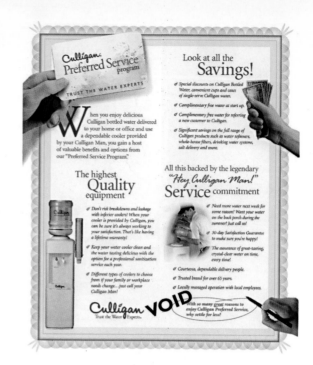

Your offer's total
potential can add up
to a big motivating
number. $100 in
"bounce-back"
coupons delivers
more sales.

Tie-in discount
program. One gives
media delivery, the
other, a value.

Integrated point-of-sale program.
Used with permission.

Display loader (wreath) commands attention, rewards retailers for placing display, and can be self-liquidated to consumers.

Make it easy and motivational to find your new location.

Game puts new spin on trade allowance. Using product as reward can sidestep corporate policies against loaders.

Sweepstakes entry also demonstrates
product and drives traffic.

Used with permission.

Stock game cards let
you customize your prize
pool, odds, and program
theme with professional
quality execution.

Provided by MCC Printing
and Promotion, LCC.

Tie-in partners share excitement, traffic,
markets, media, and great offers.

Used with permission. Dannon is a registered trademark of The Dannon
Company, Inc. ©2004. The Dannon Company, Inc. All rights reserved.

Every time you buy Velamints from now until March 15,
you could be in for a big surprise. Because the Velamints Mystery
Man will be watching at randomly selected retailers throughout
the country—and handing dozens of lucky winners $1,000 on
the spot.* So next time you reach for a mint, reach for Velamints.
With a little luck, you'll get caught in the act.

*No purchase necessary. See Official Rules for validation of winning purchase and alternate way to win. Up to
$48,000 in prize money to be awarded.

"Mystery spotter" tactic—A coupon
receives one more reason to redeem.

Used with permission.

Stock sales incentive game has variable prize levels to add
excitement, but the total prize budget is controlled in the printing.
Provided by MCC Printing and Promotions, LLC.

Financing is a powerful tool for a "considered
purchase" and no discounting perception.
Used with permission.

Your own guarantee shows quality conviction and
provides a bold, risk-free trial incentive.

Popular cause is also a collectible continuity
purchase program.
Courtesy Campbell Soup Company.

PROPERTIES AND EVENTS
(Also see "Tie-ins," Chapter 11)

INTRODUCTION:
MAKING THE RENT-OR-BUY DECISION

As explained in the following chapter, properties are audience-gathering activities around which sales promotion activities can be developed. Generally, when the marketer thinks about properties, he or she is thinking about taking advantage of the interest or attention the activity is generating among consumers as a method of building sales or enthusiasm for his or her product or service. Thus, in the strictest sense of the word, any promotion that relies on a *property* is relying on borrowed interest. That's not bad, but the promotion manager must recognize the audience came to the property not to learn about the marketer's brand or even the product category. Instead, they came because they were interested in the activity or event or the people associated with the property, whether the National Football League, the Olympics, a Rolling Stones concert, or Willie Nelson for Farm-Aid. The product or service the marketer is promoting through the property is generally a by-product of the event, not the main event. This is not to say that borrowed interest is bad, but the promotion manager needs to remember that in developing plans and programs that will help sell more stuff.

As the title of this introduction suggests, the key ingredient in developing an effective property promotional program is whether you will own the property or simply rent it for a certain period. For example, the term *soap opera* emerged from the early days of radio and television. It came from the fact that several soap and detergent manufacturers, such as Procter & Gamble, actually developed and produced the daytime dramas as a way to promote their products. They "owned" the dramatic series, which gave them exclusive rights to promote their products on the show and to use the personalities that emerged from the series to further promote their products. Today we see this same type of "ownership" in such activities as soccer clubs, basketball teams, and the like.

Alternatively, many organizations choose to rent participation in a property for a certain period. They become official sponsors of the Olympics, the World Wrestling Federation, various golf tournaments, charities, and other activities by way of agreements whereby the marketer agrees to pay a fee to have the brand or the organization represented as part of the property.

Obviously, the decision for the promotion manager is whether to rent or to buy the property. That decision is generally one that has major financial implications for the organization. Thus, the use of properties is not some spur-of-the-moment decision and shouldn't be treated as such.

The key strategic determinant in any use of properties is the audience the activity generates and for which it has appeal. In truth, participation in a property is not unlike the selection of traditional advertising media. If there is no audience match between the property and the brand or organization, the sheer size of the audience generated is of no matter. For example, in some recent analyses we conducted for a marketing organization, we found that rather than helping build the brand, the association with the property actually hurt sales. The target audience for the marketer's brand simply ignored the sponsored property. In some instances, we found the brand's involvement with the property was actually a deterrent to continued use of the brand. So the key element is to know enough about your target market and the property's audience and reputation to make sure there is a fit.

Although properties clearly can build sales for an organization, they too have a life cycle. Something that is highly desirable today may fade quickly in the face of new audience interests or changing consumer whims. Entertainment personalities are notoriously risky, as Chrysler recently learned from its association with Celine Dion, and Hertz learned several years ago with its use of O. J. Simpson. So properties can boom the product or service as well as bust it. And the problem is that it's very difficult to predict what will likely happen in the future.

Clearly, the more established the property, the higher the cost of participation but also the lower the risk.

Another factor that must be considered is the potential for piracy, or what is now called *"guerrilla marketing."* This is simply a term for marketing activities that play off the value of the property, but the marketers are not authorized to do so nor do they pay the fees required of legitimate sponsors or participants. It can be most disconcerting to spend substantial time and money developing an agreement with a property owner for participation with the assumption you will have exclusive rights to the property, only to see a competitor skirt the law in some way or other and benefit from an implied association.

The use of properties can often be a huge success, as evidenced by Budweiser's continuing participation in the Super Bowl. In fact, Bud and the Super Bowl have become almost synonymous. Consumers actually look forward to the next set of Budweiser commercials they know they will see in that venue. This ongoing association demonstrates the key point of any property evaluation. The Super Bowl audience matches the audience Budweiser wants to reach. That's when the real value of a property shows through. And in cases like this, whether you rent or buy makes little difference because the property really does help you sell more stuff. —Don E. Schultz

OVERVIEW

Put Elvis, Marilyn, or the latest teen throb on a drinking cup and it becomes a sought-after collectible, outshining your competitor's common cup. In fact, the whole sales chain will take notice. Licensed properties deliver the excitement and recognition your product or program may otherwise lack. But careful, they aren't foolproof and even award winners have been profit losers.

DEFINITION

Licensed properties are celebrities, events, leagues, entertainment packages, and the like that have their own intrinsic value, identity, *and* rights to their likenesses, which can be sold to marketers. The costs vary by the marketer's ambitions—from simple refund offers on video releases to creating character likenesses and selling them with happy meals.

COMMON LICENSING AND EVENT OBJECTIVES BY TACTIC
(Also see itemized tactics below.)

TACTIC	OBJECTIVES (Beyond Purchase)
Product placement in TV or movie	Exposure with TV/movie topspin; implied product popularity
Product affiliation	Add visibility, recognition, and possibly more legitimacy to product
Licensed premium offer	Increase/enhance product visibility, image, and demand; exclusivity
Licensed product value	Leverage existing licensed product to increase/enhance visibility, image, and demand; exclusivity
Event tickets	Leverage event/movie popularity with motivational ticket offer to consumers as well as to the trade, distributors, and other key people
Event extensions	Structure custom program to achieve unique business needs with additional topspin of event/property affiliation
Event events	Awareness and interaction during event through on-site program

ITEMIZED TACTICS

98. PRODUCT PLACEMENT

Definition   Product placed as prop in a TV or movie scene for a fee

Advantages
- Exposure to large audience in entertaining setting
- Implied product popularity
- Popular platform for a timely consumer promotion
- Exciting vehicle to motivate salesforce and the trade
- Publicity opportunities
- Can be relatively inexpensive

Disadvantages
- Impact dependent on prominence, no distractions, and observant audience
- Some say without actor interaction, virtually no product recall
- Individual scenes typically quickly forgotten
- Can be expensive, sometimes requiring payment for entire scene production
- Dependent on show's success
- Promotional timing subject to revised release dates

99. PRODUCT AFFILIATION

Definition   Licensed property appears on packaging
Examples: Flintstones Vitamins; Wheaties

Advantages
- Instantly lends recognition, enjoyable image, and appeal
- Implies product quality
- Can target to select market: children, teens, sports, etc.
- Product stands out from competition
- Encourages sales, distribution, and retailer support, particularly with coordinated incentives—autographs, appearances, tickets, etc.
- Package may be considered collectible, increasing value and demand
- Opportunity for hype, including the licenser's marketing

Disadvantages
- New packaging costs and operations

- Property may detract from brand's own identity
- Royalty adds to cost, leaving product less price competitive
- Licenser may require significant up-front manufacturing run plus royalty payment
- League may require inclusion of all teams
- Property's popularity is unknown at onset
- Trends can change during long lead time
- Competitors may engage in "property popularity contests"

100. LICENSED PREMIUM OFFER

Definition   Marketer offers exclusive licensed item with purchase of product—free or self-liquidated—often in collectible series

Examples: Fast-food "movie toys"; mail-in for character cup; free-with-purchase athlete poster

Advantages
- Added awareness, excitement appeal, and demand
- Self-liquidation offsets costs
- Lends property's image and allure to product
- Exclusivity makes retailer a destination, increasing share
- Collector appeal increases value, demand, repeat visit/purchase
- Collectible series generates repeat purchases
- Can target select market
- Added publicity through licenser's marketing

Disadvantages
- Fees, design, mold making, manufacturing, and shipping represent enormous up-front costs reliant on property's ultimate popularity
- Must consider food-safe inks, child choke tests, and other liabilities
- See "Product Affiliation" above

101. LICENSED PRODUCT VALUE

Definition   Marketer offers value on existing licensed property, such as a DVD title mail-in rebate

Advantages
- Popular, high-value consumer offer at relatively low cost

- Lends instant visibility and appeal to product
- Existing product (DVD) already has known ratings, unlike new release
- Existing premium does not require costs, operations, and risk of a custom premium
- DVD, CD, toy rebates, etc., are turnkey programs with historical results
- Can target select market
- Mail-in offers enjoy slippage economies (see Chapter 4, page 106)
- May enjoy added publicity from licenser's marketing

Disadvantages
- Common promotional tactic has less impact than other property tactics; me-too tactic
- Consumers may have already purchased nonexclusive item
- Mail-in offer less immediate and compelling than instant reward
- Requires redemption resources and expense (see Chapter 4, "Rebates/Refunds," page 109)

102. EVENT TICKETS

Definition   Marketer utilizes limited sponsorship involvement to give away event tickets as promotional rewards

Advantages
- Relatively inexpensive way to affiliate with a popular event
- May utilize property's name without expensive sponsorship fees (but not always)
- Flexibility—in-packs, handout perks, radio winners, redeem at gate, etc.
- Relatively easy execution
- Opportunity to "bond" key associates at event

Disadvantages
- Tickets may be full cost
- May require release of liability
- Weather considerations
- Does not grant right to property's images and trademarks (can't say *Super Bowl* without rights)
- May be lower visibility, value, and impact than other event tactics
- Limited to region—less economical than national program
- Future team performance or movie popularity unknown

103. EVENT EXTENSIONS

Definition   Marketer springboards off existing event to create its own event tactic
                     Examples: Match event scores and win; spot product on TV show and
                     win; sit in the Formula One car at Acme store; visit Acme's tent for
                     Mr. Hero's autograph

Advantages   • Custom program tailored to business needs while leveraging property's
                       popularity
                     • Allows grassroots extensions of national program
                     • Adds the brand's own topspin and image-building tactics
                     • Can create a treasure chest of tactical extensions so that each re-
                       tailer has an exclusive promotion—a football premium for one,
                       football cards for another, Super Bowl ticket, etc.
                     • Above advantages can saturate sponsor affiliation with the property

Disadvantages   • Substantial cost of property rights, exclusivity, and local execution
                     • Additional negotiation and coordination with property
                     • May require specialized expertise and resources
                     • Risk—reliant on ultimate popularity of property and tactic
                     • Subject to shifting release date, weather, competing events, etc.
                     • Effort—and planning—intensive

104. EVENT EVENTS

Definition   Marketer creates its own event within the event, such as tying into a
                     festival with an entertainment stage, relief tent, autograph signing,
                     etc.

Advantages   • Immediate, interactive link to the event and its excitement
                     • "Meet the market" opportunity
                     • Numerous opportunities with captive audience
                     • Brand can put on a personal face and share attendees' enjoyment
                     • Can bond key associates at event
                     • Opportunity to sell in consumer promotion through invitations
                     • PR opportunities

Disadvantages
- Planning-, labor-, and cost-intensive
- Extensive coordination with event promoters
- Susceptible to such unforeseen circumstances as weather, accidents, performer illness, etc., so have backup plans and insurance coverage
- Expensive cost per exposure compared to national events

EVENTS

Events reach right into the community, from professional sports to grass-roots festivals. The most crucial task is finding the right event from over 40,000 choices. Or you can create your own event. As always, start out by defining your objectives, then reviewing the possibilities. Some objectives to consider:

- Creating a more exciting presence
- Changing or enhancing your image
- Increasing the market's scope (e.g., children *plus* tweens)
- Publicity
- Lending credibility to the product ("Must be a good deodorant if a wrestler uses it!")
- Flexible foundation to launch diverse promotions under one umbrella
- Leveraging property's popularity for store traffic and tie-ins—with community presence
- Motivating trade, distribution, salesforce, etc. (hospitality events, incentives, celebrity visits, event-branded merchandise, perks, etc.)
- Bringing corporate image to the community level
- Prominent signage like stadium banners appearing on national TV
- Product sampling or demonstrations
- New regional distribution launch—awareness, traffic, distribution
- New product introduction—awareness (both trade and consumer)
- Product sales
- Trial—sampling handout
- Trial—experience product
- Literature distribution
- Launch diverse promotions under one umbrella and platform
- Retailer tie-ins—from parking-lot events to inclusion at your event
- Client/customer relationship building

- Sales and/or sales commitments (contracts)
- Lead generation
- Community goodwill—cause tie-in
- Countercompetitive activities
- Research
- Recruitment
- Additional revenues—refreshments, space rental, program advertising, etc.
- See "What Are 'Results'?" on page 255

The Schmooze Factor

If it isn't what you know but who you know, use your event to meet and greet key prospects. Give them the red carpet treatment, so they'll not only attend the event but also enjoy your company and appreciate your message. Have next steps in mind—from a company tour to a golf outing. Consider providing transportation—with refreshments—so it's a no-brainer to attend. Get on their calendar early—weeks in advance—and continue to send reminders as the event approaches.

WHAT CAN YOU DO AT AN EVENT?

Consider the following items the event itself might offer and you might tie in with:

Insight

"All politics is local." (Former Senator Tip O'Neil)

People tend to think of national events as one big ad buy by the sponsor. But smaller, local events project the impression that the sponsor is involved with the community.

- Signage (Place signs where photographers aim.)
- Sampling booths
- Preevent festivities
- Celebrity appearances
- Hospitality tents
- Entertainment
- VIP suites
- Autograph/photo sessions
- Premiums, novelties, souvenirs
- Programs—articles and advertising
- Exhibit items—Batmobile, future home, etc.

- Grandstanding—hot air balloon, clowns, sky divers, etc.
- Event awareness—newsletters, billboards, radio station ads and interviews, direct mailings, etc.
- Sponsor's mailing list; enthusiast organizations
- Publicity—event's plans and how to tie in
- Communication and preexisting creative—will there be a logo, posters, and the like? Can you use them?

DEFINE YOUR DEFINITIONS

Category exclusivity. What does *category* mean? Two competitors (like beers) can both be NFL sponsors—one for the regular season, one for the play-offs. And a regional beer can secure stadium rights so its cups and banners appear on TV. Soft drinks, sports drinks, carbonated juices, and noncarbonated juices may be different categories, as are fast-food and family restaurants. Some distinguish processed meat (bologna), fresh meat (branded frozen chicken), and prepared meat (TV dinners). Clearly define the terms of exclusivity in writing, and make sure the licenser lists any similar products it has lined up. Also, include the consequences of a breach of this understanding, such as voiding the agreement.

Percentage of sales. Because the licensor receives a commission on your sales, it wants to define sales in gross terms—invoiced before deductions. You want to factor in all credits, such as an 8 percent early payment discount, 2 percent advertising allowance, damaged goods allowances, 5 percent uncollected accounts, etc.

No guerrillas. Make sure your contract accounts for competitor ambushes. One proud soft drink executive, busing his business contacts to the Super Bowl, was horrified to find the bus line was sponsored and decorated by the competitor. What about the stadium?

I *nsight*

Halloween may be a spirited holiday up North, but in some regions it's devil worship. Have an alternative.

Lock in next year. Structure the contract so that you at least have first right of refusal. If your competitor offers a higher bid next year, you maintain your sponsorship by matching that bid. That way you test the event's success and lock out your competitors (though it leaves the price open).

BUDGETS AND BARTERING

- Ballpark: Sponsorships often run 4 percent of a company's total marketing budget, although some may reach 10 percent.
- Build research into your budget.
- Check the event's historical attendance numbers, and also try to verify them with actual gate receipt numbers.
- Research communication vehicles at the event—signs, booths, programs, etc.
- Remember, a brand also brings value to an event. Tally up your contributions, such as your consumer base, advertising, on-pack announcements, and retail signage. Assign a dollar value and exposure number. (See "Assigning Point-of-Sale Values" in Chapter 7, page 205.) Leverage those numbers in your negotiations to get some extras from the event manager, such as personal appearances, free posters, or more VIP seating.
- You might also "trade out" your merchandise or services, saving the event money. What's more, the products you offer will get visibility at the event.

CHECKLIST

The following checklist is reprinted courtesy of *Special Events* magazine, a Primedia publication.

____ Facility—Indoor
    ____ Usable square footage
    ____ Loading dock location and hours
    ____ Lighting controls/power availability/supplemental power
____ Facility—Outdoor
    ____ Water source
    ____ Power supply
    ____ Tent types and sizes

_____ Security
      _____ Armed/unarmed
      _____ Plainclothes/uniformed
      _____ Checkpoints/roaming numbers
      _____ Alcoholic beverages
_____ Parking
      _____ For staff, rigs, trailers
      _____ For guests
      _____ Traffic pattern
_____ Transportation
      _____ Type and number of vehicles
      _____ Driver instructions/routes
      _____ Signage
_____ Restaurant facilities
      _____ Permanent or convenience
      _____ Location and number
      _____ Supplies
_____ Lighting for load in/load out
      _____ Existing or temporary
      _____ Location
      _____ Power needed
_____ Emergency risk management
      _____ First aid/EMS/fire marshal on-site
      _____ Fire extinguishers—type, quantity; chain of command
      _____ Flame-resistant materials only
_____ Permits and licenses
      _____ Off-premise beverage license
      _____ Sound permits/special effects permits
      _____ Parking permits
_____ Insurance
      _____ Liability
      _____ Workers' compensation
      _____ Liquor liability
_____ Overall power requirements
      _____ Functional/decorative lighting
      _____ Caterer requirements—oven, coffeemaker, etc.
      _____ Entertainment

_____ Equipment list—rentals and purchases

     _____ Tables/chairs

     _____ Stage—type, size, height

     _____ Tenting—type, size, color

     _____ Miscellaneous

_____ Decor

     _____ Entrance

     _____ Ceiling

     _____ Stage

_____ Site plan

     _____ Conceptual

     _____ Blueprint of tables, staging, etc.

     _____ Blueprint of lighting and technical plan

_____ Audiovisual

     _____ Sound requirements

     _____ Screens—type of projection, size, quantities

     _____ Lighting—functional/ambient

_____ Entertainment

     _____ Dressing rooms for talent

     _____ Performance schedule

     _____ Hair/makeup/costuming requirements

_____ Food and beverage

     _____ Guest ratio for buffets and bars

     _____ Walk-up bars or cocktail service

     _____ Define traffic flow

_____ Staff

     _____ Host/hostesses

     _____ Directions

     _____ Registration

_____ Signage

     _____ Registration signs

     _____ No smoking

     _____ Restrooms

_____ Special services

     _____ Special trash pickup

     _____ List operators

     _____ Disabled needs

_____ Contingency plan

     _____ Rain/flooding

_____ Loss of power

_____ Speaker/emcee/entertainer cancels

And a few more items:

Site selection. Visit the site during another event to study traffic flow, noise, heat/air, lighting, nearby services, electrical access, and so on. Find where your competition will be and any exhibitors you may partner with. If the event is outdoors, check for underground and overhead utilities and any underground hazards if you have a tent with stakes.

Visitor profiles. Find the average profile of event attendees as it relates to your business.

Photographer. Give your photographer clear directions (with a checklist and schedule) about who and what to photograph and where they're located, targeted events, and so on. Provide a "must-have" and "would-like-to-have" list. Tell how you plan to use the photos so the photographer brings the appropriate camera—newsletters require one, posters require another. *Important:* A photographer typically retains all rights to photos, charging for additional usage. Negotiate a buyout to own your photos with documentation that transfers all rights to you. You can also compromise with partial buyout agreements.

Food. How to feed the staff and the cost?

Music and music licensing. Public performance of copyrighted music is subject to licensing under U.S. copyright law. Fees go to the American Society of Composers, Authors and Publishers (ASCAP); Broadcast Music, Inc. (BMI), and/or SESAC (once known as the Society for European Stage Authors and Composers). You may pay only one, but if you use several tunes, they'll overlap. As a guideline, for conventions BMI charges 5 cents per attendee, whether it's live or recorded. For individual events ASCAP charges a $70 minimum fee or 6 cents per attendee for recorded music. Live music fees depend on the number of people—$35 for fewer than 250, for example (plus the performers). Corporations can also buy a one-time, per-event license or a monthly or yearly blanket license that covers all music used. The music industry polices events, so work with a music management company—then it's that company's responsibility. Also consider Muzak or AEI Music, which provides musical programs to nonadmission functions like restaurants and hotels.

Event materials—planners/providers. An outside firm can provide décor, food, dinnerware, lamps, seating, and the like. These are typically charged one of two ways: (1) a flat fee for the items, which are marked up; (2) the items at cost and service charges on an hourly, daily, or percentage basis. Either may be the better deal, but the second may provide a more accurate reading of what quality to expect. For example, in scenario (1) you may expect a $100 punch bowl, when its actual cost is $75. In scenario (2) you're told up front the bowl costs $75 and you're paying $00 for the service to provide it.

Crashers and credentials. Count on the competition showing up and filling their bags with literature. Try to control literature distribution with a policy for who qualifies to receive it. When in doubt, use the fallback answer: "Give me your card, and I'll send you something." Consider a security system to keep out competitors and off-the-street people. If you have a celebrity coming, consider a high-profile security force and provide security clearance guidelines. Find out how they prevent imposters and counterfeiters. Also, find out how to correctly identify legitimate security people.

Prepare the troops. The true essence of an event is *people*—one-on-one, face-to-face. Your associates will meet your trade customers, consumers, distributor reps, field people, new prospects, vendors, even the press. Give everyone a prep sheet or kit. You might have a laminated pocket miniversion. In the larger sheet or kit include:

- A one-sentence description of your company or product for when the visitor asks: "What does your company do?"
- An event cheat sheet—what's happening, where, and when, including food and restrooms
- A top-line of what you want attendees to walk away knowing about your company, like your new product launch, your community activities, your retailer network, the 800 number, and Web site
- A comprehensive information kit available for key visitors—including the press—and let your associates know where to find it

Safekeeping. Ask the facility where to put valuables and valuable items you need frequent access to.

EVENT PROMOTION EXTENSIONS

Events offer numerous promotional opportunities. Divvy up different programs to different retail partners—radio ticket giveaways for one; celebrity appearances for another; licensed premiums for yet another; commemorative pins with another partner, and so on. Of course, explore these opportunities *before* you sign a sponsorship contract that might limit them.

LOWER-COST ALTERNATIVES

You don't have to be an official sponsor, but it has many merits, such as using the event's name and logo, access to functions and celebrities, exclusivity, and more. A less expensive option may be providing your product as an official supplier, which implies the event's celebrities eat your bread, wear your apparel, or use your soap—"The Official Widget of the Acme Games."

Licensed properties begin shopping for sponsors with a list of categories and prospects. You might approach the sponsorship like a standby airline passenger, waiting for discounting because the slot isn't being filled.

You can get high-impact visibility and customer interaction by simply sampling at an event. You'll reach the same enthusiasts. Research has shown that 70 percent of consumers who receive a sample at an event will use it, and 30 percent of those who receive a cents-off coupon will redeem it. That beats FSI and direct mail redemption.

Consider "ambush" opportunities—"Everyone who brings in an Acme ticket stub saves 10%," or purchase signs near the event like on the transit, billboards, or even at the facility itself.

WHAT ARE "RESULTS"?

You can quantify some results—exposures; samples distributed; incentive program results. But how do you quantify image building?

One corporation boils event results down to three areas: brand impact, business impact, and employee impact. It measures increased awareness—as with advertising. It measures increased revenues plus how many business relationships were initiated, tallying sales contacts and new product inquires. Last, the corporation researches how the event affects employees' perception of the company.

Here are some criteria you may use to evaluate your event, beyond good feelings and image building:

- Sales
- Contracts/order commitments/distribution gains
- Contacts/leads made

I *nsight*

Sometimes the trade buyer and the consumer are at odds. Grocery store meat buyers are often male and enjoy professional football—which is not a female consumer's first love. And if you don't satisfy the meat buyer's promotional preferences, you may not reach the consumer.

- Key prospect attendance
- Key prospect dialogs
- Retailer participation (set goals)
- Vendor participation (set goals)
- Partner participation
- Additional revenues, such as refreshment sales, vendor advertising, third-party booth space sales, third-party advertising, etc.
- Postevent traffic/sales increases
- Head count
- Samples delivered
- Literature distribution
- Research results
- Press coverage

MOVIES, MUSIC, CELEBRITIES, CARTOON CHARACTERS

In 1934, Clark Gable removed his shirt and exposed a bare chest in *It Happened One Night*. T-shirt sales nose-dived. Luckily for manufacturers, in 1951 Marlon Brando wore a skin-tight T-shirt in *A Streetcar Named Desire*. Of course, in the 1960s the Beatles did wonders for the hair-dryer business. Movies, music, and celebrities can turn trends 180 degrees overnight.

What's in It for Licensors?

Generally, for a licensed name the licensor wants 10 percent of merchandise sales, including an advance, whether you ultimately sell that amount or not. If the item is free-with-purchase, it may be 10 percent of the item's retail value (a big slice of your margin). Licensors may be flexible, based on how big a sale they foresee; 5 percent of a million dollars beats 10 percent of $25,000. They also consider how much the promotion's support budget is. You will probably commit to a minimum merchandise quantity/fee, possibly due up front and depending on whether the items sell.

Licensors strictly limit creative usage of logos, images, and characters and will provide guidelines. You'll probably be required to meet specified quality standards, including child safety precautions.

Professional sports leagues may require a premium version for every team—a T-shirt with each different team's name for each different geographical market. However, you may negotiate with an individual professional team rather than with its national franchise association. At a minimum, get *category* exclusivity to lock out competitors. (Caution: See "Define Your Definitions—Category exclusivity" above.)

For Hollywood impact and low risk, consider the familiar video release rebate tie-in. You can offer consumers a $5 savings on a popular video that may ultimately redeem at only 1 percent. (See discussion of slippage in Chapter 4, page 106.) You generally have no commitment other than the rebate fulfillment (an open liability). And you get to feature the video packaging (and star) in your point of sale and advertising.

Risky Business

There are over 300 movie releases a year coming from the top studios. Can you name ten? And a lot more music CDs are released each year doomed by tight programming. Most TV pilots nose-dive. Even with star power, new properties are risky.

Product Placement versus Product Involvement

Some industry veterans contend that simply placing a product in a scene often has no impact on recognition—it needs interaction with the actor. A verbal product mention can achieve recognition scores in the 50 to 75 percent range. If an actor simply drinks from the cola can, recognition can be 40 to 60 percent, even higher with each sip.

Product Placement Companies

These liaisons between film studios and corporations continuously strive to get products placed in film scenes that match the marketer's target. Their monthly retainers average $6,000 plus the donated product. Depending on the scene, the product's prominence, and the movie's potential, you may be asked to help fund the scene. Following are tips for directing your star product's scene:

- Get category exclusivity.
- Define inappropriate scene subjects and actions and request separation from those areas.
- Get guaranteed prominence. Don't be a background prop.
- Beyond placement, go for verbal mention and usage. Again, you may pay more, but you'll definitely get noticed.
- Be tasteful, not so brazen it turns viewers off to this obvious ruse.
- Don't tie with a property that dilutes the market with similar partner offers, even if they aren't competitive.
- If your product is being filmed, have a consultant on the set.
- Have a food stylist or other specialist on the set to put your product in the best light.
- If the movie or program is already filmed, make sure there's no competition in any scene—have it digitally concealed or removed.
- Animated or action hero films work best with premium offers and can provide a collectible series.
- Launch your promotion two weeks before the film opens—at the peak of hype.

Bartering with advertising and promotion. Negotiate your promotion's advertising and POS impressions for movie placement. You may also help underwrite the set's cost for some control over the lighting—Apple, for example, wasn't charged for its laptop's feature appearance with Sandra Bullock in *The Net.* Apple spent only about $5,000 total for the promotion, because part of the deal was donating a $2,000 Powerbook as a grand prize in a national Moviefone-sponsored sweepstakes (in turn, getting more product exposure). Apple also threw in a few dozen eWorld T-shirts as part of a *USA Today*/CNN cross-promotion and provided laptops at screenings where moviegoers could log on to the Internet.

Release dates are open. Even though movie studios try to release their film on schedule, they still may have to change that date at the last second, often because of competitive release dates. Always have a backup plan and the ability to sell it in to the field that's expecting a movie promotion.

Be careful with celebrity impersonators. If you use a celebrity impersonator to endorse your product, you're probably in for trouble, even if your intent is tongue in cheek. Use a clear disclaimer that this is an impersonator and seek an attorney's advice.

Be careful with characters. Licensors strictly limit creative usage of images and characters. For example, animated cartoon companies may let you use its characters only as drawn and posed in its guidebooks. You'll also find strict regulations governing colors, sizes, logo placement, and more.

Two-year time line. Here's a rough time line for a movie tie-in.

Time to Release Date	Activities
Two years	• Script available • Prospective marketers' review • Studio rewrites • Marketers begin initial negotiation
Eighteen months	• Staffing and casting • Product placement considerations • Marketers continue negotiating
One year	• Shooting begins • Release date set • License and manufacturer's merchandise designs begin • Trailer and logos produced • Initial merchandise artwork approvals • Point-of-sale development begins
Six months	• Studio approves point-of-purchase designs • Production ends • Marketer sell-in to trade/stores • Begin video release licensing and manufacturing process • POP to stores • Licensed merchandise in market • Video release tie-ins negotiated • Studio publicity/advertising • Marketer's TV/print ads • Marketer's FSI drops • Coordinate trade elements for video release

Do you really want your 15 minutes of fame? Some brands thrive on their own unique, even quirky, identity. If your brand has a respectable image and limited budget, you may want to focus on the long-term goal of making the brand the hero rather than focusing on the short-term, expensive, "borrowed interest" approach.

10

PREMIUM PROGRAMS

(See also Chapter 7, "Point of Sale";
Chapter 9, "Properties and Events"; and
Chapter 12, "Performance Programs")

INTRODUCTION:
ADDING RELEVANT VALUE TO A PRODUCT
OR SERVICE OFFER

Do premiums work?

Of course they do. Just think about how an entire brand, Cracker Jack, was built on the basis of an in-pack premium and how the brand has been maintained for over 100 years based on the brand promise of "Caramel-Coated Popcorn, Peanuts and a Prize" in every package. Or the dozens of cereal brands that have relied on premiums to build sales and profits. Or perhaps the most productive kids' promotion of all, McDonald's "Happy Meals," fun food but for kids the most important ingredient—a small gift or premium to enhance the value.

Premiums do work. But to generate maximum benefit, premiums must be developed and implemented correctly. Simply sticking an inexpensive prize or premium in the pack doesn't make much sense or provide much ongoing consumer value. And it certainly doesn't help to build the brand.

For premiums to work, they must be related in some reinforcing way to the key brand value proposition. Washcloths or towels in detergent boxes make lots of sense. Toy cars with breakfast sausage may not.

Premiums, like many other sales promotion tools, are considered short-term motivators to create immediate purchase. But in many cases the premiums live on long after the promotion has occurred and the sale consummated. For example, for years our family has had what was originally a premium, a ceramic A&W Root Beer mug. My mother received it with a purchase of the root beer when she was a girl, and I inherited it from her. I have now passed it along to one of my sons; and he likely will pass it on to one of his children. The mug is going on 75 years old, but it still reminds all of us of A&W and the "real root beer taste" the product provided then and now. So if you think a premium is just a giveaway, think about the A&W root beer mug. And if you doubt that premiums work over time, just check out the 10- to 15-year-old rock concert premium T-shirts you see walking through the mall on Saturday morning.

As more and more products become impulse items (research now shows that up to 70 percent of all consumer purchase decisions made in retail stores are impulse purchases), a premium offer at the shelf can often mean the difference between marketplace success and being an also-ran. And as retail stores move more and more to the "clean store" approach (i.e., few signs or flashing red arrows or cluttered displays), in-pack, on-pack, or banded-premiums become a critical differentiator for the marketer.

Premiums are generally described as short-term, generally low-cost, controllable motivators to purchase. For the consumer, the premium becomes an immediate reward for selecting a particular product from among a host of others. In other words, buy now and get the immediate reward of the premium. If you delay, the desirable premium may be gone.

Here are four key elements in developing any type of successful premium promotion:

1. Making sure the premium has some relationship to the product or service. For example, for several years, Union 76 gasoline has offered various types of premiums tied to NASCAR with the purchase of its gasoline

(e.g., a pin, a cap, a T-shirt, etc.). Clearly, there is an association between gasoline and auto racing, and the premiums offered by Union 76 have paid off at the pump.

2. Making sure the premium has an acceptable level of quality. A Marlboro jacket that rips at the seams or fades in the sunlight can do more harm than good for the brand. Many premiums become treasured mementos of events or activities or brand usage. Be sure the premium lives up to the reputation of the brand.

3. Picking premiums that have lasting value. A premium that is tied to a "hot" rock group can disintegrate quickly if the group fails to perform or is replaced by another fad. Fad premiums can be risky—what if you were a marketer betting your premium budget on Ben Affleck and Jennifer Lopez's *Gigli!*? Although fad premiums may sometimes work and marketers can generate huge sales increases if they guess right, a box office failure can leave marketers stuck with more character dolls than can ever be disposed of.

4. If possible, try to develop "interactive" premiums, that is, premiums that involve the customer and require additional or ongoing activity to receive full value. Collecting premium programs, such as the venerable Betty Crocker prize points that allow the consumer to obtain cooking equipment and kitchen products, continually reinforces the marketer's brand. These types of programs can range from saving points for school playground equipment and classroom computers that appeal to large groups to the more esoteric approaches tied to specific products that provide logoed merchandise and collectibles. The key element: Although the marketer may consider the premium to be a short-term incentive to buy now, the consumer may well consider the premium an emblem or icon of his or her relationship with the brand.

Premiums work. But they work best if they are planned and implemented so they accomplish the strategic goals of the brand and the organization, not just offer some type of prize or gimmick that has short-term appeal. Steve provides more details on premiums in the following chapter. —Don E. Schultz

OVERVIEW

This chapter overlaps with other chapters because premiums are the promotional rewards other tactics offer. A premium program can be a continuity program, a sales incentive program, a display program, or other type of program. Premiums are also a discipline unto themselves, as you'll see in this chapter.

DEFINITION

Premium is promotion-speak for merchandise—T-shirts, licensed character items, footballs, glassware, pens, keychains, and the like. The differentiating factor: premiums are used motivationally as rewards for purchases or achieving goals. *Merchandise* is sold by marketers directly for profit. Still, both words may be used interchangeably. (See "Three Merchandise Types" below.)

COMMON PREMIUM OBJECTIVES BY TACTIC

(Also see itemized tactics below.)

TACTIC	OBJECTIVES (Beyond Imprint Brand Registration)
On-pack/In-pack	Motivate purchase; deliver product sample; ensure prominent shelf position/visibility
Premium pack	Motivate purchase through reusable package; better shelf position/visibility; create new, higher price SKU (stock-keeping unit)
Near-pack	Motivate purchase; display presence (bin and sign)
Self-liquidator	Motivate single, multiple, or continuity purchase; slippage to defray premium cost; in-store signage (loader)
Loaders	Display and prominence
Collect and get	Short-term continuity; multiple purchase; traffic and repeat traffic
Loyalty	Long-term, ongoing purchases/traffic; long-term program efficiencies
Free with commitment	Encourage sustained purchase commitment; future full markup purchases; lock out competitor
Collectibles	Short- and long-term continuity; stand out through exclusivity; reinforce brand

TACTIC	OBJECTIVES (Beyond Imprint Brand Registration)
Licensed properties	Generate excitement; leverage property's advertising, publicity, awareness, and image; purchase motivation; exclusivity; offer retailers popular property with no fee
Exclusive offers	Build brand image and equity; higher perceived value than other premium offers
Catalog (print or Internet)	Accommodate all tastes; increase participation through performance levels; motivate goal setting; prolong incentive program; turnkey redemption process
Tie-in	Economize on premiums; leverage partner equity, image, and reach; leverage partner's distribution; utilize partner's fulfillment capability (redeem at Acme Stores); tap into partner's franchise (and traffic)
Sales incentives	Motivate staff and salesforce; prep staff for promotion; achieve incremental sales goal; economize over cash; provide a permanent reminder of achievement and sponsor's appreciation

TACTICS ITEMIZED

105. ON-PACK/IN-PACK

Definition
Premium is inserted in, or attached to, package, like cereal in-box toys or snifter attached to brandy

Advantages
- Instant gratification purchase incentive
- Adds value without discounting perception
- Can reinforce product attribute
- Increases visibility
- Breaks tie with adjacent product
- Can encourage trial
- Can promote new usage
- Can economize through partner product

Disadvantages
- Operational and cost issues—packaging, shipping, manufacturing delays, distribution, etc.
- Timing issues; may cannibalize same unpromoted product on shelf
- May require USDA- and FDA-approved inks plus secure wrap
- Odors may seep into product
- Premium may compete with retailer's inventory
- New packaging may require alternative shelf space and plan-o-gram

106. PREMIUM PACK

Definition   Product packaging doubles as a premium—tin, tote, decanter; offered
                     as a free or value-priced premium

Advantages   • May economize, combining packaging and premium costs
                     • Instant gratification purchase incentive
                     • May not require alternate shelf space (like On-pack may)
                     (see "On-Pack/In-Pack" above)

Disadvantages   • Premium must fit product dimensions
                     • May not accommodate different package sizes
                     (see "On-Pack/In-Pack" above)

NEAR-PACK

See "Point of Sale," Chapter 7, page 188.

107. SELF-LIQUIDATOR

Definition   Premium is sold at "value price," typically through a mail-in offer with
                     proof(s) of purchase; ideally, offer pays for itself

Advantages   • Motivates display placement (see "Loader" in Chapter 7, page 187)
                     • Premium purchase requirement offsets cost
                     • Allows higher-value premium
                     • Economies—premium's value perception can be greater than cash
                     alternative
                     • Can require single or multiple product purchases
                     • "Clean"—communicated with a simple tear pad or print/Internet
                     media
                     • Premium can be dramatic display element
                     • Premium can reinforce product attribute
                     (*Note:* Self-liquidator results are often measured in display placement,
                     not premium sales.)

Disadvantages
- Paperwork and mailing delays lower response versus instant gratification tactics
- Costly and involved display if premium is mounted
- Premiums purchased up front and warehoused accrue costs and risk losses if response is low
- Fulfillment, processing, and tracking expenses
- May compete with retailer's inventory
- Single premium limits scope of market

LOADERS

See "Loader" in "Point of Sale," Chapter 7, page 187.

COLLECT AND GET

See "Collect and Get—Merchandise/Service" in Chapter 6, "Continuity," page 156.

LOYALTY

See different loyalty descriptions in "Continuity," Chapter 6, pages 158, 159, and 160.

FREE WITH CONTRACT/COMMITMENT/ACCOUNT

See "Club/Contract" in Chapter 6, "Continuity," page 162.

108. COLLECTIBLES

Definition
Free or value-priced series of premiums offered with ongoing visits/purchases—fast-food cartoon toy characters, in-pack baseball cards, holiday ornaments, etc.

Advantages
- Immediate plus ongoing reward builds sustained visits/sales
- May defeat competitor's better higher value; consumer may not even shop competitors

- Popular property builds excitement and awareness
- Can target specific profile
- Premiums may cost less than perceived value

Disadvantages
- Collectible appeal may rely on licensed property, which requires expensive royalties (and higher price)
- Custom-made premiums require expensive designs, molds, production, etc.
- No guarantee of collectible's popularity
- Target limited to collectible's target
- Occasional users less motivated—cannot collect all
- May be vulnerable to competitive price promotions
- Retail-delivered premiums consume valuable space and may require additional staff tasks

109. LICENSED PROPERTIES

(Also see "Licensed Premium Offer" and "Licensed Product Value" in Chapter 9, "Properties and Events," page 244.)

Definition
Premium incorporates a licensed property, like action hero cup, NFL team lapel pin, cartoon character toy, etc.

Advantages
- Property lends appeal and attention to product and promotional media
- Implied endorsement and quality
- Property may lend itself to numerous promotional vehicles— posters, toys, prizes, stickers, etc.
- Premium may become valued collectible
- Can reinforce product attribute
- Breaks clutter, stands out from competition
- Encourages retail participation through popular property without fees to retailer (manufacturer absorbs fees)

Disadvantages
- No guarantee a new property release will succeed
- Royalty fees increase price—less competitive
- Property may change release dates
- Property often requires long lead time

- Licensors strictly limit creative usage
- Possible clutter of other same property tie-ins
- Custom items require exceptional commitment, timing, and liabilities
- Risk that movie release becomes controversial or offensive
- Properties may have restrictive policies

CATALOG

See "Loyalty—Premium Catalog Program" in Chapter 6, "Continuity," page 160.

110. TIE-IN

See "Tie-ins," Chapter 11, page 283.

Definition
Premium is provided by partner, usually in exchange for sponsor's complimentary assets or benefits—sampling distribution, display placement, consumer target, etc.

Advantages
- Partners benefit from each other's assets
- Lowered (or no) premium costs
- Motivates purchase
- Share partner's respective consumer base
- Implied partner endorsement
- Can leverage mutual usage occasions, like picnic holidays, Easter, back to school, Super Bowl, etc.
- Economies and efficiencies, pooling costs and resources
- New product category can introduce itself with promotion—like free electronic games with purchase of newly launched game hardware

Disadvantages
- Reliant on partner's respective objectives, timing, ability to execute, target, regionality, distribution, etc.
- Extensive up-front groundwork, negotiation, meetings, and paperwork
- Extensive logistics from sell-in to distribution
- Joint advertising creative approvals may be difficult
- May require significant lead time and presell to retailers
- Plans and work may be rejected by new management

III. SALES INCENTIVE

(Also see "Performance Programs," Chapter 12, page 311.)

Definition	Premium(s) used as motivational reward for sales and performance

Advantages
- Premiums offer greater perceived value per dollar than does cash
- Premiums are remembered and ultimately valued more than cash
- Premiums can be imprinted
- Range of premium values can motivate greater performance for greater rewards and allow all participants to achieve reward
- "Breakage" through unused "points"—200 earned for 185-point premium
- Can target prospect—sportsman, fashion, music, etc.

(see Chapter 12, page 311)

Disadvantages
- Limited selection has limited appeal
- Cash is most requested reward
- If reward seems unattainable or too difficult by some participants, program suffers
- Warehousing, order forms, processing, ordering instructions, etc. compared with straightforward cash reward

(see Chapter 12, page 311)

Insight

Practical or aspirational? The customer may already own a flashlight or cooler. But he or she may consider Godiva Chocolates or a personalized wallet more motivational—a luxury a customer may not buy but would love to indulge in.

PREMIUMS OR CASH?

Cash is the most popular reward. But it's also the most uneconomical and least memorable. (See "Prizes" in "Sweepstakes and Contests," Chapter 2, page 34.)

SHHH! DON'T SAY LOADER WITH LIQUOR

Loaders are not allowed in the distilled spirits business. However, you can use the words *display enhance-*

ment to mean virtually the same thing. Your display enhancement must be a part of the display theme—a football for a Super Bowl theme, a punch bowl for a party theme. It cannot appear to simply be a gift for the liquor store manager.

THREE MERCHANDISE TYPES: PREMIUMS, AD SPECIALTIES, AND LICENSED MERCHANDISE

1. **Premiums.** Name brand manufacturers often have independent offerings specifically for premium programs. Sometimes, their color, feature, or style variations are exclusive to the premium community. These premiums are available to businesses through a separate division that may also offer a turnkey catalog program handling processing and redemption. Typically, the discount is only 10 percent, so it's possible to find the product for less at retail. Many premium divisions allow imprints; some, however, like designer apparel, do not.

2. **Ad specialties (versus premiums).** Some refer to ad specialties as *novelties* or *trinkets and trash,* but they overlap with premiums. Some distinguish a premium as a brand-name product, while an ad specialty brand is recognized only by your imprint. There are imprinted T-shirts. And there are Fruit of the Loom T-shirts. Regardless, ad specialty merchandise is set up specifically for promotional programs with professionals and systems that accommodate your needs.

   ASI—Advertising Specialties Institute is an organization of manufacturers, vendors, and importers who offer imprintable products to businesses, *not* the general public. Each ASI provider has its own catalog with an assigned ASI number, offering anything from buttons to umbrellas to business portfolios to truly original and novel creations. The trinkets and trash label sometimes fits, but ASI also offers high-quality and highly unique items. Only licensed companies can sell ASI merchandise and their customers are businesses. The system's computerized search capability can source items by keyword, color, price, quantity, even theme word, plus combinations—from tens of thousands of items.

Insight

Good buy! Good-bye! You may get an excellent price overseas, but be sensitive to "Made in America" sentiments, especially if you have a patriotic theme.

ASI discount codes—An ASI salesperson might boast, "I sold 3,500 on a C and, if they reorder, on an A." That's ASI-speak for margins—how much the salesperson marked up the original cost of the product. There are two parallel codes—"A" through "H" and "P" through "W." They work identically, according to the following chart.

Industry Code	Margin	Seller's Net Cost
A or P	50%	50%
B or Q	45%	55%
C or R	40%	60%
D or S	35%	65%
E or T	30%	70%
F or U	25%	75%
G or V	20%	80%
H or W	15%	85%

3. **Licensed merchandise.** Licensed merchandise programs add value to premiums through pop culture tie-ins. They're particularly effective for parity competitors, adding a dramatic point of difference. (See "What's in It for Licensors?" in Chapter 9, "Properties and Events," page 256.)

BREAKAGE AND SLIPPAGE

Breakage and slippage are two ways that premium programs add economies through *non*redemption. (Incentive programs also enjoy breakage.)

Breakage refers to leftover, unspent points, like change after a purchase. Say you earned 10,300 points, but all the rewards are in 500-point increments. You can only get the 10,000-point reward, so 300 points fall through the cracks. And if you prefer the 9,500-point item, 500 more go unredeemed.

Slippage refers to the fact that most people never get around to the required paperwork to redeem their reward. (See Chapter 4, page 105.)

PERCEIVED VERSUS ACTUAL VALUE

Premiums deliver more bang for the buck. See this topic under "Prizes" in Chapter 2, "Sweepstakes and Contests," page 34.

POINTS VERSUS MONEY

Premium programs often deal in points instead of cash. Points obscure the reward's cost and how much is required to achieve the reward. They also allow flexibility for bonus point incentives for busy or slow periods, even for slow-moving premiums. You can also mix things up, assigning different point values for different premium rewards and achievement levels; and the accounting is simple. As described above, points enjoy the economies of breakage. (See "Points Pay for Programs" in Chapter 12, "Performance Programs," page 331.)

ORDER FORMS

Here's an order form checklist. You may not need it all, but at least consider each item.

_____ Prominent proof-of-purchase requirements—cash register tape required, price circled, dated between ___ and ___, store name, etc.

_____ Original UPC code (if appropriate)

_____ Prominent expiration date and/or when P.O. box closes

_____ Quantity limitations (one per name/address and so on)

_____ Whether official order form copies are OK

_____ If requests for order forms will be fulfilled, returned, or ignored

_____ Exclusionary copy—"Void where prohibited," "Open to entrants 21 or older," and so on

_____ Length of time for processing and delivery

_____ Payment options (check or money order only, no cash, etc.); credit card payments should specify type, card number, and expiration date

_____ Allow time for checks to clear the bank before filling orders

_____ "Available while supplies last" or "Offer may be withdrawn without prior notice"

_____ Premium may be replaced by a similar product of equal value

_____ Geographical limitations—for example, good only in 48 contiguous states, APO/FPO addresses OK, etc.

_____ "Offer may not be assigned or transferred" disclaimer

_____ Establish a cash value for the certificate/order form (see "Coupons," Chapter 3, page 77)

_____ Stipulate no orders will be sent to a P.O. box or that the item is being delivered by another service (that cannot access P.O. boxes)

_____ Whether group orders will be honored or disallowed

_____ "Not responsible for lost, delayed, or misdirected mail"

_____ Allow enough space on the form to print information; too little space means more time and work for fulfillment company

_____ Have a qualified attorney review your form

Reply Copy Example—Version One   This guideline suggests how you may want to structure your order form. In this case, the premium is being sold, such as a self-liquidator offer.

ACME COOKWARE
LIMITED EDITION HOLIDAY DOVES FIGURINE OFFER
Treasure it for $25
A $50 value!

It's easy to receive your collectible figurine.

1. Fill out the information on this form.
2. Cut out and include the UPC codes from *any two* Acme Cookware boxes.
3. Indicate how many figurines you want and the price.
4. Choose one easy form of payment.
5. Mail your UPC codes, payment, and this form to:

   Acme Cookware Holiday Figurine Offer
   111 White Velvet Way
   Brainerd, MN 00000

Enclosed is this amount:

Please send me ____ figurine(s) at $25.00 each plus $4.50 shipping and handling for each figurine. (Minnesota residents add 6.5% sales tax.) My total payment is $_____.

Choose one of these two easy payment methods:

Mail a check or money order: Payable to Acme Cookware Holiday Figurine

OR

Charge by mail: Please charge my _____VISA _____MasterCard

Card Number _____ Exp. Date _____

Please send my figurine(s) to:

Please print legibly:

Ms./Mrs./Mr. _____

Address: _____

City/State/Zip: _____

Telephone: (_____) _____

e-mail: _____

Signature:_____

Offer valid in the United States. Illegible forms or addresses without zip codes cannot be honored. Offer void where prohibited, licensed, taxed, or restricted by law. Allow 4 to 6 weeks for delivery after receipt of funds. Offer good while supplies last.

Orders must be received by 00/00/00.

Would you like us to send you regular updates about other exciting offers?

____ Yes—To my mailing address

____ Yes—To my e-mail address

____ No thank you

ACHF-500

Order Form Copy Example—Version Two
This example folds shipping and handling into the price and alerts buyers they're covered. It also offers multiple premiums and does not allow credit card purchases.

Mail-in Certificate
Offer Expires 00/00/00

ACME COOKWARE
LIMITED EDITION HOLIDAY DOVES FIGURINE OFFER
Here's how to order!

I wish to order the following:

Prices include shipping and handling

ITEM	QUANTITY	TOTAL $
Calendar(s) @ $1.95 each		
Ornament(s) @ $3.95 each		
Collector Figurine(s) @ $29.50 each		
SAVE $1.00—Buy the Calendar and Ornament for $4.90 per pair		
Minnesota residents add 6.5% sales tax		
TOTAL (+ 2 Acme White Velvet UPC Codes.)		

NOTE: Calendar, Ornaments, and Figurines are shipped separately and will arrive at different times. OFFER EXPIRES 00/00/00 or while supplies last. Offer good only in United States. Illegible forms or addresses without zip codes cannot be honored. Offer void where prohibited, licensed, taxed, or restricted by law. Please allow 4 to 6 weeks for delivery.

Please make check payable to: Acme Cookware Holiday Figurine Offer.
(Only offers postmarked by November 1 can be delivered in time for Christmas.)

I have enclosed **2 labels** with a check or money order for $_____.

Please send your order to: Acme Cookware Figurine Offer
                            111 White Velvet Way
                            Brainerd, MN 00000

Ms./Mrs./Mr. _____

Address: _____

City/State/Zip: _____

Telephone: (_____) _____

BUDGETING

What Should a Profit Margin Be?

In the advertising specialty business (and in many retail businesses) a 40 percent margin is the goal for a premium sale; 35 percent is good; 30 percent is getting borderline; and 25 percent better be high volume and a simple, inexpensive execution (like a bulk shipment). Shipping is extra.

But if a 5¢ premium ships to only one factory destination, filling a few million cereal boxes you may sell at an even lower margin, which includes prototyping, molds, tools, dies, and overseas manufacturing and shipping. You're functioning as an importer with little overhead for your margin to cover.

If the premium is a promotional vehicle to generate product sales, you may even offer it at cost. Be sure to factor in warehousing, fulfillment, cartons, and other costs, including a 5 to 10 percent contingency for unforeseen glitches.

You Get What You Pay For

A vendor's higher price may reflect higher safeguards, like inventory reserves, backup programs, inevitable last-minute requests, return policies, and more. Cutting the vendor's margins may cut your own program safeguards.

Shipping and Handling

Shipping and handling make up a gray area. Should you bill it additionally so your price is low, or fold it into the price so the price is high? Should you mark up shipping, handling, or both? Warehouses are profit centers with major overhead. Shipping is typically billed at cost, whereas handling is marked up. Here is some suggested copy once you've made your decision:

- Please add $0 shipping and handling.
- Value price includes shipping and handling.
- Order more and save on shipping and handling.

- Free shipping and handling if . . . (you order now, order this many, allow six weeks, join our club, refer a friend, etc.).
- Free bonus gift to cover your shipping and handling costs.
- Free shipping and handling [covered in your full markup].

(Also see "Refund Fulfillment," page 109, and "Shipping and Handling and Much More," page 108, in Chapter 4.)

Spoilage

Count on a percentage of your order being lost, damaged, or defective; and factor that percentage into your quantity. Some ad specialty and premium specialists factor in 0.5 percent spoilage for wearable goods and 1 to 2 percent for electronic goods. Printers often have a standard 10 percent overrun backup in their estimate. Generally, lower-priced promotional goods made overseas have higher spoilage rates. Get your supplier's spoilage rate and policy.

Overseas versus Domestic Manufacturing

You'll save considerably and still offer quality by manufacturing your premium overseas. Plan a year ahead, however, to gear up the manufacturing and allow significant "on the water" shipping time plus customs. Air freight saves time but is expensive. Hire a professional bilingual representative in the manufacturing country to monitor progress and quality. For manufacturing and quality control plus reduced shipping costs, use a domestic company.

Made in America: Pat Buchanan rolled into Motor City (Detroit) in a Mercedes. Not good! And imagine the street talk when Merrill-Lynch boasted "Bullish on America" with ads made in Mexico. Many companies demand promotional products be made in the United States. And if you're a proud U.S. Olympics sponsor, you may eat crow if the tag says the product was made overseas.

Insight

Your toy car may pass the choke test. But what if the child removes the wheels? Get expert advice.

Employee Pilferage
(See "Guidelines and Cautions" and "Near-Packs," below.)

GUIDELINES AND CAUTIONS

In-packs/on-packs. This may sound like a free delivery vehicle, but it can be very expensive, possibly requiring new packaging and equipment. Also, game pieces on food products must be overwrapped, boosting production costs. (However, most specialty printing companies offer FDA-/USDA-approved inks.)

Some retailers discourage on-pack promotions because of pilferage. Other retailers welcome it, so you may incur the cost of warehousing separate inventories. If the new package is bigger, consider changes in shelf placement. If the retailer complains of less profit per square inch, show increased volume and profit projections. Also, consider a self-shipper display.

Near-packs. Near-packs can be difficult as retailers resist the additional space requirement, especially for a free, nonprofit item. In your sell-in materials, show increased volume and profit projections, especially with multiple purchase requirements. Consider assigning a price and SKU for the near-pack item so the retailer can sell it at a 100 percent margin while you offer it free with purchase. It also deters employee theft as a profitable SKU.

Kid safe. The most common concern is choking, but a choke test device is simple and inexpensive. If the toy has parts, they can be broken off and pose a danger. Toys need kid-safe paints, nontoxic materials, no sharp corners or extrusions, no removable parts, and more. Rely on an independent testing laboratory. There are also environmental concerns about toys with built-in batteries that kids play with then throw away.

Order extra? See "Spoilage" above. Also, count on several premiums being pulled for photographs, internal meetings, field sales presentations, and so on. Some marketers prefer running out of premiums versus overstocks. In this case, consider a system for reimbursement or reorders (with "Due to popular demand . . ." notifications). Always say "While supplies last."

Out-of-stock policy. Don't assume vendors will have sufficient quantities, even if they promise they will. Find out how long before reorders are available. Often vendors will substitute a similar product valued at the same price. State clearly to your customers: "If quantities run out, a similar product of the same quality and value may be substituted."

Cartons and pick-and-pack cost! Stock cartons cost, and you'll probably need some customization, especially for the inner packing. Your premium may be accompanied by a cover letter, catalog, imprinted novelty (like a refrigerator magnet), new product sample, bonus surprise gift, newsletter, or others. Pick-and-pack people have to read the packing and labeling instructions; retrieve each item from storage; assemble the packing materials; insert each premium, cover letter, catalog, and so on; pack the carton with the proper partitioning; seal it; label it; log it; and place it in the master shipping carton. Whew!

Mailing without an order. It is illegal to mail merchandise to consumers that they haven't ordered and then bill them for it. Federal regulations state that any unordered merchandise may be treated as a gift by the recipient, who has the right to retain, use, discard, or dispose of the merchandise in any manner in which he or she sees fit.

Disclosure of country of origin. You must reveal on the premium itself where the premium was manufactured—the familiar "Made in Somewhereia."

CHECKLIST FOR PURCHASING PREMIUMS

_____ Return policy on damaged goods

_____ Return policy on unused goods

_____ Spoilage rate

_____ Reorders

     _____ How quickly and reliably

     _____ How many can be reordered

     _____ How long those quantities are good for—and what guarantees that they be sufficiently stocked

_____ Out-of-stock policy—how long to restock or what will be substituted

_____ Length of current pricing policy

_____ Discounts for quantity orders

_____ Shipping and delivery time details

CHECKLIST FOR SOURCING WAREHOUSES

_____ What types of programs and merchandise they specialize in—quantities, package sizes, volume per day, duration of program, etc.

_____ Who their customers are, particularly any with needs similar to yours

_____ What their capabilities and facilities are—data entry, computer tracking, report generation, labeling, pick and pack (above), carton design, and fabrication

_____ Lead times, from premium receipt to carton fabrication to pick and pack to shipment

_____ Quality control (Usually one of a set number will be randomly inspected and they may also weigh a control carton, then see that all other incoming/outgoing cartons are consistent.)

_____ Internal procedures and reports for receiving, warehousing, order processing, packing, and shipping

_____ Determine what reports you'll need and ask if they can deliver them (They'll say yes, so ask for samples.)

_____ Who will be responsible for your project and their background

_____ Pilferage prevention

_____ Insurance coverage

_____ Security provisions for winning sweepstakes cards, sensitive mailings, etc.

_____ Affiliations and organizations

_____ References

CHECKLIST FOR FULFILLMENT OF PREMIUMS

_____ How shipments are logged, tracked, and verified

_____ What your order form should say, such as "Please allow 4 to 6 weeks for delivery"

_____ Mailing list management and security processes

_____ Presorting (for economies), drop shipping, UPS, or other shipping processes they will use, and how they will impact cost and timing

_____ Backup systems for unforeseen labor needs, computer breakdowns, loss of power, rush jobs, depleted inventory, etc.

_____ Lead times or schedule; how long it will take to ship your program from order receipt to loading dock

_____ How long quoted prices are good for

_____ Any anticipated rate increases from the vendor and services like UPS

FINALLY, A WORD ON BEHALF OF YOUR VENDOR

If one vendor answers your questions quickly and another keeps asking more questions, the latter may be the better. Eager or inexperienced salespeople may not know the right questions to ask and will make false assumptions. Good vendors ask questions. It may seem suspect if you ask "How much?" and the reply is "How much is your budget?" But try answering a straightforward question yourself: "How much is a car?"

11

TIE-INS

(Also see "Properties and Events," Chapter 9)

INTRODUCTION:
TIE-INS: IT'S A MATCHING PROCESS

Tie-ins, more than most any other promotional technique, depend on matching. Matching of potential sponsors. Matching of potential customers. Matching of similar promotional interests and goals. Matching of resources. In short, tie-ins, to work, must align, and be integrated, on a number of fronts. Many of those needed matches are discussed in the following chapter.

Strategically, however, all tie-in marketplace success begins with two basic matches: (1) a match between the promotional partners and (2) a match between their respective customers and prospects. If there is no strategic fit between the prospective partners, no matter how logical, innovative, or creative the tie-in appears to be, little marketplace success will likely follow.

One of the best tools we have found to evaluate this tie-in matching is through an initial strategic screening of partner customers and prospects. A worksheet for this process is shown in Figure 11.1.

FIGURE 11.1 *Tie-in Matching Model*

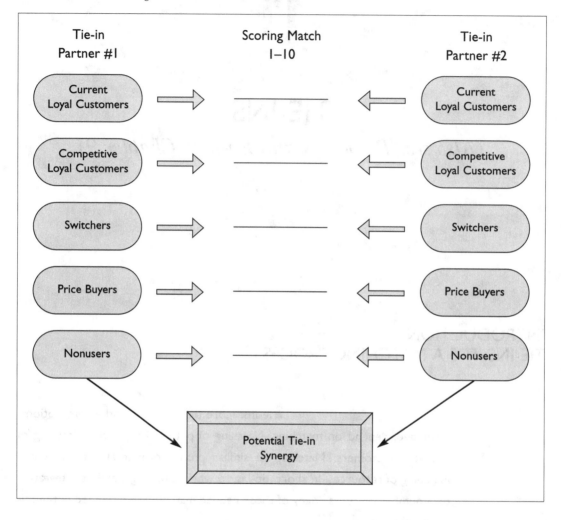

The matching of potential tie-in partners is simply the matching of custom- ers and prospects each with the other. In Figure 11.1, we've set up a 10-point scale, 10 being the highest. For example, are the brand-loyal customers of Tie- in Partner #1 similar to those of Tie-in Partner #2? Score them 1 to 10, and do the same for competitive loyal customers, switchers, price buyers, and so on. Clearly, if there is a good match, there's potential synergy between the two brands. If not, few potential incremental sales are likely to occur for either. Gen- erally, we've found a score of 75 or above is needed to assume tie-in success.

A key part of the matching process has to do with the promotion responsiveness of the two partner audiences. If Tie-in Partner #1 relies heavily on promotion activities to generate product sales and Tie-in Partner #2's customers and prospects all but ignore any type of promotional offer, little will likely occur as a result of the tie-in program.

It is this matching process that really drives the success of any tie-in promotion. Thus, tie-in success is the result of up-front, strategic analysis, not how colorful or impressive the promotional tactics are. Time spent in identifying the best potential tie-in partners makes the implementation much more relevant and reduces many of the glitches that often occur once the program is developed.

In my experience, one of the key problems of the naïve promotion manager is that he or she too often falls in love with a creative tie-in idea. For example, the attempt to bring together two radically different tie-in partners with the idea that mixing oil and water will result in some magical promotional elixir. Generally, that doesn't happen. It's the alignment of the tie-in partners that creates success.

Proven marketplace success is the best example of why and how promotional tie-ins work. "Intel Inside" was a natural matching of marketers with similar customers and prospects, similar needs and interests, and similar concerns. The computer manufacturer needed ways to build consumer confidence in a very rapidly changing and dynamic product category. Intel needed ways to differentiate itself from other chip manufacturers. The tie-in of the computer manufacturer and Intel was a natural. Customer and prospect matches and alignments were key.

The real success story of "Intel Inside," however, was that the tie-in program was carried out all across the promotional marketspace—advertising, in-store displays, sales presentations by both Intel and retail salesforces, and, of course, the most visible and differentiating tie-in of all, the "Intel Inside" sticker on the computer itself: a continuous reminder of the alignment of two major forces in computing.

The "Intel Inside" tie-in program has been in place for more than a decade now. Most important, the promotional partners generally haven't relied on price discounts or promotional deals or big red flashing arrows saying "Buy a computer with an Intel Inside today!" Instead, it has relied on providing benefits to the three key players in the tie-in: the manufacturer, the retailer, and the consumer. And it has provided benefits to all through a clearly identified offer, a solid in-market promotional program, and continuity over time.

Tie-in promotional success begins with the matching process illustrated by Intel Inside. If the alignment is right, marketplace success will likely follow.
—Don E. Schultz

OVERVIEW

Tie-ins allow marketers to increase their sales more efficiently, effectively, and economically. They can stretch budgets and increase a promotion's results several ways. It sounds idyllic; however, they are often complex, time consuming, and unwieldy; and after all the well-intentioned planning, tie-ins can fall through at the last second.

This chapter outlines the many forms of tie-ins, their advantages and drawbacks, and, most important, guidelines to help the partnering process proceed in an orderly fashion with open communication, clear objectives, and all the details covered.

DEFINITION

A tie-in joins two or more marketers together by uniting their complementary marketing assets and opportunities, such as media, distribution, advertising, traffic, fulfillment, target, joint usage, display activity, and more. Ideally, a tie-in both saves money and increases impact by uniting forces.

COMMON TIE-IN OBJECTIVES BY TACTIC AND DELIVERY
(Also see itemized tactics below.)

TACTIC	OBJECTIVES (Beyond Purchase)
Cousage	Leverage partners' combined usage to reach and motivate each other's target
Coupons—joint drop	• Share media cost • Higher value, more motivational offer • Tap into one another's consumer base • Cross-store/trade signage and shopping

TACTIC	OBJECTIVES (Beyond Purchase)
Co-refunds	• Share printing, fulfillment, point-of-sale, and other costs • Higher value, more motivational offer • Tap into one another's consumer base
Coupons/Refunds—on-pack/in-pack	• Give product extra value • Tap into one another's consumer base • Leverage cousage • Targeted offer delivery at minimal cost • Deliver offer in a partner's trading area
Bundling	• Higher value, more motivational offer • Tap into one another's consumer base • Share printing, point-of-sale, media, and other costs • Leverage cousage • Joint sales call/distribution • Prominent retail display through combined consumer offer and higher retail price point
On-packs	• Immediate purchase incentive at partner's cost • Economically deliver sample to target via partner's package • Add value and draw attention to package
Near-packs	• Immediate purchase incentive at partner's cost • Deliver sample through partner's display • Prominent display
Cross-merchandising—cross-store	• Vendors: Drive traffic to each other • Encourage retailer participation • Share point-of-sale costs • Retailer: Cross-store shopping
Vendor/Retailer tie-in	• Preempt competitors as partners combine for an offer their respective competitor cannot match acting alone
Comarketing	• Create strategic alliance by uniting retailer's and vendor's respective resources and capabilities to achieve their respective marketing objectives
Cobranding	• Combine two brands' equities into a single product that appeals to both brands' markets
Trade-outs	• Economize by exchanging each partner's complementary products or marketing asset(s)
Sponsorships	• Awareness through event/property • Sampling/demonstration opportunities • Increase perceived value through affiliation
Co-op programs	• Encourage retailer marketing activities that support the vendor brand • Route advertising and promotion funds directly to the sales arena—retail, distribution, and sales

TACTICS ITEMIZED

112. COUSAGE

Definition
Promotion supports two products' combined usage, particularly through in-, on-, near-pack offers
Examples: Free DVD with player, free soft drink with pizza delivery; nonoffer examples: "Intel Inside," "Protected by ScotchGard," "Real Cheese"

Advantages
- One party offers product, the other distribution
- Provide greater consumer offer at less cost to each partner
- Economical sampling vehicle
- Can introduce new product entry to early adopters, like free software with new game system
- Efficient targeting through partner's franchise
- Implied, credible endorsement by partners
- Share media, POS, and other costs
- Distinguish product quality—"Made with Thinsulate," "Real Cheese," etc.

Disadvantages
- Requires ability to efficiently distribute both products together (except for refunds or coupons)
- New packaging configuration (on-pack) has cost, operational, and stocking concerns
- Possible resistance from retailer who may prefer to mark up promoted product
- Locking into one partner risks losing its competitor's market (tie into Apple computers at the expense of losing PC users)
- Each partner is reliant on quality and dependability of other's product
- Products must share common seasonality, target market, distribution, etc.
- Lengthy prenegotiation and coordinated timing, logistics sell-in, distribution, etc.
- Cocreative execution may be compromised
- Dilutes branding

113. COUPONS—JOINT DROP

Definition   Partners share coupon drop; can be multiple single-product coupons or one coupon requiring multiple-product purchase

Advantages
- Partners share media cost
- Encourages combined product usage
- Leverages joint usage occasions—picnic theme, family health, etc.
- Adds to greater immediate savings and purchase motivation, possibly group purchase
- Retailer sells multiple products and gets cross-store shopping
- Economical joint display opportunity
- Joint sell-in
- Partners tap into one another's customer base
- Hard copy reminder of offer

Disadvantages
- Must share common seasonality, target market, distribution, etc.
- Locking into one partner risks losing its competitor's market (dedicated Coke drinkers won't respond to Pepsi tie-in)
- Lengthy prenegotiation and coordinated timing and logistics sell-in, distribution, etc.
- Cocreative execution may be compromised
- Dilutes branding
- Relies on scrutiny of retailer cashier
- Subject to misredemption—wrong sizes, products, line extensions, etc.
- Reach limited to coupon clippers
- Difficult redemption projections with additional variables

114. CO-REFUNDS

Definition   Partners share in refund offer; can require purchase of all partner products or choice from selection (possibly with escalating discount)

Advantages
- Partners share media cost and may use other's packaging and point of sale for delivery
- Can encourage products' usage together
- Adds to greater savings and purchase motivation

- Escalating value version (buy more, save greater percentage) encourages multiple purchase without discouraging lesser purchases
- Slippage economies
- Virtually no execution for retailer
- Retailer can combine vendor offers, spearheading its own high-value flyer

(See "Coupon" advantages above.)

Disadvantages
- Mismatched distribution can frustrate consumer seeking tie-in product
- Greater administration costs than for coupons
- Larger value lessens slippage economies
- Complex refund form may discourage participation and/or lead to mistakes
- Delayed reward discourages participation
- Requires exceptional up-front negotiating

(See "Coupon" disadvantages above.)

115. COUPONS/REFUNDS—ON-PACK/IN-PACK

Definition
One partner delivers the other partner's coupon or refund on or in its package

Advantages
- Couponer/refunder receives free media vehicle
- Delivery partner receives value-added offer at no charge, no redemption costs, no executional requirements (except delivery)
- Breaks tie with competitors
- Solo coupon/refund delivery for higher awareness and redemption
- Can be highly targeted
- Coupon/refund can be delivered in trade classes the partner does not normally access

(See "Coupon" and "Co-refund" advantages and disadvantages above.)

Disadvantages
- On-pack/In-pack application can be costly with operational concerns
- Printing offer on package requires separate press run
- Limited delivery compared with mass media
- Shelf life may outlast coupon life
- Delivery product must reach retail shelf in a timely manner

(See comments in "Coupon" and "Co-refund" advantages and disadvantages above.)

116. BUNDLING

Definition   Two or more related products combined into one package as a
promotional offer
Examples: Student dictionary, thesaurus, and book of quotations
bundled into three-pack at special price; airline, hotel, and rental car
package; free printer with computer purchase

Advantages
- Adds to greater immediate savings and purchase incentive
- Excellent value over competition
- Partners share point-of-sale and other costs
- Can encourage product usage together
- Can leverage partners' customer bases
- Commands attention at shelf
- Can be account-specific offer for key retailer participation
- Implies mutual endorsements

Disadvantages
- Costly custom packaging
- May require new plan-o-gram and retailer approval
- Doesn't move current retail inventory
- Dependent on consumer's desire/need for all items
- Products must share common seasonality, target market,
distribution, etc.
- Requires significant negotiating and logistics
- Cocreative execution may be compromised
- Dilutes branding

ON-PACK

See On-Pack/In-Pack in "Premium Programs," Chapter 10, page 265.

NEAR-PACK

See "Point of Sale," Chapter 7, page 188.

117. CROSS-MERCHANDISING—CROSS-STORE

Definition   Display program with cross-store partners
Examples: Picnic theme signage appears with beans, ketchup, hot dogs, plates, etc.; tactical choice(s) open

Advantages
- Encourages display placement and multiple sales through cross-store traffic and offer
- Adds to greater immediate savings and purchase incentive
- Shared costs
- Partners tap into one another's target and section
- Extends and promotes usage
- Implied partner endorsements
- Can leverage peak sales periods

Disadvantages
- Extensive up-front negotiating and coordination, including joint retail sell-in for multiple signage
- Tie-in partners must match distribution, regionality, seasonality, etc.
- Cocreative execution compromised
- Promotional offer must unite objectives and resources as well as retailer issues
- Additional signage consumes space, adds clutter
- Potentially large multiproduct display may become series of small shelf signs

118. VENDOR/RETAILER TIE-IN

Definition   One or both partners contribute a unique promotional offer exclusively to the other
Examples: Multifood company imprints grocer chain name on recipe/coupon book—retailer distributes with flyer; hardware chain offers advertising and signage for lawn tractor's prize contribution

Advantages
- Vendor receives exceptional retailer support
- Retailer receives exclusive offer, preempting competitors
- Partners share respective costs while giving consumer added value

- Can build relationship
- Implied partner endorsements

Disadvantages
- Up-front negotiating and coordination
- May alienate other chains; open to competitor programs (see Robinson-Patman Act in the Glossary)
- Limited to partners' reach and market
- Can become parity practice as others receive similar programs
- Cocreative execution may be compromised
- Less economical than national program
- May dilute branding

119. COMARKETING

Definition
Retailer's and vendor's *strategic* alliance, uniting resources and capabilities to achieve each partner's marketing objectives

Examples: Soft drink company codevelops fast-food partner's menu board based on mutual traffic and food preference research; tool maker and hardware chain co-sponsor housing cause for joint community drives

Advantages
- Partners maximize their respective marketing assets in mutually rewarding program
- Partners assured of each other's exceptional participation
- Partners share costs
- Vendor receives strategic advantage over competitors at partnering retailer, possibly long term
- Can reach community level
- Builds bond in the often conflicting vendor-retailer relationship

Disadvantages
- Requires extensive information sharing, analysis, and planning
- Resultant program may be costly, including capital expenditures
- Limited to one chain versus national "sizzle"
- May alienate other chains; open to competitor programs (see Robinson-Patman in the Glossary)
- May dilute branding

120. COBRANDING

Definition	Two compatible brands unite equities and products to form a third combined brand
Examples: Dairy Queen Oreo Treat, movie-themed video game, "cola float," branded recipes
Advantages	• Cobranded product reaches two established products' consumer bases
• New products built on existing products' success and marketing
• Immediate recognition and quality perception
• Can command a high price point and margin
• Partners share costs
Disadvantages	• New food product may cannibalize original products
• Requires two distinct brands to negotiate, develop, agree on, manufacture, and market a third
• Requires negotiation on responsibilities and remuneration
• Risks jeopardizing each brand's image
• Cocreative execution may be compromised
• May dilute branding

121. TRADE-OUTS

Definition	Two (or more) partners exchange their respective products and/or marketing assets in a joint effort
Examples: Automaker contributes car as prize in exchange for exposure in soft drink sweepstakes advertising and point of sale; radio station gives advertiser concert ticket prizes—concert gets exposure, station gets media buy
Advantages	• Partners receive free products/services and exposure
• Cost minimized as brand's own product or service cost or existing marketing budget (like advertising)
• Partners tap into one another's market and trading area
• Adds new, exciting spin and value to program
Disadvantages	• Extensive time and negotiation

- Requires matching objectives, markets, regions, distribution, etc.
- May be difficult to assign values and determine a fair exchange
- Each partner is reliant on the other partner's responsibilities and capabilities
- Partner is reliant on the other partner's product quality
- May require distribution considerations—messenger delivery of tonight's concert ticket prizes or delivery fees for the automobile prize
- May require legal liability considerations

SPONSORSHIPS

Definition Marketer ties in with event or licensed property to add value, visibility, excitement, and promotional offerings (See "Properties and Events," Chapter 9, page 239.)

122. CO-OP PROGRAMS

Definition Retailer (or distributor) accrues funds via cumulative vendor purchases, which are applied toward mutually beneficial marketing initiatives

Examples: Retailer's purchases earn funds toward local advertising that must include vendor logo; distributor earns NFL premiums to pass on to its customers based on total product purchases

Advantages
- Encourages ongoing purchases by retailer/distributor
- Funding is applied to business-building practices for both parties

Disadvantages
- Complex with extensive claims, verification procedures, reconciliation processes, etc.
- Frequent misunderstandings on how program works, what qualifies for how much, current fund balance, etc.
- Requires efficient tracking and communication system
- Can be parity with competitor programs
- Dilutes retailer branding
- Featuring one or two brands in advertising may give impression retailer only carries those brands
- Vendor has minimal creative quality control regarding how retailer advertises its products

FINDING AND NEGOTIATING WITH PARTNERS

Can You Two Even Tie In?

Before you even contemplate a tie-in, a little research may reveal it's impossible from the get-go. Consider a national house-paint partner, for example. There are national paint companies but not really one national paint brand, because different brands are assigned to different retailers. If you defer to 3M sandpaper instead, you may find it's in and out of a chain as retailers switch to whatever brand has the best deal for a specific period.

Few national retailers are actually in each state. Some are only in urban areas, others in rural. As of this writing, the largest retailer—Wal-Mart—is just now entering urban Chicago.

Find out the chain of ownership of your potential partner. You may find it also owns your competitor.

Negotiating Advertising for Prizes or Rewards

Trade-outs save money and gain exposure. If your sweepstakes prize is a car, you'll be showcasing it in your advertising. Try trading out that advertising value for a free car from the manufacturer. Or if your auto lube chain is running a sales incentive, you might service a sporting goods company's fleet in exchange for its products.

Media trade-outs often run from a ratio of 7 to 1 to 10 to 1 in media value as related to prize cost, though it could run as high as 25 to 1 or higher for something as commonly sought after as a car. In the 10:1 example, you may be able to negotiate $20,000 in an apparel brand with $200,000 in advertising media—or more. But a $20,000 car may require at least a $500,000 media buy that features the prized car. Nonetheless, there are many variables:

- Advertising support levels and demographics
- Marketing topspin—you'll get its car in a movie scene or event appearance
- Point-of-sale coverage (very important if a partner wants exposure in your retail arena)
- Popularity of the partner's prize—does partner really need to give a product away and is it back ordered?
- Demographics and image matchup—BMWs or Chevy trucks?

- Seasonal matchups
- Is the partner popular and available in all your regions? Can you help it?
- Franchise tie-ins: Independent, regional groups may not agree to a head-quarters program without regional considerations (no swimming pools in the inner city).
- Prominence of the prize in the advertising
- Product image (no cigarettes, please)
- Timing of promotion (maybe it helps a new product launch)
- Prize provider's budget status
- Who is authorized to negotiate prizes in which corporate department? Corporations have several departments, each of which can give you a "yea" or "nay"—advertising, PR, promotion, events, sales, retail relations, different brands; try them all.
- Executional opportunities—field force, salesforce, event marketing, display placement
- Overall marketing plans

Negotiate your unique assets. Apple's iTunes provided 99 free mp3s with the iMac launch. Record labels received a sampling of the artists—from well-known to semiknown (that's where the bartering got interesting). Apple received a high-value freebie for purchasers, which also demonstrated its iTunes. The iTunes launch was so successful that Apple eventually bought its own record company.

Point-of-sale signage can be a powerful bargaining chip. Point of sale can be surprisingly effective because some brands value key stores. For example, convenience stores cater to blue-collar males, who love Beer Nuts. So Stanley Tools delivered a rebate offer on the Beer Nuts package and signage. Bull's-eye! Some brands can't afford point-of-sale promotions, so a back-to-school notebook may partner with a candy bar.

Calculating a point-of-sale trade-out value. Calculate the value of your signage as either a dollar figure or an exposure figure ("impressions").

Dollar value:	Number of displays × cost per display (including shipping, retailer payment, etc.)
Exposure value:	Number of displays × total traffic exposures per store = Impressions (Remember, unlike advertising, displays reach consumers with wallets in stores.)

Also consider all the variables, such as the display's location, prominence, the store's importance to the partner, and so on. (See Chapter 7, "Point of Sale," page 181.)

WHO'S BRINGING WHAT TO THE TABLE?

Consider the following attributes you or your partner can bring to the negotiation table:

Product compatibility	Pizza and cola—maybe one needs trial; DVD player and DVDs; rental cars and restaurants
Market	Blue-collar male, nurturing mother, young m/f professional, tweens: They don't have to match—husband-wife, parent-children, purchasing agent–end user, company head–employee
Distribution	Match or provide access to outlets, like the Beer Nuts/Stanley example above
Cross-merchandising	Get your offer and your partner's offer in another store aisle—a salty snack offer in the soft drink aisle, a sandpaper offer in the paint department—retailers love cross-store traffic
Salesforce	Can your partner augment your sales effort and vice versa? Does salesforce offer direct sales versus broker?
Point-of-sale capability	Is there store delivery to assure execution? Do you have a merchandising service your partner could use? Can one provide display space?
On-pack/In-pack delivery	Can one product carry a partner sample or offer?
High value	Can one partner deliver an exceptionally high value for the customer, like a rebate, travel discount, or free-with-purchase combination?
Demand	Does one partner offer a mass market and exposure?
Advertising and media	Can either provide advertising support or deliver new media categories?
Regionality	Can one partner's strong distribution enhance the other partner's efforts in that region?
Seasonality	Can you bolster one another's strong or weak seasons, or get a jump on the competition?

Traffic and   Can one fulfill the other's offer in exchange for traffic?
fulfillment

TIE-IN PARTNER CRITERIA AND CHECKLIST

_____ Mutual interest:
     _____ Value added
     _____ Distribution—access to partner's franchise, accounts, and trade area
     _____ Delivery through partner packaging
     _____ Exposure: signage, collateral, advertising, package bursts, etc.
     _____ Cross-store merchandising
     _____ Redemption/fulfillment (i.e., fast-food redemption of package goods prize—win free fries with burger and soft drink purchase)
     _____ Added promotion impact
     _____ Shared costs and economies
     _____ Target market
     _____ Seasonality
     _____ Regionality
     _____ Brand image/positioning
     _____ Mutual product usage
     _____ Turn
     _____ "Windows" in promotional/advertising calendar
_____ Execution
_____ Respective executional lead times—sell-in, distribution, packaging, etc.
_____ Redemption, slippage, breakage, etc.; promotional history
_____ Late redemption grace policy
_____ Liabilities:
     _____ Overredemption
     _____ Misredemption (consumer, sales, and trade)
     _____ Partner reliability in execution
     _____ Potential injury or damage claims
     _____ Product quality
_____ Partnership roles:
     _____ Contributions—costs, salesforce activities, point-of-sale capabilities, creating and printing materials, advertising, creative, events, other assets
     _____ Liabilities

_____ Manufacturing considerations:

     _____ On-pack/in-pack, package burst, instant redeemable coupon (IRC) on package, package fabrications, product shipping container, lead times, etc.

     _____ Separation of promoted and unpromoted product

_____ Trade considerations:

     _____ Motivation to participate

     _____ Chain-specific versus all chains (in-store coupon versus newspaper FSI)

     _____ No conflict regarding taking alternate sale away or diminishing trade's profitability

     _____ Allowance funding

     _____ In-ads, shelf positioning, floor space, postoffs, etc.

_____ Sales:

     _____ Motivation to participate

     _____ Training

     _____ Capability to participate (ample time, know-how, resources, etc.)

     _____ Joint sell-in and timing

_____ Logistics:

     _____ Fulfillment (and costs)

     _____ Timing regarding product in field and on shelf

     _____ Timing regarding mutual sell-in process

     _____ Timing regarding other promotional activities

I *nsight*

TropArtic® Motor Oil could not convince car companies to give it a car for a sweepstakes prize. After calls to several General Motors departments, it finally scored a free Trans Am. Why? Trans Am wanted point of sale in "gear-head" stores that TropArtic had access to.

THE BASIC STEPS TO A TIE-IN

Step	Description	Create These Items
Take stock	Identify objectives; itemize brand's relevant assets and marketing dynamics—timing, distribution, media, target market, regionality, executional capabilities, sales process, etc.	Brief fact sheet
Identify partner prospects	Companies with complementary assets and marketing dynamics—you each have what other needs	A grid with your criteria and prospect matchups; use industry reference publications, the Internet, or sales rep
Contact partners	Identify whom to talk to—director of marketing, promotion, etc.; brief initial contact; allow for wrong initial contacts and getting rerouted	Phone call, letter, or e-mail with a top-line introduction and concept; fact sheet if the party's interested. Include brief on your business, product, and promotional overview, including partner contributions and benefits. Do not provide information unless there's interest
Additional negotiations	Narrow your prospects and work out the finer points	Address questions, share more data, possibly meet in person
Finalize partner selection	Agree on the partner and overall structure of the promotion	Letter of intent providing an overview so both parties are on the same page; include who's responsible for what. *Make this clear:* This is not an obligation to tie in, only a preliminary understanding
Contract	Agreement on program	The contract plus a comprehensive attachment specifying roles, contributions, tasks, timing, and responsibilities

Partner Prospect Letter—Example 1 (Brief Intro)

Dear _____:

This letter is to explore your initial interest in a tie-in promotion with our Acme Baked Beans and Smith Potato Chips for the three summer holidays.

We would like to share creative, media, and production expenses for an FSI, while giving consumers an exceptional value by combining coupons. Baked beans and potato chips are a natural combination during the prime picnic season, and by uniting our efforts, we can both increase sales and reduce costs.

If you are interested in a brief background, I will provide a document detailing how Acme Baked Beans is a leader in the picnic market with excellent trend indicators.

I will follow up with a phone call to ascertain your initial interest in a tie-in promotion.

Thank you for your attention.

Best regards,

Steve Smith
Promotion Manager

Partner Prospect Letter—Example 2 (Harder Sell Than #1)

Dear ___:

This letter is to explore your interest in a potential tie-in FSI with Acme Baked Beans for the July 4th period this year. At this point, we simply request your expression of interest (or lack thereof) in pursuing further discussions.

We are contacting Smith's Potato Chips as a potential partner because your brand is a leader in our targeted region and an excellent complement for our brand.

Acme is the fifth leading brand in the canned beans category and number two in the Smith Potato Chip southern region. Our baked bean variety is only two years old, yet it has already achieved a 20 percent share in your region. This growth is compounded by the fact that the baked bean variety is enjoying a 4 percent annual growth. What's more, consumers prefer Acme to the leading brand three to one according to independent taste research. Clearly, we are establishing the trend in your market.

The timing is excellent for your brand: baked bean sales peak in the three summer holidays. The product is a favorite for family occasions, and Smith Potato Chips would tie in with a major store shopping destination.

Acme has an aggressive marketing plan for the upcoming year with half of its $1 million advertising support committed to July 4th and Labor Day. In addition to spot TV and radio, Acme will spend an additional $500,000 on consumer promotion.

These funds will be targeted to women who are 35+ years old, are high school graduates with a household income of $45,000, have older children at home, and are living in C and D counties.

Though July 4 is six months away, we are already under time pressures with an April 30 insertion deadline. I appreciate your expedient review of this letter and will phone you soon for your comments.

Thank you for your consideration.

Best regards,

Steve Smith
Promotion Manager

Partner Prospect Letter—Example 3

Dear ____:

This letter is a preliminary exploration into a possible tie-in promotion with your wall cleaner line and Jones Decorative Paint Applicators. I would appreciate your initial comments as soon as possible as we are finalizing the initial concept presentation.

Jones Decorative Paint Applicators is launching a new product in the do-it-yourself home decorating category. The primary target is female home decorators. This launch will be supported with:

- Prominent point of sale in 6,000 home improvement locations, such as Home Depot, Sears, Sherwin Williams, etc.

- $1 million in TV and print ads in June and July

- $500,000 in infomercials

We would like to offer a free or discounted value on your cleaning product to our purchasers. We would insert your coupon or rebate certificate inside our product package.

This offer would be mentioned in the above media. It would also be promoted in the retail chain Sunday flyers and on package bursts.

We believe our target matches yours—conscientious female homemakers who are constantly striving to improve the appearance of their home.

I will follow up with a phone call to see if you wish to explore how Jones Company can deliver your product information and promotional offer to a highly targeted, heavy-user consumer.

Thank you for your initial consideration.

Best regards,

Steve Smith
Promotion Manager

GUIDELINES AND CAUTIONS

The deal-breaking/deal-making third party: the retailer. You cannot simply deliver a free product coupon on a partner's product, because retailers want to *sell* products. (See "Free Product Coupons" in Chapter 3, page 78.)

The best laid plans oft go astray. Try to get both parties' upper managements' commitment up front as well as involvement from every participating department. Consider the following potential problems:

- Sudden budget cuts by one partner
- Personnel changes
- Company reorganizations
- Product release delays—especially with movie tie-ins
- Logistics and operations, including new tasks beyond the routines of current personnel
- Retailer glitches and policies
- Vacations, maternity leaves, layoffs, or strikes
- You name it—"If something can go wrong, it will."

Lots of approvals. Getting decision makers from two companies on the same calendar is a feat. Often, the first tie-in contact isn't empowered to approve a program. The promotion department may not be in sync with marketing's plans. The VP of marketing will wait until you've laid out the whole plan and then change it. The creative development needs both brands' approval, and the promotion agency may weigh in. Legal is the last to see it and will have its imprint.

Prepare fallbacks. Always assume a tie-in program will fall apart at the last second, so have a backup plan in place.

Robinson-Patman Act. By law, you must give all same-size retailers equal value programs. (See the Robinson-Patman Act in "Co-op Glossary" and in "Discounts," Chapter 5, page 139.)

Fred Meyer Corollary. See the Glossary.

Timing is everything. Tie-ins take time. Marketers prefer a 12-month lead time but may act with a 6- to 9-month window. Less than that and you have little time to make up for unforeseen circumstances. Following is a guideline for your tie-in process:

Task	Allow This Much Time
Identify and seek out partner prospects; allow for prospect's availability and time to route and respond—even time to forward your request to alternative contacts	30 days
Negotiations (involve marketing, sales, and operations)	30–60 days
Draw up agreements and get approvals from each side's marketing, sales, and legal department (may then lock in dealer promotion period)	45 days
Develop and approve creative	30–60 days
Produce promotion materials and ready them for shipment; brief each partner's salesforce (retailer period should be locked in)	30–60 days
Salesforce sells program into trade depending on trade's commitment scheduling policy (Try to do this prior to POS print production for accurate quantities.)	60 days
Execute final details, including reserving media time/space, distributing promotional materials, and dealing with logistical issues that arise	30–60 days
	TOTAL: 255–375 days, though some tasks may overlap in timing

CO-OP PROGRAMS

Co-op programs are designed to support retailers when dealers support their vendor's product. If a dealer's advertisement includes a vendor's product or logo, the vendor may contribute to the cost.

Typically, the manufacturer credits a specified amount for every product unit the retailer or distributor purchases. The amount may also be based as a percentage of a quota. In retailer programs, these are "co-op funds," but in distributor programs, they may be called marketing or brand development funds (MDF or BDF).

Distributors may use the funds to promote the vendor's products in sales contests, logoed merchandise for corporate buyers, and so on. On the retail side, vendors might allow co-op dollars to fund storefront signage, radio advertising with vendor mentions, Yellow Page and newspaper advertising with the vendor's logo, and the like. Generally, there are several options.

Your competitor may be running a co-op plan with the same dealer or distributor network, so unless your strategy is to spend more money than your competitor, you need to spend more wisely. What's best for both you and the retailer? Cofund Yellow Pages if they include your logo? Provide an employee sales contest? Fund employee training on your product? Provide professional radio spots your dealer can personalize?

CO-OP PROGRAM DEVELOPMENT CHECKLIST

_____ Define the objectives for yourself and your retailer (or distributor), preferably something you can measure and evaluate

_____ List what activities you'll cofund—display fixtures, advertising, salesforce programs, consumer promotions, training, premiums, and more

_____ Consider a percentage allocation for each specific dealer or distributor activity

_____ Identify which products qualify and how much funding each generates

_____ Define how the retailer qualifies for the program

_____ Define how the retailer earns co-op funds

_____ Define when and where the advertising can run and your brand exposure requirements

_____ Determine how participants know what they've earned

_____ Determine how and when to submit claims

_____ Create a system to process and validate claims—tear sheets of ads, invoices, receipts for materials, audits, etc.

_____ Create a payment system

_____ Define periods—seasons, months, year-end

_____ Any special provisions—how to carry funds over to a new season; limitations; bonus funding; etc.

_____ State a notification time for changing or terminating the plan

_____ Determine how to resolve disputed claims

_____ Consider an auditing service

_____ Determine how to communicate the program to different layers—launch and ongoing—progress reports, instructions, specials

_____ Review the following glossary

CO-OP GLOSSARY

accrual Amount of money earned by dealer or distributor.

ad specs Criteria for an ad design, such as logo, trademarks, and sizes, for the advertisement to qualify for co-op dollars.

advertiser's checklist Products qualifying for co-op.

assignment of funds A process to assign co-op funds to distributors or retailers; also a process to pay for a multiple listing ad that requires assigning funds by specific product—for example, when a manufacturer's ad lists several retailers.

audit services Companies that monitor co-op ads for manufacturers.

barter co-op Using merchandise from the manufacturer to pay for advertising; usually used by companies without regular co-op plans.

billback allowance An accrual that's held from the retailer until it provides proof it has complied with all requirements.

co-op action plan (CAP) A program developed by the Newspaper Advertising Bureau to facilitate handling co-ops.

claim period Deadline for claims to be filed, usually 30, 60, or 90 days after the ad date.

clear separation A layout specification requiring a separation line between products.

competing merchandise provision Manufacturer's policy that ads containing competing merchandise do not qualify for co-op reimbursement.

credit memo Payment method that allows advertiser to deduct a certain amount of funds from the *next* manufacturer's invoice; usually has a deadline.

deal sheet A sheet outlining the deal in a special bonus co-op plan.

deduction Subtraction by a dealer of co-op charges from a manufacturer's merchandise invoice; forbidden in most plans.

development money Funds outside the normal co-op budget for things like store openings and new product launches.

distribution affidavit Affidavit from the U.S. Postal Service or publication distributor identifying a publication's circulation. Also a means in direct mail and some shoppers guides to qualify for co-op payment.

electronic tear sheet In broadcasting, a statement placed on a script telling when a commercial aired and at what cost.

format Advertising guidelines on how the product is presented while maintaining the retailer's dominant identity.

Fred Meyer Corollary See the Glossary at the back of the book.

front-ending Contacting the manufacturer before an ad is run to make sure the co-op allowance will be paid.

graduated percent participation A plan based on the number of ads run; the first ad may be 50 percent paid, the second 75 percent, the third 100 percent.

ingredient co-op An accrual plan based on the product's ingredients; a computer maker may have co-op available from the chip manufacturer.

manufacturer's accrual notice Regular notices of accrual earnings that may be required to submit claim.

manufacturer's claim form Form for the advertiser to claim reimbursement.

maximum and minimum ad size Required sizes some manufacturers require for qualifying co-op ads.

multiple listing ads A manufacturer's single ad listing several retailers. Dealers may pay jointly for the ad through co-op funds.

omnibus ads Retail ad page format containing multiple products.

open-ended An accrual method to initiate in-store distribution that permits a special amount of co-op funds with the first purchase of product.

participation The percentage of a specific ad for which the manufacturer will reimburse the dealer.

pass-through co-op Funds available to dealers even if they purchase from a wholesaler or other indirect source.

performance date The last date an ad can run to qualify for co-op—typically the date the magazine hits the street.

prior approval A manufacturer's requirement to review and approve the advertiser's ad.

prior approval media A manufacturer's requirement to approve the advertiser's media selection when it doesn't fit qualifying media policies.

proof-of-product purchase Documentation to claim pass-through co-op, such as from a distributor to a retailer; typically filled out by the distributor or a copy of the retailer's invoice.

qualifying media Predesignated media that don't require approval for co-op; media typically have an outside audit.

rate-based accrual Accrual value based on the prevailing media rate.

Robinson-Patman Act Regulatory act covering co-op that outlines the responsibilities of all parties in the process of using co-op funds. See the Glossary at the end of the book.

supplementary funds Same as development money, except they are often part of the *manufacturer's* co-op budget.

tear sheet A copy of the print advertisement that must include the name and date of the publication.

tie-in ads Co-op ads designed to tie in with the manufacturer's national advertising. These regionalized ads use local co-op funds to communicate where the products can be purchased.

unlimited accrual A manufacturer's plan that cofunds an unlimited number of ads at a specific participation percentage.

vendor rate A rate a retailer establishes when billing cooperative advertising to manufacturers.

12

PERFORMANCE PROGRAMS

INTRODUCTION:
BASIC PRINCIPLES OF MEASURING SALES
PROMOTION PERFORMANCE

The following chapter deals with performance programs—those incentive and motivational activities developed to encourage key people or organizations to make an extra effort to support a product, service, or brand and, in particular, a specific promotion. The people whose performance might be encouraged can be inside or outside the organization, and the performance programs can be short term or long term.

The key element in performance programs is how the rewards will be determined and distributed. Remember: nothing kills enthusiasm for a promotion among the salesforce (employees or external associates) as does a badly planned or confusing performance reward system. Therefore, the key elements are the nitty-gritty details of planning and measurement. You'll find substantial information in the following chapter on that. To develop an effective performance pro-

gram, you'll need to determine the basis for the performance improvement reward. For that, you need a basic understanding of how sales promotion works
in the marketplace. If you don't understand promotional effects, you risk expensive mistakes in performance program design.

The illustration below shows the typical impact at retail of two sales promotion programs.

As shown, during a 13-week period the marketer employed two retail promotions. If we only looked at the bar chart, we'd assume the promotions were
successful. They increased sales for a limited time—in weeks 3 and 10. The important part of the chart, however, is not the weekly promotional sales result.
Instead, the real impact of those two promotions should be based on what is
called the *baseline*, that is, the average sales per week during the entire measurement period.

Clearly, from the chart, overall product sales, or the baseline, is essentially
flat during the measurement period. Yes, sales did increase during the two promotional periods, weeks 3 and 10, but those were offset by declines in other
weeks—that is, sales were below what would have been expected. As a result,

FIGURE 12.1 *Baselining Store Level Data*

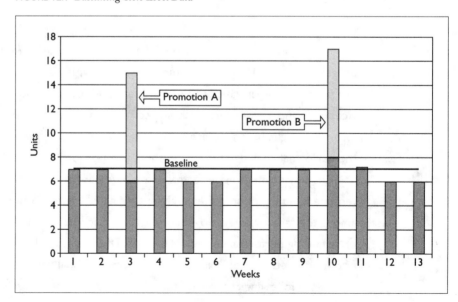

for the entire period there was no ongoing or residual impact from the sales promotion programs.

The flat baseline in this example raises some questions on how performance programs should be structured.

If, as above, no longer-term sales increase was achieved, the sales promotion events should be judged only on the incremental sales increases achieved during weeks 3 and 10—that is, how much more was sold than would have normally been expected. Those incremental sales would have to increase profits sufficiently to cover the performance program's cost and other associated activities. If the increased sales didn't provide sufficient profit to cover those costs, the marketer would likely have a net loss—not an attractive scenario for a promotion planner.

If, however, the promotional program succeeded in driving the baseline, or the trend line, up in a positive way, then the promotion planner might be justified in evaluating the performance program over the longer term.

Let's suppose that rather than being flat, the baseline, as shown in the chart, actually trended upward over the course of the 13-week measurement period. Let's say that at the end of the 13 weeks, unit sales were averaging a level of eight rather than the starting unit volume of seven. With this increasingly trending upward baseline, the promotion manager might say the performance program incentive could be justified over time rather than simply being evaluated on the results of the two weekly sales increases. The two promotions, although they did increase incremental short-term sales, also appear to have had some longer-term sales impact as well. Therefore, the promotions and the performance program could be evaluated on the entire 13-week period, not just on the incremental sales in weeks 3 and 10.

Understanding how promotions work and the basic concept of baselining are two of the most important areas for the promotion planner to understand, not only in planning promotions but in designing performance programs as well. Performance programs work, but you must be sure they provide profits as well as merely short-term incremental sales. —Don E. Schultz

OVERVIEW

Performance programs answer the overriding question: "What's in it for me?" Without performance incentives, "The pay's the same" mentality can stagnate your business. And if your product is one of several a salesperson or staff member has on his or her plate, it often pays to "grease the wheel." You may also motivate people to learn about your product, even "suggestive sell" it. A good program motivates overachievers and underachievers and high- and low-volume areas. In the end, one of the greatest motivators you can enlist is also one of the least expensive: recognition. A certificate, trophy, or simple thank-you note works wonders.

DEFINITION

A performance program motivates key people to make an extra effort in supporting a product or service by defining goals and rewarding achievement. Performance programs are typically for sales but may also reward quality control, speed quotas, safety practices, punctuality, and the like.

Note: Although some consider purchase incentives to be performance, this chapter deals only with sales or tasks (with the Casino Night exception). Other tactics and chapters cover purchase incentives.

COMMON PERFORMANCE OBJECTIVES BY TACTIC

(Also see itemized tactics below.)

TACTIC	OBJECTIVES
Quota	Meet and exceed sales projections; set benchmarks; motivate and reward all participants, either individually or collectively
Contest—greatest volume	Sales by the best performers; no outlays for lesser performers; fewer rewards; foster competition
Contest—volume and percentage increase	Sales increases by all participants, low and high performers; foster competition
Qualifying sweepstakes	Economical, rewarding a few but motivating all

TACTIC	OBJECTIVES
Strategic performance	Achieve objectives that lead to sales, such as placing displays, new accounts, up-selling, etc.; discipline sales staff
"Casino Night"	Economically reach a great number of small targets, like mom-and-pop stores; bonding opportunity
Customer submission = sales entry	Leverage consumer program to simultaneously and economically motivate sales performance
Group competitions	Build targeted trading area sales; unite and motivate regions/groups
Mystery spotter (shopper)	Demonstrate and reward model practices at work site when they occur; sustain quality staff practices, anticipating spotter; employee education
Recognition	Economically motivate employees and recognize model performance; cost savings on insurance, medical benefits, handling errors, returns, and other employee operations

TACTICS ITEMIZED

123. QUOTA

Definition	Motivating performance (sales) through rewards for specified achievement level(s); may offer cumulative catalog reward points or program-end merchandise, trips, etc.
Advantages	• Establishes benchmarks and helps achieve or exceed sales projections • Can motivate and reward all participants • Several goals can be weighted with different reward levels to address several objectives • No added costs if budgeted through incremental gains • Straightforward and easy to implement.
Disadvantages	• Lesser performers (or regions) may not be motivated by unachievable quota • If open-ended, rewards may exceed budget • If funded by incremental profits, rewards and motivation may be limited • Participants may revert to old ways once the program ends

- Salesperson may forestall immediate sales opportunity anticipating program
- May require auditing and possibly subject to fraud
- May not factor in sales that are subsequently returned (which is also subject to collusion by seller/buyer)

124. CONTEST—GREATEST VOLUME

Definition

Participants compete, but only the top performers are rewarded; performance can be sales or tactical, such as a display contest—most displays placed

Advantages

- Motivates the best performers where the "critical mass" is generated
- Spurs competition and determination to sell and win
- Less expensive as fewer are rewarded
- Fewer rewards allow more exciting selection
- If budgeted through incremental gains, no added costs

Disadvantages

- Lesser performers (or less-developed regions) may not be motivated
- Less flexible in combining different tactical goals
- May upset strong performers who didn't win
- Competition may foster ill will, even suspicion of unfair competition
- Salesperson may forestall immediate sales opportunity anticipating program
- May not factor in sales that are subsequently returned (which is also subject to collusion by seller/buyer)

125. CONTEST—VOLUME AND PERCENTAGE INCREASE

Definition

Participants compete in two platforms—greatest volume increase and greatest percentage increase

Advantages

- See "Contest—Greatest Volume," above, but lower performers and regions can win greatest percentage increase (see "Motivating *Everyone*" on page 325)

| *Disadvantages* | • See "Contest—Greatest Volume" and its disadvantages; however, lesser performers can be motivated by greatest percentage increase |

126. QUALIFYING SWEEPSTAKES

| *Definition* | Prize drawing entry earned for each performance achievement (such as unit sold); drawing alternatives: win a scratch card, a pull-tab pull, a wheel-of-fortune spin, etc. |

Advantages

- Motivates all participants as everyone can win, but better performers have better odds
- Fewer rewards allow more exciting selection
- Easy, accountable budget—the fixed-prize cost
- Can increase odds/participation with numerous lower-cost prizes
- Several objectives can be entry criteria
- Budgeting through incremental gains eliminates costs (earn entry only after achieving quota)
- Drawings (or pull tabs, wheel spins, etc.) at weekly sales meetings generate enthusiasm

Disadvantages

- Minor performers may win as major performers go unrewarded
- May require greater materials cost, such as scratch cards, pull-tab boards, etc., for each sales center
- More administration
- Salesperson may forestall immediate sales opportunity anticipating program
- May not factor in sales that are subsequently returned (which is also subject to collusion by seller/buyer)

127. STRATEGIC PERFORMANCE

| *Definition* | Program rewards participants for achieving business-building objectives—display placement, new accounts, trading customer up, selling service warranty, etc.—rather than for sales |

Advantages

- Establishes business-building disciplines that build sales

- Rewards salespeople for professional, strategic practices
- Corporate planning objectives extend tactically to field level
- Focus on long-term business-building disciplines versus short-term sales bursts

Disadvantages

- May be difficult to monitor and verify performance
- More complicated for participants to understand and act
- May not deliver immediate sales results
- Salesforce may not want to jeopardize current practices, customer relationships, and commissions with unfamiliar new practices
- May require training, materials, manager programs, and monitoring system
- May be less accountable without direct sales criteria
- Predicated on the success of new tactics versus direct sales objectives

128. "CASINO NIGHT"

(Note: This is a purchase versus sales incentive program but still an effective sales program)

Definition

Numerous accounts earn "point-money" toward a future group event, such as a casino-themed evening, and "spend" their points on rewards, prize games, auctions, etc.; targets are often diverse, scattered small operators who cumulatively represent significant business; can be any entertaining event theme from sports to Hollywood

Advantages

- Reaches, motivates, and brings together a large and profitable, but fragmented, territory—businesses that may not otherwise warrant attention
- Gives salespeople "news" for each account visit
- Event gives sales organization opportunity to fraternize with several smaller customers at once
- Night on the town for smaller rural businesses
- Everyone earns something desirable with accumulated point-money
- Strategic reward can build goodwill in family values communities— family zoo trip, ice capades, etc.

Disadvantages
- Requires extensive planning—entertainment venue, events, point-money distribution, verification
- Extensive, ongoing communication materials
- Point-money requires an accountable system
- Casino/gambling theme may offend some
- May require liability insurance, particularly with alcohol
- Difficult to schedule event for all participants
- Check local/state codes—point-money format may or may not meet gambling/lottery restrictions

129. CUSTOMER SUBMISSION = SALES ENTRY

Definition
Participant earns prize-drawing entry for every customer redemption his or her efforts initiate.

Example: Restaurant employee gives acquaintances coupons with his or her name—redeemed coupons enter drawing, and consumer may also win

Advantages
- Motivates employees to generate sales and satisfy customers
- Extends salesforce size
- Motivates everyone, since anyone can win, while greater performers earn better odds
- Sweepstakes economies—many participants, few winners
- Can be simple administration
(See "Qualifying Sweepstakes" above)
- Can merge volume and percentage increase (above)

Disadvantages
- Requires process to credit performers for redemptions
- Minor performers may win whereas major performers go unrewarded
- Competition may cause friction in environment of close-knit employees who target mutual acquaintances
- May not factor in sales that are subsequently returned (which is also subject to collusion by seller/buyer)

130. GROUP COMPETITIONS

Definition   Performance competition pits group against group, region versus region, shift versus shift, store versus store, etc.

Advantages
- Fosters a groupwide spirit
- Encourages teamwork
- Utilizes existing internal systems and personnel
- Organization can share and learn successful practices
- Organization can better evaluate its sales dynamics
- Can reach and motivate both the sales and the support organizations

Disadvantages
- Group effort may not motivate individuals who prefer personal control
- Doesn't motivate weaker or disadvantaged groups—requires level playing field
- May be competing with the wrong target—internal versus the external
- May foster internal ill will, suspicion, and resentment
- Requires fair accounting system

131. MYSTERY SPOTTER (OR SHOPPER)

Definition   Employee is spotted practicing quality standards and is rewarded immediately

Advantages
- Recognizes and rewards model practices at work site when they occur—in front of other employees
- Sustains quality staff practices, anticipating spotter visit
- Motivates employee learning
- Gives on-site managers a performance tool
- Vendors may tie in

Disadvantages
- Can be time, cost, and labor intensive
- Limited by spotter coverage capabilities
- Requires effective up-front communication of required practices
- May suffer apathy if employees believe they will not be visited
- May foster resentment as one lucky employee is spotted and re-warded for behavior the others also practice

132. RECOGNITION

Definition
Employees rewarded by recognizing their personal, professional, and admirable achievements—typically awards (versus rewards) such as plaques, trophies, pins, or rings; rewards may be engraved items, gift certificates, or paid time off, even an employee-of-the-month parking space; may be business-to-business rewards, such as a retailer honoring its best vendors

Advantages
- More bang for the buck—very inexpensive program delivers one of the greatest motivators: recognition
- Builds employee morale, acknowledging individual tasks and achievements and demonstrating employer appreciation
- Reward (plaque, trophy, etc.) is permanent personal reminder often prominently displayed
- Platform to communicate ideal employee practices
- Recognition meetings provide "feel-good" breaks and remind employees of their value

Disadvantages
- Requires a system of identifying and tracking employee performance
- Susceptible to subjective criteria—or the perception of such criteria
- Requires reward-meeting organization and tasks
- Employee-initiated submissions can be unfair, such as stuffing the ballot box
- Some deserving employees may feel resentment for being unrecognized
- May foster perception of favoritism
- Should acknowledge diverse employee services—tenure does not necessarily mean outstanding performance
- Requires ongoing communication
- Program often gets neglected, taking second seat to daily business priorities

CONSIDERATIONS

Common Performance Objectives

- New product launch
- Liquidate product for new product launch
- Increase overall volume
- Increase margins—trade up
- Increase share of market
- Increase product/services mix
- Distribution—new accounts and/or channels
- Account penetration—more products in existing accounts
- Product/display placement
- Bolster slow season
- Enhance professional skills
- Increase product knowledge
- Support consumer promotion
- Offset competitive activities
- Build dealer traffic
- Improve morale, show goodwill
- Lead generation
- Productivity
- Reduce turnover
- Safety, health, reduced sick time, etc.
- Recognition (quality performance, tenure, punctuality, safety, etc.)
- Teamwork

For safety and quality objectives, specify goals—for example, proper safety procedures, reporting potential hazards, proper lifting techniques, and so on.

Setting Up

- Keep it simple. Limit the number of goals, and try to coordinate them, like goals that can be achieved in one sales call. Make instructions concise.
- Base goals on previous performance, factoring in traditional slow and peak periods plus industry trends and activities.
- Are the rewards achievable and motivational enough to inspire the extra effort?

- Ask vendors their return policy to limit unearned rewards warehousing costs. Or run a drawing for unrewarded prizes—or make them employee recognition rewards.
- Set parameters to track performance. Tracking current sales can be difficult with the lag between orders and shipments, canceled orders, returns, overlapping territories and accounts, forward buying, and the like. A safety program may be measured by accident reductions, quality in returns' reductions, and so on.
- Rules should specify how performance will be monitored and judged so no one can question the results. (Remember the 2000 presidential election?) Consider an outside agency whose decisions are final.
- Try to integrate other departments into the program with roles for salespeople, order processors, administrators, shipping, and so on.
- Objectives should also be coordinated with company objectives, policies, and upcoming programs.
- Look for loopholes and conflicts. Ask everyone for advice—sales, administration, order processing, and all managers.

The Feeding Chain

Imagine if the person taking the calls for orders is actually pushing the salesperson to perform! Consider motivating everyone involved. Following is a list of common motivation targets:

When pushing product

- Company salesforce—directors, managers, reps
- Manufacturer's rep/agents
- Retailer salespeople
- Wholesaler/jobber principals and salespeople
- Employees involved in the sales and distribution process
- Customer service
- Field services

When pulling buyers

- Corporate/company buyer
- Institutional/facility buyer

- Purchasing agent
- Chain buyer
- Store owner/franchisee/manager
- End user (the IT person versus the corporate buyer)
- Consumers

WINNING WAYS

Incentive magazine (©2004 VNU Business Media, Inc. Used with permission of *Incentive*.) cites the following performance criteria for additional motivation:

Open-Ended

Basic: Earn 500 points for every case of product sold

Bid and Make: Predict the percentage increase of sales and receive a corresponding reward when the goal is reached

Qualifier: Earn 1,000 points if the person recruited stays on the job a year

Retroactive: Reach a minimum goal before earning points but receive retroactive payment that includes all sales once the goal is passed

Team Bonus: Each participant is eligible for a 5,000-point bonus each quarter if everyone meets goal

Two for One: Participating distributors earn 10,000 points per $1,000 in incremental purchase increases, provided they buy a certain number of points to pass along to customers

Up and Over: Reach a minimum goal of 1,000 points before beginning point accumulation

Close-Ended

Lucky Squares: Make a sale and write name in a square. Winning squares picked at the end of the week

Make Your Own Odds: Earn a sweepstakes entry or game card for every case of product bought/sold

Only the Top Win: The top 50 achievers (and their spouses) win award, or the three customers who submit the best ideas win

Pick 5: Every fifth purchase earns an entry into a sweepstakes drawing

Unequal Thirds: Participants are divided into three groups and the top 20 participants in each group win

Short-Term Rules

> *Beyond the Sale:* In addition to rewards for sales, earn bonus points for prospecting (or demonstrations, calls, expense-control efforts, etc.)
>
> *Fast Finish:* Every sale made in the final two weeks earns double points
>
> *Fast Start:* Every sale made in the first two weeks earns double points
>
> *On-Target Bonuses:* For every quarter the goal is met, win an additional 5,000 points
>
> *Sprint:* Earn bonus points on every deluxe-grade product sold during the next six weeks.
>
> *Win Two Ways:* Earn 1,000 points redeemable for merchandise per case sold, plus the top 50 performers will win a trip.

MOTIVATING *EVERYONE*

There are always high, average, and low achievers as well as regions. Following are ways to level the playing field so everyone can win and is motivated.

First, *always* motivate high performers. Keep all-important high performers motivated and happy. Consider a separate prize pool for highest volume or guarantee rewards for volume quotas.

Each sale equals one entry. Every person who sells a unit has another chance to win. High performers earn more chances.

Volume versus percentage gained. High-volume salespeople usually don't register a high *percentage* sales increase. If they sold 1,000 units last period, 25 more is a 2.5 percent increase. If a low performer sold 100 units last period, 25 more is a 25 percent increase. Motivate both with two criteria, one for highest volume, the other for highest percentage increase.

Volume and percentage increase combination. Each salesperson earns points or entries based on sales volume multiplied by percentage increase.

Example: 1,000 sales @ 3% increase = 30 points (or entries)
100 sales @ 30% increase = 30 points (or entries)

Volume and percentage increase ranking combination. Each salesperson earns a point ranking based on sales volume multiplied by sales volume ranking.

Example: The highest-ranking volume seller sells 1,000 units.
1,000 units × number 1 ranking = 1,000 points/entries

The lowest-ranking volume seller (#20) sells 25 units.
25 units × number 20 ranking = 500 points/entries

The midranking volume seller (#10) sells 150 units.
150 units × number 10 ranking = 1,500 points/entries

A variation adds the sales volume ranking to the percentage increase ranking to determine the final score.

Example: Low-volume salesperson places 90th of 100 in volume sales but number 18 in sales percentage increase. He places 108. (90 + 18.)

High-volume salesperson places 5th in volume but 85th in percentage increase. She places 90. (5 + 85.)

"Best effort" category. This category recognizes people who make the effort but don't win, especially given their unique circumstances. Consider several best effort rewards acknowledging persistence, toughest odds, new accounts, even the toughest customer. It recognizes effort and it's fun.

Tiered reward levels. Both earn rewards, but high achievers earn higher-value rewards than do low achievers. If lower-level rewards aren't sufficient motivation, include a sweepstakes overlay with sales also earning entries.

Weighted objectives. Assign different values for each objective. (See "Common Performance Objectives" above.)

HOW WILL YOU VERIFY PERFORMANCE?

Here are some guidelines in establishing a measurable program.

- Hold meetings with people directly involved in tracking sales—computer programmer, order processing, telesales, sales managers, and so on.
- Review how sales are reported in the system and how these documents can double as performance reports.
- Determine how frequently sales reports are issued—daily, weekly, monthly, or other. Look for peaks or other aberrations, like one dealer's excessive order. Also, use them as progress reports—the more frequently, the more top-of-mind.
- Use existing, controllable vehicles. For example, for display placement put a different number on each display, which becomes a drawing number when it's placed.
- Make goals simple, such as accounts opened, clients serviced, dollar sales.
- Make a policy on issues like returned merchandise—does the salesperson still get credit or is it the salesperson's job to maintain purchases? Was the merchandise defective?
- *Always* mention an audit will be conducted and violations may result in penalties—even if you don't plan to audit.

REWARDING PRACTICES

Rewards versus awards versus prizes. In general and as previously noted, performance programs give *rewards*—vacations, stereos, apparel. Recognition programs give *awards*—plaques, trophies, medals, pins. Sweepstakes and contests yield prizes.

Does your reward vendor really have the rewards? Make sure the supplier has a sufficient reward stock or will when the reward date rolls around. Suppliers rely on vendors too. Make provisions in the rules for reward substitutions.

Warehouse versus drop ship. If you're offering custom imprinted rewards, consider the control a dedicated warehouse service offers. However, you're buying the prizes up front and may have warehouse costs for leftovers. To avoid additional warehouse costs and up-front purchases, have the manufacturer drop ship the rewards, although this gives you less control and may not accommodate custom-imprinted rewards.

Aspirational. For the greatest impact, desirability, and memorability, make rewards "luxuries." The program is an opportunity to own what we dream of having but otherwise wouldn't indulge in.

Trophy value. Recognition programs thrive on *trophy value*—the plaque on the wall (that cost mere dollars). Give winners a plaque along with the reward. If it's a group trip, have professional photos taken and frame them for winners.

Psychographics and demographics. Consider the participants' lifestyle, age, gender, geography, income, education, family status, and so on.

Reward formats:

Stock catalog—Performance agencies offer stock catalogs that you can customize with your company imprint. The reward ranges meet everyone's taste and several achievement levels. They're turnkey with a self-administered fulfillment process in place. These rewards typically don't allow imprints, and they're commonplace—not particularly exciting or brand reinforcing.

Retailer catalog—Many retailers and catalogers offer a reward catalog program, but you can probably shop for better values than their standard 10 percent. You may also consider the exact catalog to fit your target, from Eddie Bauer to Omaha Steaks.

Custom catalog—You can shop suppliers directly for your own reward selection. Many agencies offer custom programs. You might imprint the merchandise.

Sponsorship merchandise—If you sponsor a league or property, you might create a custom catalog with imprinted rewards to increase the merchandise's perceived value. (Review what your sponsorship allows and what specifically you can imprint.)

Travel—Travel ranges from cruises to destination packages to weekend get-aways. Be cautious with hotel chain vouchers because many chains have independent franchises that may not honor the offer. Domestic trips generally run $1,800 to $2,300 per person.

Group travel—It may be pricey, but group travel can bond your customers and salesforce with an experience they'll always remember—*and* associate with your company.

Retail gift certificates/cards—Certificates are easy to stock and send; they accommodate numerous achievement levels; winners choose their reward (which is instant); and the retailer handles warehousing fulfillment. However, rewards are limited to the retailer's category and selection, and you might do better than the standard 10 percent discount.

Cash—This is the most popular reward but least efficient. You get more for your buck with merchandise, even if it's only a 10 percent retailer discount. (See "Prizes" in "Sweepstakes," Chapter 2, page 34.)

Credit card credit—You can give credit cards charged with buying power. Offer any level of reward, and there's virtually no administration but this can be a costly service. And although it may cost more than cash, it suffers the same drawbacks.

On the spot—This is a discretionary bonus or gift given as a reward for excellent performance right when it happens. It should be as objective as possible for prespecified achievements.

Recognition—Even a simple certificate of achievement winds up on the recipient's wall. Recognition should be for specific accomplishments so employees know the criteria for quality performance.

Reward claims. Set up a simple process with vouchers or certificates to claim rewards. Include:

- Name and company ID
- Location
- Performance claim
- Reward(s) and quantity (itemize rewards with a checklist)
- Where to ship
- Any liability disclaimers
- Details: Allow 0 weeks; if damaged . . . ; return policy; etc.
- Monitoring and fraud practice
    - Phone or e-mail for questions
    - Signature, possibly with truth claim

I *nsight*

It's remarkable how the 80/20 rule rings true—20 percent of the market represents 80 percent of sales. Consider an objective of increasing the 20 percent figure and increasing your most profitable customer base.

BUDGETING

Ballpark Allocations

Incentive programs are typically funded by incremental sales—profits beyond those you would achieve without a program. Program budgets usually boil down to the following:

- Rewards
- Communication
- Administration
- Training possibly

The following rules of thumb may vary with each situation:

Incremental sales increase: Incremental sales goals average 15 to 20 percent; however, they vary greatly by industry. Base your projection on history plus the current sales climate, new products, new accounts, and other factors.

Total performance budget: Consider 10 percent of *incremental* sales. To generate $100,000 in additional sales, allocate $10,000 to your program.

Another formula is to devote 20 to 50 percent of your projected incremental profit (not sales) to the program. Of that figure, spend 60 percent on rewards and 40 percent on administration and communication.

Consider using the following allocations:

Rewards: 50 to 75 percent of your total incentive budget. (This includes warehousing, shipping, etc.) Higher-income, more experienced participants expect more valuable rewards. Sales or dealer rewards may total from 3 to 5 percent of the participant's annual income.

Communication: Consider 15 to 20 percent to communicate the program (folders, tip sheets, rules, teaser mailings, posters, progress reports, etc.), which includes creative, production, and shipping.

Administration: Consider 5 to 15 percent of your budget for this area, which has a lot of variables: how many employee hours are needed, how detailed your analysis will be, what your tracking and verification processes will be, and so on.

Contingency: Allow 5 to 10 percent for the unexpected.

Training: If you include training, you'll need to adjust the above figures or tap into a separate budget.

Open-Ended and Close-Ended Budgets

An open-ended budget has no limit on the values that can be awarded. Keep selling—keep earning. It's geared to sell more product, but the reward system has to keep paying for itself or you'll risk going over budget. Also, you can't budget your total costs up front, such as projecting reward quantities and cost.

A closed or fixed budget program sets a limit on rewards. Fewer people can earn high-value rewards, which may not motivate lesser achievers. However, you can establish a firm budget up front, knowing you have the funds.

Incremental volume requirements. See "Discount," "Budgeting Guidelines," page 146, and apply the same principles.

SWEEPSTAKES ADD TOPSPIN AT LOW COST

Because most participants don't win, the cost is limited primarily to the prizes. Add some motivational sizzle by making every sale double as a drawing entry, so each sale earns points and can win a big prize at program-end. Minor prize drawings every week help keep things interesting.

POINTS PAY FOR PROGRAMS

You must assign a value to your points, and that value ultimately finances the entire program. (See "Points versus Money," page 273, plus "Breakage and Slippage," page 272, in Chapter 10 on the benefits of a point system.)

If a reward is a mini-TV that costs $100.00, the budget for that reward is actually $133.33 if you allocate 75 percent of your budget to rewards. (The other 25 percent [$33.33] is for communication and administration.)

$$\$100.00 \div .75 = \$133.33$$

At .005 cents/point, it takes 26,667 points to achieve a $100.00 prize (with $33.33 [25%] left for administration and communication).

$$\$133.33 \div .005 = 26,667 \text{ points}$$

Because $133.33 represents 10 percent of your sales,* you needed $1,333.33 in sales to generate a $100.00 prize (and $33.33 for communication and administration).

$$\$133.33 \div .1 \ (10\%) = \$1,333.33$$

*Assumes you've allocated 10 percent of incremental sales to fund the program.

I *nsight*

Scrutinize your structure. Bonus points, for example, could break the house, turning a fixed budget into an open one.

Because 26,666.66 points represents $1,333.33 in sales, each point represents 5¢ *in sales*. (The .005 cents/point above represents the value of a point.)

$$\$1,333.33 \div 26,667 = \$0.05$$

So your salesperson earns 20 points for every dollar sale.

$$\$1.00 \div \$0.05 = 20 \text{ points}$$

To check your math:

$1,333.33 sales goal × 20 = 26,667 points (which equals $133.33—see above)

or

$1,333.33 in sales = 26,667 points (1,333.33 × 20), which earns a $133.34 performance budget (26,667 × $0.005), of which $100 goes toward the TV ($133 × .75).

Bonus Points: You can offer bonus points for specific achievements. Again, assign a percentage of your budget for those points and calculate the increased point value.

Yearlong Pricing Average: Consider your yearlong price plan when you calculate point values. If you base your points on your full wholesale price, promotional discounts to distributors and retailers will throw off your payout.

Note: Also see the discussion of budgeting in "Continuity," Chapter 6, page 164.

BREAKAGE

Breakage can save you money on unspent points. If you have a performance agency, ask for breakage credits. See "Breakage and Slippage" in Chapter 10, "Premium Programs," page 272.

TAX STATUS

Items valued up to $400 for safety and length-of-service awards are tax deductible to the company and excluded from an employee's taxable income. Issue tax form 1099 to recipients of rewards valued over $600.

SAFETY, TENURE, PUNCTUALITY, AND THE LIKE

The goal of these areas is to save money. ("A penny saved is a penny earned.") Ask the human resources department to calculate how much is lost in productivity from absenteeism, employee turnover (and new training), and insurance claims. Begin your budget based on a percentage increase of improved behavior—fewer days off the job, less turnover/hiring/training, lower insurance premiums, and so on. Recognition rewards can be very economical, from plaques to movie tickets.

SCAMS AND FLAWS

Ask *everyone* from shipping clerks to salespeople to computer freaks to order processors: "If you were a thief, how would you rob me?" Offer a reward to any successful scenarios.

Red flags. Identify indicators to discover misconduct, system flaws, and irregularities; and then establish how to monitor them—who commits them and how often. Consider such items as these:

- Exceptional sales activity (or inactivity) by a salesperson
- Exceptional order activity (or inactivity) by an account
- Duplicate addresses, invoice numbers, orders, etc.
- Any mechanical reproductions of key materials
- Previously unlisted purchasing agents or buyers

Trial runs. Run every element of your program through a reality check with every person who'll encounter that element from order forms to tracking reports.

COMMUNICATION

Give your program a theme that can be a rallying cry. Make it one word or phrase so it's memorable and instantly recognized. Managers should be able to say, "Hey, how you doing in the *Hit the Beachfront Drive?*" so the salesperson instantly identifies the Hawaiian vacation incentive.

Constantly keep the program top of mind. Consider the following:

- **Teaser mailings:** Pique interest before the program
- **The company newsletter, payroll stuffers, statements, and other existing vehicles**
- **Announcement packet:** Usually distributed at sales meetings with all the information salespeople need—performance requirements, rewards, duration, and official rules; consider training materials
- **CD-ROM:** Salespeople can review the program, see training programs, even make sales presentations
- **Web site:** Use it for training, updates, logging and tracking points, and more
- **Faxes and e-mail:** You communicate with these anyway—tag on your communication
- **Audiotape or CD:** For salespeople who spend a lot of time in their car
- **Ongoing mailings:** Create exciting, fun mailings that can vary from clever postcards to novelties; consider attaching progress reports
- **800 numbers, voice mail, and text messaging:** Keep everyone posted on their respective cell phones
- **Progress wall charts:** Foster competition by posting everyone's status, which also sets benchmarks as top performers begin setting the pace and others see what's achievable
- **Home base:** Consider mailings directly to homes, so families rally behind the program and prize

TOP-LINE COMMUNICATION POINTS

Don't let these important points get buried in the official rules. Highlight them in the program overview:

- Rewards/prizes
- Who can win—titles

- How they can win/earn—how many ways
- Eligibility—tenure, region, division, employment required before and after program period, etc.
- What products are eligible
- Promotion period
- Enrollment process and deadline
- Performance requirements and resultant points/entries
- How to report performance
- How to monitor progress
- How to receive rewards
- Who they go to for answering questions

COMPLETE RULES

Issue to everyone a complete rules sheet that succinctly spells out every program detail. Envision the unforeseen, such as what happens with ties; if a winner leaves the company; if rewards become unavailable. Include all the dates—invoice dates, invoice submissions, reward claims—everything. Consider an independent agency so you can defer disputes. For travel or motorized vehicles, include a "not responsible" clause as well as waivers of liability for winners.

Some of the topics your complete rules should include:

- Who's eligible—specific titles, territories, requirement to be employed throughout program duration, etc.
- Which products qualify
- Which accounts qualify
- Criteria and rewards
  - What must be accomplished—be precise
  - What each accomplishment earns
- How entries are submitted, including proper documentation (invoice photocopy, display photograph, buyer signature, etc.)
- Entry deadline
- Program dates—all of them
  - When performance begins and fails to qualify
  - How to document performance timing
  - Submission deadlines
- How entries will be verified

- Penalties for improprieties
- Policy on returns and canceled orders
- How to submit for rewards
- How rewards will be fulfilled—and timing
- Tax responsibility (typically the participant's responsibility)
- Damaged or depleted rewards policy
- Cash option policy (typically none)
- Limitations on rewards, such as the top five salespeople; cap on points; first five to achieve goal, etc.
- How to register disputed performance claims
- Independent judging agency whose decisions are final

SELL-IN AND COMMUNICATION PROCESS

Here are seven approaches to selling in and communicating a performance program. In these scenarios, a manufacturer is selling through a distributor, who in turn sells to retailers or corporate buyers.

1. Sponsoring regional sales manager secures half-hour meeting with distributor principal:
   - Distributor signs enrollment/authorization.
2. Sponsoring regional sales managers meet distributor sales managers (DSMs) to introduce program.
   - Introduce distributor sales manager's incentive—DSM rewarded for salesforce enrollment and performance
   - Introduce salesforce incentive program
     - Enrollment/authorization form with names and addresses of participants
     - Inventory count for subsequent reward audit
3. Sponsoring regional sales manager and distributor sales managers introduce program to salesforce; enrollment forms signed; introductory kits distributed to salesforce
4. Sponsoring regional sales managers fax enrollment/authorization form to headquarters (or agency), which sends kits according to enrollment form information (unless kits were distributed in step 3); performance-tracking kits may be sent to distributor sales managers

5. Distributor sales manager receives kit to monitor program
6. Regular mailings sent by sponsor to remind and motivate various participants
7. Regular sales reports submitted by distributor sales manager to sponsoring regional sales manager to claim point earnings; sponsoring regional sales manager processes information and forwards to headquarters (or agency) for verification and fulfillment

REPORTS

Depending on your organization, you won't need all the following reports. Check off what you need.

Enrollment forms:

- Distributor principal
- Distributor/regional sales managers
- Salesforce

Current sales and inventory (to benchmark performance):

- By distributorship
- By distributor/regional sales manager
- By salesperson

Activity reports:

- Distributor principal
- Distributor/regional sales managers
- Distributor/field salespeople
- Brand national sales director

Redemption reports
Budget recap
Tax report—1099s

EVALUATION

Beyond sales, answer these other important questions when the program ends:

- How did you do compared to your objectives?
- What did it really cost? What was the ratio of incremental profits to cost?
- How much administration time was consumed?
- How many participated—who?
- What type of participant did or did not succeed and why?
- How did participants compare with nonparticipants?
- Were there regional variations; if so, why?
- Were there product line variations; if so, why?
- What did participants think of the program—those who did and did not receive rewards?
- How was the execution throughout the organization?
- Would an open- or close-ended program have done better?
- Was there a competitive program going on simultaneously; if so, how did yours compare in terms of scope, rewards, performance requirements, and results?
- How might other tactics have done—increased advertising, discounting, consumer promotion, etc.?
- How can you build on this model to make next year's even better?

CHECKLIST
(See details above)

_____ Groundwork
    _____ Current sales and inventory (to benchmark performance)
    _____ Performance objectives
    _____ Sales objectives
    _____ Criteria for success
    _____ How to measure success
    _____ Participants—roles and responsibilities
    _____ Targets
    _____ Timing

_____ Program structure

_____ Math—quota, point values, budget allocations

_____ Reporting system

_____ Performance verification

_____ Process blueprint—how program rolls out

_____ Program rewards

_____ Reward claim and fulfillment process

_____ Reward backup plans

_____ Rules

_____ Creative development

_____ Communication plan

_____ Targets

_____ Vehicles

_____ Schedule

_____ Budget (including postage)

_____ Sell-in process throughout system

_____ Inventory counts, sales histories, or other auditing measures

_____ "Red flag" alerts

_____ Sales activity report forms (to submit sales and then to tabulate and track)—by salesperson, sales manager, distributor, region, etc.

_____ Reward redemption reports

_____ Tax forms for prizes and IRS follow-through

_____ Program recap that reflects original objectives and projections

13

TRADE PROGRAMS

(Also see "Point of Sale," Chapter 7 (page 181);
"Tie-ins" ("Co-op Programs"), Chapter 11 (page 306);
and "Performance Programs," Chapter 12 (page 311)

INTRODUCTION:
WHEELING AND TRADE DEALING

How important is trade promotion in the marketplace success of products and services? It depends on whom you ask.

Ask the retailer and he or she will say that without manufacturers' trade promotion support, sales would fall, as retailers simply couldn't afford to offer the specials, features, short-term promotions, and the like that drive retail sales in almost all categories. There simply isn't enough retailing margin to cover the consumer-expected promotional costs.

Ask the manufacturer and you get a different answer. Manufacturers say that as the marketplace power has shifted to retailers, trade promotion has become more of a legitimized bribe or, worse, some are even calling it extortion. For example, if you as the manufacturer want space in the retail store, you have to pay up in the form of trade deals, promotions, slotting allowances, or the like—in short, "trade promotions" to get retail support. Without trade promotions, your products will languish on the shelf or, even worse, your products may never reach the shelf.

So whether you love trade promotions or hate them, they're a fact of life in today's promotionally driven environment. The challenge is knowing how to make the best of them whether you're a manufacturer or a retailer.

The complicating factor with trade deals is the differing goals of the retailer and the manufacturer. The retailer wants store traffic and doesn't care what brand is sold, only that something is purchased during the consumer visit. Alternatively, the manufacturer doesn't care from whom the consumer buys; the only concern is that his or her brand is purchased.

Thus, the opposing views of the retailer and manufacturer generate ongoing controversy.

Whether developed by the manufacturer or conducted by the retailer, trade deal effects are generally short term. That is, there's commonly no long-term impact or residual brand value for the manufacturer. From the retailer's view, last week's promotion is worth less than yesterday's newspaper. The retailer needs a continuous stream of promotions to keep shoppers coming into the store. Thus, both the manufacturer and the retailer judge the value of a trade promotion on short-term, incremental results.

Clearly, trade deals work. They do generate short-term incremental sales for both manufacturer and retailer. And depending on the deal, the volume, the consumer offer, and the like, a trade deal can be profitable or unprofitable for either party or both. It is the combination of the offer and how it is promoted and merchandised that really determines the value to each.

The big question in trade promotion is which consumer buys what. Do trade promotions generate new sales or simply reward current product users?

Based on some recent marketing-mix analysis in food store studies developed by PDI, an analytical consulting firm, 46 percent of the incremental volume from a trade deal comes from trial by new brand consumers. The other 54 percent comes from repeat purchasers. That compares with 83 percent of incremental volume coming from new purchasers who are influenced by advertising versus only 17 percent coming from repeat purchasers. So trade deals do impact consumers, but they tend to reward present users rather than attract new users. That's important to know when developing a trade promotion program.

Perhaps the most important ingredient in a trade promotion is the support provided by the salesforce in selling the promotion to the retailer. Today, given the commoditized nature of many products, what the salesforce often has to "sell" to the retailers to get their support is the trade deal. That's why it's important that the promotional material supporting the trade promotions is what the salesforce needs, wants, and can use. A promotion planner who develops support materials that never make it out of the trunk of the salesperson's car or never get out of the retailer's backroom has wasted a golden opportunity for increased sales and profits.

We can summarize trade promotion planning with a few potential objectives. Is the trade deal designed to achieve the following three things:

1. Gain new distribution? If so, it will likely be necessary to replace a competitor's product on the shelf—a major change for a retailer. It will require the removal of the competing brand, shelving your brand, make changes in computer systems for stocking and logistics, and so on. So gaining new distribution by replacing a competitor is a major task and requires an integrated trade program, not just a one-time off-price deal.

2. Optimize a product mix? Often, a trade deal is designed to encourage the retailer to stock the full range of sizes, colors, flavors, and so forth of the product line. As above, that will require (1) reducing space from competitors or (2) rearranging the available shelf space for your product line. Either will require aggressive trade dealing.

3. Exploit peak seasonal demand periods? Almost all products and even most services have some sort of seasonal purchasing pattern. Two common reasons for a trade promotion are to enhance normal purchasing patterns or to offset seasonal declines. But these too require thought and consideration.

Of course, there are other reasons to develop a trade deal. Your creative instincts will likely lead you to develop a multitude of others. Steve will spark those ideas in the chapter that follows. —Don E. Schultz

OVERVIEW

Fifty to 75 percent of a manufacturer's budget may be spent strictly on trade allowances—money to "grease the way" and get the product to market. Smaller brands may allocate 90 percent. Packaged goods brands pay to get in the store, more for shelf space, more for end-aisle, more to get a promotional display, and more for retailer services, including co-op funds. Managers and salespeople get "spiffs" (bonus money for each sale), not to mention dinners and tickets.

DEFINITION

Trade programs in this book are business-to-business programs that allow manufacturers to secure additional services from the trade and the trade to secure additional funds or marketing support from the manufacturers.

Retail (trade) promotional programs appear throughout this book. However, this chapter on trade deals with business-to-business activities as opposed to consumer programs.

Note that the words *retailers* and *wholesalers* may be used interchangeably in many of these program descriptions. In other words, you may apply retailer principles to wholesalers and vice versa. Also, manufacturers simultaneously motivate their distribution arms and their retail network.

COMMON TRADE OBJECTIVES BY TACTIC
(Also see itemized tactics below.)

TACTICS	OBJECTIVES (Beyond Purchase)
Slotting program	*Manufacturer:* • Get new product placed on retailer shelves *Retailer:* • Counter risk of new unproved product • Make up for lost sales if new product replaces a profitable product • Turn shelf space into profitable real estate
Allowance program	*Manufacturer:* • Secure services from retailer, like signage, in-ads, etc. *Retailer:* • Secure marketing funds and services from manufacturer • Leverage ongoing marketing practices to secure manufacturer's funding

TACTICS	OBJECTIVES (Beyond Purchase)
Account-generated program	*Manufacturer:* • Secure assured participation in a retailer's program • Turnkey execution *Retailer:* • Offer an exclusive consumer program funded by vendors • Continued traffic through ongoing program
Account-specific program	*Manufacturer:* • Exceptional retailer support and partnership *Retailer:* • Receive exclusive program that stands out from competitors • Awareness and excitement of a vendor's property or sponsorship without licensing fees
Comarketing program	Address both the retailer's and manufacturer's respective marketing objectives to maximize the joint capabilities and resources of both; build fruitful relationship
Co-op program	*Manufacturer:* • Encourage retailer to feature brand in its newspaper advertising, Yellow Page advertising, signage, etc. • Employee training and performance *Retailer:* • Defray cost of marketing practices • Showcase high-recognition manufacturers
Performance incentive program	*Manufacturer:* • Motivate retailer and staff to perform and achieve specific tasks and goals *Retailer:* • Receive reward for business-building program while increasing sales • Improve staff performance

ITEMIZED TACTICS

133. SLOTTING PROGRAM

Definition	A fee the manufacturer pays the retailer to provide shelf space for a new product entry
Advantages	• Secures space for a new product • Reimburses retailer for potential revenue loss and displacement of original profitable product

Disadvantages
- High cost limits small brands from reaching retail
- May replace a profitable product with a new, less profitable product
- New product must generate exceptional sales to cover slotting fee
- Limits new product offerings and consumer choice

134. ALLOWANCE PROGRAM

Definition
Discounts or funding from manufacturer to trade or wholesaler in return for a service like additional stocking, display space, flyer inclusion, etc.

Advantages
- Retailer receives higher margins or marketing funds in exchange for sales-generating services manufacturer receives
- Increased retailer orders through allowance
- Consumer purchase motivation if retailer discounts product
- Manufacturer gets some return for discount, even if it isn't passed on to consumers
- Allows timely correlation between orders and in-store promotional activities

Disadvantages
- Diminishes manufacturer's margin
- Can become a routine cost of doing business
- Retailer may not pass discount on to consumer
- Requires negotiations, paperwork, and follow-through with each chain, plus communication to sales, distribution, and outlets
- Requires administration, including verification of performance requirements
- Manufacturer's objectives may compromise retailer's marketing

135. ACCOUNT-GENERATED PROGRAM

Definition
Program the retailer creates and invites vendors to participate in; ranges from frequent buyer card to cause marketing to sponsorships, etc.

Advantages
- Retailer efficiently pools vendor funding into one focused program
- Reduces brand promotion clutter

- Cumulative offers provide greater traffic motivation than single vendor offer
- Vendor partners encourage cross-store shopping
- Ongoing program can build loyalty
- Multiple vendors broaden appeal—can leverage one another's market
- Vendors may tie in with a retail sponsorship or cause otherwise outside their reach
- Turnkey program for vendors through retailer's signage, flyer support, advertising, etc.
- May give small-size vendors a competitive edge
- Vendors assured the program will be executed by all the account's units

Disadvantages
- Retailer-driven program may not address vendor's marketing needs
- Dilutes manufacturer's branding in glut of products and parity execution
- Vendors may forgo their objectives and programs
- Vendor may lose the marketing competition to competitors exercising their own programs
- May be less cost-efficient than a national vendor program

ACCOUNT-SPECIFIC PROGRAM

See "Point of Sale" programs, Chapter 7, page 190.

COMARKETING PROGRAM

See "Tie-ins," Chapter 11, page 293.

CO-OP PROGRAM

See "Tie-ins," Chapter 11, page 295.

136. PERFORMANCE INCENTIVE PROGRAM

(Also see Chapter 7 "Point of Sale," page 181, and Chapter 12, "Performance Programs,"
   page 311)

Definition   Program targeted to trade (or to/through distributors) by manufacturer
                        to encourage displays, signage, price features, stocking, etc.; may
                        include display-building contest, display number drawing, rewards for
                        orders, sales incentive, etc.

Advantages   • Manufacturer can specify sales objectives and reward/spend accordingly
                        • Motivates strategic performance
                        • Can reach the most result-driving target, like the store manager or
                          staff versus the corporate director
                        • Particularly effective in franchise-controlled versus corporate-
                          controlled chains
                        • Provides salespeople with a "quality appointment"
                        • Opportunity for a coordinated program for sales, distribution,
                          trade, and consumer

Disadvantages   • Many corporations do not allow vendor performance programs
                        • Manufacturer's objectives may not support retailer's marketing needs
                        • Complex programs must encompass and coordinate several levels
                        • Budgeting and payout may be difficult to project and evaluate
                        • Considerable, ongoing communication requirements
                        • Expense and logistics of tracking performance, processing, database,
                          administration, verification, and reward fulfillment
                        • Requires system to avoid abuse and misredemption and refute
                          contested decisions

SPENDING MORE MONEY OR SPENDING MORE WISELY

At first blush, a manufacturer may get the idea that retailers (especially
the grocery, drug, and mass merchandising categories) constantly have their
hands out asking for more money for this, more money for that, from slotting
fees to flyer advertising demands to conversion costs to display allowance

funding (see the Glossary). It may seem that retailers make more money buying products than selling them, and there may be some truth to that. On the other hand, many of these fees have legitimate claims. Why should a retailer replace a known seller with a manufacturer's new product entry? The slotting fee is its insurance policy. A retailer's end-aisle space is valuable real estate that every brand covets—why not rent it to the highest bidder?

But, what if both retailer and manufacturer look at it from another perspective—good business? I once worked with a salesperson who sold major program concepts to savvy Frito-Lay brand managers with just one tool—a calculator. He simply demonstrated the increased profits his program would generate at the bottom line. Retailers and manufacturers alike should consider the same approach with trade programs. Both have something to offer the other beyond blatant buying and selling of store space and flyer ad insertions. When you design and negotiate trade programs, consider some of the following business-building assets, capabilities, and strategies you mutually may bring to the table:

- Store traffic
- Display traffic
- Cross-store shopping
- Access to alternative communication media—infomercials, bus stop signage, packaging, event programs, mall advertising, and so on
- Multiple product sales
- Niche markets you both need
- Licensed property affiliations
- Sponsorships
- Signage expertise (which soft drink companies often apply to fast-food customers)
- National caliber creative resources
- Concepts to combat each partner's competitor activities
- Research tie-ins, testing various programs together
- Research studies on shoppers, shopping behavior, products, complementary product usage, trends, etc.
- Other marketing partner affiliations you can bring to the program
- Training programs
- Coadvertising opportunities, especially local media
- Targeted direct mail
- Community events—fairs, leagues, school programs, and the like

- Causes
- PR
- See Chapter 11, "Tie-ins," page 283

SAMPLE TRADE PROMOTION BUDGETS

PROMO's Promotion Trends Report 2003 reports the following marketing fund allocations:

Spending per Discipline

Consumer promotion	30.6%
Trade promotion	26.6%
Media advertising	37.6%
Other	5.2%
Total Marketing Budget	100 %

Source: *PROMO* magazine (http://www.promomagazine.com, a Primedia publication)

Other studies have shown trade spending representing 40 to 60 percent, consumer promotion 20 to 25 percent, and advertising 20 to 35 percent. A small but national candy company spends 90 percent against the trade.

ALLOWANCES AND OTHER FUNDS

Slotting allowances. Slotting is money paid to retailers (grocers) to get a new product on the shelf. Because most new products fail, grocers won't pay the penalty for their vendor's miscalculations. What's more, a new shelf slot replaces an existing product, and slotting fees can be staggering. In New York it can cost over $100,000 to introduce an SKU into supermarkets and wholesalers covering 73 percent of the metro ACV (see the Glossary). Many brands forgo introducing their otherwise successful lines in major metro markets like Chicago and New York.

FIGURE 13.1 *A Square Foothold on Profits*

Turn/Profit Calculations for Displays

Turn/Profit Ratio Example

Product	Turns per period (month, 3 months, year, etc.)	Profit per unit sold	Turn/profit ratio	Square feet to display	Turn/profit per time period
A	14	× $6	= 84	÷ _____	= _____
B	40	× $3	= 120	÷ _____	= _____

Even though Item A offers a higher profit per sale, item B has a higher turn/profit ratio—more total profit per time period. The next example factors in square footage.

Turn/Profit Ratio per Square Foot Example

Product	Turns per period (month, 3 months, year, etc.)	Profit per unit sold	Turn/profit ratio	Square feet to display	Turn/profit per time period
C	75	× $10	= 750	÷ 25	= 30
D	30	× $ 5	= 150	÷ 3	= 50

The calculation above determines each item's profitability in terms of space. C has more turns, more profit per sale, and a higher turn/profit ratio. However, D delivers the greater turn/profit ratio per square foot.

(Also see page 144.)

MDFs, BDFs, street money. Marketing Development Funds (MDFs) and Business Development Funds (BDFs) are funds allocated to a sales organization to spend toward each unique business environment. Some fund sales incentive programs, others retailer flyer ads, and still others coproducing storefront signage. "Street money" is spent at the individual salesperson's own discretion and may go toward floor sales spiffs, to retail managers for "favors," for event outings, and so on. A beer salesman purchases $2,000 worth of Best Buy gift certificates to pass out among bar owners, managers, and wait staff at his discretion. One study reported that 35 percent of these funds "get lost."

Display charges. Many retailers charge for display space *if* they even grant it to you. Charges vary, especially if you're bartering co-op advertising or other support. In the grocery store category, expect to pay in the hundreds, depending on where the sign appears. You may pay less for a small shelf sign. In fact, you may have to purchase that space from an in-store media company. Think of it as a large flea market, and you're trying to get the best table spot available—it won't be free. You rent your space. Even universities receive cash for vending machine placement. You can get creative: The $400 merchandiser fee might be handled as a $200 donation to the store's cause (for some PR value) and a case allowance makes up for the other $200. Still, you may not even qualify for the space as so many compete for it.

Conversion costs. Grocers often charge significant fees when a manufacturer makes a packaging change. They incur costs reprogramming and moving a package through the system. In 1997 the total conversion costs in the densely populated New York metro market for one SKU totaled $36,000.

Co-op funds. See extensive description in "Tie-ins," Chapter 11, page 306.

Profit calculator. See "Selling in a Discount to the Retailer" in Chapter 5, "Discounts," page 144.

RETAILER DISPLAY PACKAGES

Before it displays your product, a major mass merchandiser might charge $75,000 for your product to appear in the Sunday flyer, then request a 20 percent discount. But the flyer may cost less than a periodical, and it reaches shoppers. And 70 percent of shoppers use a shopping list.

TRICKS OF THE TRADE

- **Trap captive audiences:** Escalators, elevators, lanes, even bathrooms give people time to ponder signs. Promote popular but pricey items—perfumes, jewelry, imported spirits.
- **Wandering wallets:** Place popular, profitable products like cosmetics or digital cameras near the ground-floor entrance; other high-impulse items are usually nearby. "Destination" departments, like furniture or appliances, are better on higher floors or further walls. Grocers often lead with the produce department, which shoppers feel is the section that most differentiates grocers. And you won't stop shopping after getting your greens.
- **Glass says class by a wide margin:** Display luxury items under glass with comfortable spacing. For expensive items, turn the price tag over so a salesperson has to "reveal the true value."
- **Implied bargains:** Simply posting a large price gives shoppers the impression it's a sale price, even at full markup. Some pricey, prestigious retailers use "dump bins" to suggest a deal.
- **"New" sells:** Because many new items can sell at full price and enjoy advertising support, showcase them.
- **Accessorize sales:** Place batteries by flashlights, dip by chips, earmuffs by caps.
- **Loss leaders:** If you break even on a popular item and it results in traffic, you come out ahead.
- **Impulsive behavior:** Place high-turn, high-margin, impulse items by the cashier. Small is good—stock more—candy bars, magazines, breath mints, digestives.
- **Stoppers or shoppers:** Price-focused retailers may lead with bargains to stop consumers as they enter. Pricey retailers may lead with pricey products.

Insight

Performance and consumer marketers think differently. An ad specialty firm eyeing huge sales to a sporting goods brand was dismayed to learn the consumer marketer wanted slippage—minimal premiums. After all, in performance programs premium orders represent strong sales performance.

CATEGORY MANAGEMENT

Category management is a fact-based, diagnostic approach for manufacturers and retailers to get more unit sales based on historic movement per item, per shelf position, per store location, and more. The idea is to give fast movers more prominence while placing each in the best store location given its particular shopping occasion—breakfast, after school, baking, and so on.

Opinions differ, and many variables are at work. Should high-priced, high-margin, slower-turn Equal sugar substitute be placed with other sugars, though it's rarely used for baking? Should it be near tea, coffee, and cereal? Diabetic supplies? Fitness products? If it's low turn, it shouldn't be prominent. If it's high margin, it should be visible. If it isn't seen, it can't mature. Category management attempts to address these overlapping categories and subcategories statistically, but the right answer may be a moving target. As Mark Twain observed, "There are three kinds of lies: lies, damned lies, and statistics."

(Also see the glossaries in the chapters discussing point of sale (page 208) and tie-ins (co-op) (page 306)

account-specific A manufacturer's promotional or advertising program that's tied specifically to one retail account.

ACV *See* all commodity volume.

ADI *See* area of dominant influence.

Advertising Specialties Institute *See* ASI.

all commodity volume A basis for measuring retailer distribution that factors in the relative importance of each retailer. Example: Brand X has distribution in only one store, but that store represents 25 percent of market sales; therefore, Brand X has 25 percent ACV. Brand Y has distribution in 100 stores, but they represent only 10 percent of market sales; therefore Brand Y's greater distribution represents only 10 percent ACV.

allowance Discount or funding offered by manufacturer to distributor or retailer. May be an off-invoice rebate for order submission, or case allowance, such as five cases delivered for four ordered.

area of dominant influence A geographic division of markets by a service named *Arbitron* that is based on the preponderance of television viewing by county.

ASI Advertising Specialties Institute. An organization of merchandise manufacturers, vendors, and importers who sell imprintable merchandise to businesses, not consumers. Computerized system searches from among tens of thousands of items by theme word, color, price range, size, etc. Businesses must order ASI merchandise through authorized ASI resellers.

back haul allowance (BHA) Money manufacturers pay retailers who will pick up shipments at manufacturer's own plant or distribution center.

BDF *See* business/brand development fund.

best food day An opportunistic day of the week for food marketers when the newspaper runs editorials on food topics and weekly grocery specials begin—usually Wednesday or Thursday, depending on the market.

BHA *See* back haul allowance.

billback Additional money paid by the manufacturer to the retailer for the retailer's display, ad, or price feature. The retailer performs the services, then bills the manufacturer back (versus off-invoice).

BOGO Buy one–get one promotion. Typically, buy one, get one free, though it could be buy one, get one at half-price or other configurations.

bounce-back A coupon the shopper receives *after* the store visit (in the package, at checkout) that "bounces the consumer back" to the brand and store.

brand equity The level of awareness consumers have of a brand and the degree to which it is favorable. Schlitz beer once had tremendous equity, then fell to a more "commodity" perception.

branding The science and art of building a singular identity and image of a brand. What makes Coke, Coke and Pepsi, Pepsi and 7 Up, 7 Up when insiders refer to them as sugar water. Marlboro was originally a female brand until Leo Burnett himself rebranded it. Ice cream was a commodity until Häagen-Dazs; before Nike, they were tennis shoes.

brand switchers *See* switchers.

breakage Points and dollars that go unredeemed; "leftover change." *See* "Premiums Programs," Chapter 10.

buckets A relationship marketing database term for groups (buckets) of consumer profiles. One bucket may be young, active, single male, sports enthusiasts; another may be mature, 40+-year-old, higher-income male parents, with travel replacing sports interest. Each requires a different communication strategy.

bundle Packaging two or more related products or services into one package. Example: a video player cleaner, CD player cleaner, and DVD player cleaner in one bundled pack; local, long-distance, and Internet services bundled in one price.

burst an obtrusive deal announcement on a package or sign ("Save $00!"), often a star burst. *See* snipe.

business/brand development fund (BDF) Money spent by manufacturers on a field or account level earmarked for problems and opportunities for the brand (versus geographically focused market development fund). Fund may be applied to new account development, introductory offers, performance incentives, etc.

buy-back allowance Manufacturer's discount to retailer/distributor based on amount remaining from previous deal purchase.

C&P Convenience and petroleum store. *See* definition of each.

cannibalization Selling one brand extension at the expense of another. Example: "Dr Pepper Free tastes just as good as Dr Pepper" ad campaign, which may rob Peter to pay Paul.

cash value What a coupon is worth in cash, since some states allow coupons to be redeemed for cash; cash values are low—1/20¢ or 1/100¢. *See* face value.

Catalina A service that, among other things, reads purchases at the cashier and then prints out corresponding coupons. Example: A cat food purchase generates a cat litter coupon or a competing cat food coupon.

category The grouping of several similar products and brands; the soft drink category, the automobile category. Categories can be broken down further, such as the automobile category's SUV category.

category development funds (CDFs) Money targeted to drive a specific category supporting all brands at once, and in the process increasing the sponsoring brand's sales. Cheese, milk, and other groups unite to promote their category.

category management A fact-based diagnostic store-stocking approach for manufacturers and retailers to get more unit sales based on historic movement per item, per shelf position, per store location. It attempts to manage product categories as business units and customizes them on a store-by-store basis to satisfy individual store shoppers' needs.

cherry pickers Shoppers who visit only for the promotional offers and, as a result, hurt bottom-line results.

chain A retail operator with 11 or more stores.

churn The defection of current users to a different brand. A term common in some industries (cellular service providers) but not others (packaged goods = switchers).

CMA *See* cooperative merchandising agreement.

comarketing A retailer and vendor combining their marketing objectives and resources to create a custom program that better accomplishes their mutual goals.

company owned *See* franchise.

consignment An agreement by a manufacturer and distributor or retailer that unsold goods can be returned to the manufacturer with no purchase obligation.

continuity Continued purchases. A program that promotes ongoing purchases of a product, such as collect and get. *See* loyalty.

convenience store (C-store) Compact, easy-access store offering a limited line of popular items. Over half sell gasoline and some sort of fast food. Their roots are not founded on petroleum but rather on packaged goods retailing. *See* petroleum store.

conversion cost Fees grocers charge when a manufacturer makes a packaging change on a product already in distribution; offsets costs incurred reprogramming and moving a package through the system.

cooperative merchandising agreement (CMA) Annual incentive contract to get a retailer to commit to ad display or price feature for a brand for a specified period.

corporate sales program (CSP) An umbrella promotion across a marketer's total brand portfolio. Corporation may unite several brands under one promotion with a picnic, Super Bowl, or other theme. Products often shipped direct from plant on ready-to-display pallets.

corrugated Commonly called cardboard, which is a broader term. A popular display construction material with two stiff cardboard laminates reinforced by a rippled inner layer; exceptionally strong, versatile, and lightweight.

cost of good What a product actually costs a manufacturer/reseller as opposed to the marked-up sell price. A restaurant giving a free soft drink may spend only a nickel to offer a 99¢ value.

cross-dock or pedal runs Cash incentives for placing full-pallet orders for four or five stores and distributed by a single truck; marketer saves distribution costs.

cross-ruff Coupon(s) delivered on one product package that is good for another product purchase. Example: Scotch tape coupon delivered inside a Post-it note package.

CSP *See* corporate sales program.

dayparts Segmenting a retailer's business activities by the time of day. Restaurants try to boost slow midday dayparts; mall stores target seniors on morning walks, moms and preschoolers from 10:00 to 2:00 weekdays.

deal The deal cut between the salesperson and the retailer, distributor, or other buyer. The terms vary greatly as they "horsetrade" quantities, allowances, advertising, flyer features, display activity, and so on. *See* terms. "On deal" means an offer is available.

demographics A way of analyzing a particular market by quantifying its average household income, age distribution, family makeup, ethnic makeup, and so on. Also *see* psychographics, geodemographics, and segment.

detail person Part-time person hired to hand out samples, coupons, literature, entries, and so on, or to assemble and place displays or perform other temporary field tasks.

direct distribution *See* store-door.

disclaimer Small print specifying exceptions beyond your control or ground rules, such as, "Not responsible for lost, stolen, or misdirected mail."

display Exact definition varies according to participant. The marketer's broader interpretation includes promotional signage highlighting prominently placed product. Field salespeople and retailers (particularly grocers) define *display* as the product stacking itself (versus on the shelf). "Display and feature" refers to a product stacking with a price feature sign. A salesperson might refer to a marketer's *display* as *signage*—the promotional signs that accompany the display (or product stacking).

display allowance A manufacturer's price discount (or payment) to receive the retailer's support for displays.

display-ready cases and pallets Marketers pay retailers for using these cost-efficient shipments ready for immediate display.

diverting *See* forward buying.

donut A commercial (typically radio) that sandwiches one message between two others (the "Intro" and the "Outro"). It may be a national advertisement followed by a local dealer announcement in the middle, then closed with a continuation of the national advertisement. Example: National car ad—local auto dealer announcement—national car ad close. It could also be the opposite: Local dealer announcement—national advertisement—local dealer announcement. *See* tag.

door-to-door *See* store-door.

double coupon Some grocers in some markets routinely double the value of a manufacturer's coupon; if a manufacturer's coupon is 35¢, they'll discount the purchase 70¢, picking up the other 35¢ cost. They typically limit the manufacturer's coupon value to 55¢ ($1.10 total shopper discount). So if your coupon is 65¢ and your competitor's is only 45¢, the competitor beats your offer on double coupon days (65¢ versus 90¢).

drive periods Scheduled timing for a promotional drive. A packaged food marketer may have five promotional drive periods—the three summer holidays, Christmas, and Thanksgiving. A snow blower marketer may have three drive periods—preseason (World Series timing), peak (holiday gift timing), and postseason (March Madness).

drop When a promotional element, such as a coupon or magazine insert, hits the newsstand.

drop ship allowance (DSA) Money to retailers who bypass a grocer's distribution center for preplanned orders or customized pallets.

EDLP Everyday low price. A price positioning retailers take (especially some mass merchandisers and grocers) as opposed to short-term sales features/ events (high-low); *see* temporary price reduction (TPR). Wal-Mart is a classic EDLP retailer.

efficient consumer response (ECR) A retail industry concept for more efficient distribution and shelf management systems. Theoretically, it predicts and responds to product movement in-store with more efficient shelf allocation, restocking, departmental categorizing, and distribution through the manufacturing-warehousing-store delivery process. Ideally, it's a distribution system that responds more efficiently to consumer behavior.

end user The person who ultimately uses the product or service and often not the same person who purchases it. The purchasing agent may buy the computer software, but the end user (the Web master, for example) may influence that decision as the end user. The software salesperson should consider both targets.

exposures The number of times in a specified period that consumers are exposed to an advertisement, point-of-sale display, or other communication piece.

face value How much the coupon discount is on the specified product; a "Save 50¢" coupon has a 50¢ face value. *See* cash value.

facings The number of packages of an item on the front line of the store shelf. This does not include the number of packages stacked behind that front line. *See* SKU.

feature A retail price reduction "featured" at point of sale and/or in store's flyer.

field The business world outside headquarters' four walls—the outside arms and legs that may refer to the outside salesforce that has to oversee sales and stock product, and implement headquarter programs; distributors doing the same, or retailer's regional representatives.

field marketing Marketing plans and operations specifically intended for the field. Examples: in-store sampling program; regional event sponsorships; local cause tie-in; local radio promotions.

flexible coupon Agreement by the advertiser that allows the FSI service to place the coupon at the top or bottom, left or right of the page to avoid damage if the opposite side's coupon is clipped. A "guaranteed position" costs more.

flyer The weekly (or less frequent) publication featuring price reductions and other special offers; prevalent as Sunday newspaper inserts.

forward buying Practice by some regional distributors buying manufacturers' products offered on a deal for that region, then diverting (or reselling) some of those products to nondeal markets. Also termed *diverting*.

franchise (1) A retail operation in which the store operator buys into a franchise brand name (as opposed to company-owned operations). Some franchise operators are very independent, like Dairy Queen, where the corporation has limited control over operator practices. McDonald's franchise agreements give corporate greater control than others. Hardware franchisees (Ace, True Value, etc.) typically are highly independent. Company-owned retailers like Target or Sears have complete control. Most companies have a combination of company-owned and franchise stores. Franchisees also often operate as groups for clout—the Chicagoland Ford Dealers, the Florida McDonald's franchisees.

franchise (2) A company's existing group of consumers—actual purchasers of its products.

Fred Meyer Corollary A court decision that requires manufacturers and wholesalers to offer the same co-op plan to all advertisers within a market area. It also requires that they notify all their known outlets that the plan is available. They must also provide supporting documentation for reasonable opportunity to use those co-op funds. *Also see* Robinson-Patman Act.

freestanding insert *See* FSI.

frequency How often an advertisement will reach a person or household. *See* reach.

FSI Freestanding insert. The promotional section most commonly distributed freestanding in Sunday newspapers filled with manufacturers' coupons and other promotional offers. The significance of freestanding is the flexibility for regional versions, positioning in the insert, and custom printing unavailable in the run-of-press (ROP) newspaper format (like improved color, scratch-off games, custom-seeded numbers, etc.)

FTC Federal Trade Commission. Establishes laws for marketing and sales practices.

geodemographics Quantifying a market by a combination of demographics (and sometimes psychographics) within geographic clusters, such as regions, zip codes, and neighborhoods.

grocery store Any retail store selling a line of dry groceries, canned goods, or non-food items plus some perishable items. *See* convenience and supermarket.

header Prominent point-of-sale card (typically corrugated) that sits on top of a display stacking, floor stand, gondola end-aisle, or the like. *See* glossary in Point-of-Sale chapter.

high-low (versus EDLP) High-low pricing. A price positioning retailers take (especially mass merchandising and grocery trades) featuring short-term sales on numerous select items. Although most products remain at higher prices, weekly advertisements lure shoppers with a host of special low prices on select items. The practice sacrifices margins on featured items, while enjoying high margins on other impulse sales during the shopping trip. Alternative to EDLP, everyday low pricing positioning.

home meal replacement (HMR) Food/packaged food category term for food-service outlets offering traditional "home-prepared meals," taking share from traditional grocery shopping.

impressions The number of times advertising and/or promotional signage exposes a brand to a consumer; 100 impressions mean it was exposed to consumers 100 times but doesn't necessarily mean 100 *different* people were exposed to it.

impulse items Products that have high appeal for immediate, unplanned purchases. Strategically placed by retailers at high-traffic areas.

impulse purchase Making an unplanned purchase. Two-thirds of grocery store purchases are impulse.

impulse sales Plus sales for retailers because they're unplanned extras by shoppers, for example, beyond the sale items in the retailer's flyer.

in-ads Ads within retailer ads. For example, a vendor, like Hills Brothers, buys an in-ad in Kroger's newspaper ad. The in-ad is usually a price feature designed by the retailer for consistency.

independent A retail operator with up to ten stores.

insert An advertising or promotional page or folder inserted into a publication, such as a newspaper. Research reveals inserts gain greater readership and response as they stand out from the clutter. *See* FSI.

in-store media Music, radio, and TV media "piped in" by the store and available for advertising.

IRC Instant redeemable coupon placed on the package that can be redeemed immediately at checkout.

licensed property Copyright-protected, registered, or trademark-protected property that marketers may tie in with to add sizzle, sales, and event opportunities to their product. (Examples: Super Bowl, Disney, movies/videos, TV programs, NASCAR, Miss America, etc.) Marketers must negotiate rights to work with a licensed property, which also spells out the usage limitations.

limited assortment store A store with fewer than 1,500 items, primarily dry grocery with few, if any, perishables. Small gross margin and workforce and virtually no service.

line extension Offshoots of the flagship brand, such as the diet extension, caffeine-free extension, cherry-flavored extension, and the like.

load A marketing strategy to "load the consumer's pantry." By getting the consumer to stock up, the competition is locked out by the lack of demand. It also seizes timely high-demand opportunities (like season changes or holidays) to generate multiple sales.

loader Merchandise item that's used in one of two ways: (1) a promotional gift to a retailer (or business-to-business target) for participation in a program—a manufacturer's beach-themed promotion might include an inflatable beach ball for the retailer—and (2) a part of the display that helps command attention and becomes a retailer gift after the promotion (the above beach ball is "lugged on" the display, which the retailer may keep after the promotion).

loss leader An item a retailer sells at or below cost to drive store traffic in hopes of selling additional profitable items during the visit.

loyalty Customer loyalty to a product or service. Continuity may promote a few ongoing purchases (McDonald's Monopoly), but loyalty programs strive for a long-term, even permanent, customer retention (American Airlines Aadvantage Miles; credit card rewards).

lug-on A merchandise item or dimensional display element that's attached to the point-of-sale signage. An actual inflatable beach ball might be lugged onto a corrugated display depicting a beach scene. Or a cardboard representation of the beach ball may be lugged on as a dimensional element. *See* loader.

mandatories Small print items legally required in the communication, such as copyrights, corporate identification, or disclaimers.

margin The dollar or percentage amount a product is sold for compared with what it costs. Also "markup," "mark," or "MU." (The *true* cost of a product is complex—materials, manufacturing, system tracking, sales process, packaging, distribution, returns, etc.)

market development funds (MDFs) Money spent by the brand, usually via the retailer, to expand brand sales in given markets; used to increase share in markets where category growth is high and a brand's share is low. *See* business/brand development funds.

markup The dollar or percentage amount added to a product's cost to establish the sell price. Also "margin," "mark," or MU.

mass merchandisers/merchants Large retail store carrying numerous mass-appeal product categories with a discount image (real or perceived); fewer frills than a department store and more frills than a warehouse store.

media The vehicle that delivers the advertising and communication—print (magazines and newspapers), broadcast (radio and TV), outdoor (billboards), Internet, direct mail, and so on.

merchandiser A display that showcases a product, often demonstrating its benefits.

merchandising (1) Retail store designing and decorating; a retailer will merchandise a store for seasonal events like the Easter sale and the holidays.

merchandising (2) Retail store fixturing and product display. Stores may supply their own fixtures to stock and display merchandise; or manufacturers may hire merchandising agencies to design permanent or semipermanent fixtures. Merchandising is more permanent than point of sale, made with styrene plastic, wire racks, wood, vacuform, and the like. Examples: cigarette stocking fixtures; Timex watch plastic rotating showcases; mirrored cosmetic displays.

merchandising (3) *See* trade-out. Radio merchandising means bartering a media buy for items the station can provide, such as CDs or concert ticket prizes.

modeling In database programs, building a predictive model of common customer behavior patterns to help predict future behavior. Also see "Profiling and Modeling" in Chapter 6.

MU Markup.

off-invoice allowance A discount for retailers when the order is placed; deducted from the bill.

overlay A tactic (often optional) "laid over" the foundation tactic. A coupon may have a sweepstakes entry overlay; a point-of-sale signage display may have a self-liquidating offer overlay.

packaged goods Broad-based term for everyday usage prepackaged products. Generally refers to grocery, convenience, and mass merchandiser products—packaged foods, soaps, health and beauty, some automotive (like motor oil), some hardware (like cleaning aids), and so on.

pack-out The quantity and configuration of products in a shipping carton.

pedal runs *See* cross-dock.

petroleum store Compact, drive-to store founded on the gas station class and evolved to include the convenience store format with packaged goods. Petroleum stores still have the vestiges of gas stations and are not as focused on retail/packaged goods/food and snacks as are their convenience store counterparts. They are often perceived to have higher-quality gasoline than do convenience stores, whereas they lack the retail sophistication of convenience stores.

plan-o-gram A schematic design for a store's merchandising plan or a product line section. A major retailer will design a plan-o-gram for a seasonal theme, then for individual product sections like electronics, then CD players within the electronics section. Packaged goods marketers offer plan-o-grams to stores with ideal shelf locations for their product's various sizes, extensions, and suggested quantities. Plan-o-grams vary regionally. For example, some regions prefer 12-ounce cans, whereas others prefer one-liter plastic bottles, so the same brand's plan-o-gram changes by territory.

point-money A consumer or sales incentive currency.

point of sale The location where the shoppers shop, products are displayed, and sales are consummated. While sales can be by phone, Internet, mail, etc., point of sale refers to a physical location with products and shoppers present.

POP Point of purchase.

POS Point of sale.

postoff A price reduction in store—dollars "off," "posted" at retail. A manufacturer attempts to get a retailer to run a postoff, passing the trade discount on to consumers.

producing plant allowance (PPA) An incentive to retailers to buy full or half-truckloads direct from the factory. Saves manufacturer's distribution costs.

profiling In database programs, assembling lifestyle and behavior patterns of individual customers to build a profile of that customer and create a closer "relationship" with targeted messages and offers. Also see "Profiling and Modeling" in Chapter 6.

profit calculator A sheet the salesperson uses to close the sale with a retailer. It lists the various products and has blanks for filling in the cost, discount, sell price, quantity, turn, and, finally, the profit. *See* "Selling in a Discount to the Retailer" in Chapter 5.

program learning Tactic(s) that informs participant of product attributes, promotional activities, training tips, and so forth. A drawing entry may ask for the product's slogan, or a staff incentive may have answer-and-win product questions.

proof of purchase The proof required in some promotional offers that the consumer purchased the required product, such as a receipt, UPC symbol, package logo, and the like.

property *See* licensed property.

psychographics Quantifying a particular market by its psychological patterns, such as activities, lifestyles, and opinions. Also see demographics, geodemographics, and segments.

push-pull A marketer's coordinated program to push the product into retail while pulling consumers into the stores for the product. For example, it may be a united sales incentive, trade deal, and consumer promotion with advertising support.

reach The number of people or households an advertisement will reach. *See* frequency.

reconciliation The final accounting of a program that reconciles all costs and payments among partners.

redemption A consumer (or other incentive target) cashing in on a promotional offer, such as a coupon purchase, a reward-for-performance claim, or a refund claim. Redemptions are also quantified figures used to project and evaluate results, such as the percentage of certificates redeemed from the total of certificates distributed.

retrofitting Adding or replacing an element to an existing display fixture. Many permanent display fixtures are designed to accommodate new replacement signage for promotional offers or display upgrades.

Robinson-Patman Act An antitrust act that requires proportionately equal co-op and promotional offerings to retailers by manufacturers. A manufacturer may offer greater program values to proportionately larger-sized retailers. It may offer different programs to the same size retailers as long as they have similar values. It may also offer singular programs for testing purposes. *Also see* Fred Meyer Corollary.

ROP Run of press. Refers to newspaper printing process in which all pages are printed in one run of the press, with virtually no customized printing capabilities such as finer-line screens, better color, scratch-off games, or match and win symbols.

route person The sales and/or stocking person who makes the routine route to the individual stores in the area.

rub-off card *See* scratch card.

run of press *See* ROP.

scan-downs Price discounts programmed into grocer's computer and registered when a product is scanned at checkout. (Retailers may legitimately add up to 25 percent to the scanned amount when they bill manufacturers, mostly to cover rainchecks and sale days not covered in the data period.)

scratch card Also rub-off card. A sweepstakes card with an announcement concealed beneath an ink layer the participant must scratch off to reveal.

secondary display A second (or third, etc.) display in a separate location in the store. The primary display might be a mass cola stacking at the store entry with a Super Bowl theme. The secondary display may be the same cola next to the pizza case for a Super Bowl tie-in offer.

segment A portion of the overall market that a marketer might target, such as single male, African American, 18 to 35 years old; or female homemaker, C-D county, 25 to 35 with children. (*Also see* demographics, psychographics, and geodemographics.)

self-liquidator (SLO—self-liquidating offer) A consumer offer by a brand that liquidates its own cost. Example: "Buy five packages of Acme Candy, send in your proofs, and receive this Candy Decanter for just $5.99." The $5.99 covers the offer's cost.

self-shipper A shipping container that houses both the display and the product. The display often includes the floor stand, the bin that stocks the product, and the header card sign. Also called a prepack.

sell-in The plan, materials, and process of selling a product or program to a business audience—the retail buyer, the distributor, the store manager, and so on. A sell-in plan could be multitiered—first to the distributor management, then the distributor sales reps, and then the retailer. It may range from a simple sell-in brochure showing the product's popularity and profitability to a sales incentive program.

set-sell Countertop version of self-shipper.

share The percentage of total retail purchases expressed in dollars or units for a specific brand within its product category. If one quarter of all widgets sold are Acme Widgets, Acme has a 25 percent share of market. Share may also be used to express the percentage of other factors, such as regional market, "voice" (advertising exposure), or total dollars (because 25 percent of unit sales doesn't mean 25 percent of dollar sales).

shelf-keeping unit *See* SKU.

shelf life The length of time a product will remain on a shelf. A package's promotional announcement should not be on the shelf longer than the promotion itself.

shrinkage The amount of merchandise received but not sold, typically because of pilferage (either by shoppers or employees).

signage *See* display.

SKU Shelf/stock-keeping unit. Pronounced skew, this is a territorial term for the number of product units on a retailer's shelf. The goal is more SKUs that will be at the expense of the competitor's SKUs on the finite space. SKUs are designated for each variety of the product, from extensions to package sizes. *See* facings.

slippage Typically a percentage figure that expresses the difference between consumers who purchase a product with the *intention* to respond to its offer and those who *actually act* on the offer; common in refund programs where many consumers never get around to the paperwork.

SLO *See* self-liquidator.

slotting allowances Money paid to the retailer simply to get a slot on the shelf for a new product. Because most new product launches fail, grocers don't want to pay the penalty. Adding a new product requires system modifications plus removing the previous product, which may have been profitable. Slotting fees can be staggering.

snipe *See* burst.

spiffs Money to motivate salespeople to focus efforts on sales of the manufacturer's product versus competitors' products. A consumer electronics manufacturer may offer a $5 to $20 spiff for every sale by a retail floor salesperson.

spoilage The percentage of lost, damaged, and defective goods that should be factored into a premium order quantity.

stacker card A card designed to prominently showcase a stacking of product. It may be mounted on top of a floor pole or a gondola fixture or posted on a product-stacking case. (See "Point of Sale," Chapter 7.)

store-door Refers to the ability some manufacturers enjoy of having their own salespeople or route people deliver the product and any display materials directly to each retail location. Most rely on less reliable third parties, like distributors. Also door-to-door and direct delivery.

street money Cash spent in the field at street level to get more features, display, sales, and so on. It's used at the field salesperson's discretion—sales spiffs, gift for the customer, crew event tickets, contributions to retail community causes, and so on.

suffix code An additional code in the ordering and distribution system to assure special promotional product is only distributed to eligible regions and countries.

supercenters Large food/drug combination and mass merchandisers under a single roof offering a wide variety of food as well as nonfood merchandise. Average more than 150,000 square feet and typically devote as much as 40 percent of space to grocery items.

supermarket Any full-line, self-service grocery store with annual sales of $2 million or more.

superstore A supermarket with at least 30,000 square feet doing $12 million or more of business annually and offering an expanded selection of nonfood items; offers specialty departments and extensive services.

switchers "Unfaithful" consumers who switch brands based on best price, easiest access, or other benefits.

SWOT Popular analysis and planning acronym: strengths, weaknesses, opportunities, and threats. (Don't let the clever convenience limit the scope of your thinking.)

tag Also dealer tag. Five- to ten-second spots at the end of a broadcast commercial for the tie-in retailer or vendor to add its promotional message. *Also see* donut.

temporary price reduction (TPR) Short-term retail discounts offered in exchange for manufacturers' trade funds. Allows significant consumer discount on select, popular items to entice traffic. (*See* EDLP.)

terms All those fundamental and fine points in a sales agreement made in each party's interest—pricing, duration of pricing, payment method, return policy, and so forth. (*Also see* deal.)

30:30 radio Radio ad by manufacturer that allows an additional 30 seconds for the retailer's ad. No charge to retailer for media as an encouragement to participate in the program as well as guide consumers to point of sale.

touchpoints Areas where a marketer can reach and "touch" a particular consumer—favorite TV programs, ballparks, beauty parlor, and the like.

trade Term used by specific industries for their specific distributors, dealers, publications, and so on.

trade area One or more counties, usually within a central metropolitan market, in which residents transact most of their retail purchases.

trade-out Swapping something you've got and your partner needs for something your partner has and you need. You can trade out your home electronics products for their appearance as prizes in your partner's sweepstakes advertising.

traffic Shoppers visiting a store or chain, expressed in numbers and often broken down by calendar period, days, and dayparts.

translight Back-illuminated, plastic sign most often seen as fast-food menu boards.

turn The average number of unit sales for a product in a specified time period.

turnkey Simple. Easy for the participant to participate and the sponsor to execute.

UPC Universal Product Code. The bar code on packaging that identifies the product as well as retail price and other information. Scanned at the cash register in retail and used for product tracking in warehousing and distribution applications.

UTC Under the cap. A term for sweepstakes in which prizes are revealed under the product's lid—soft drinks, yogurt, canned goods.

vendor The company supplying the next sales link's product. A grocery store's food manufacturers, an auto lube chain's motor oil supplier, a bar's spirits suppliers.

viral marketing Refers to utilizing the Internet's ability to spread e-mail (from friend to friend and associate to associate)—to replicate and spread your message across the Web.

warehouse store Store with more than 1,500 items, primarily dry grocery with some perishables. Small gross margin and workforce; no frills with pricing focus; limited service.

wholesale club A business and consumer membership retailer/wholesaler hybrid with a varied selection and limited variety of products. No-frills warehouse setting. These 90,000-plus square-foot stores have 60 to 70 percent general merchandise and health and beauty care products as well as a grocery line dedicated to large sizes, limited brand selection, and bulk sales.

Share the message!

Bulk discounts
Discounts start at only 10 copies and range from 30% to 55% off retail price based on quantity.

Custom publishing
Private label a cover with your organization's name and logo. Or, tailor information to your needs with a custom pamphlet that highlights specific chapters.

Ancillaries
Workshop outlines, videos, and other products are available on select titles.

Dynamic speakers
Engaging authors are available to share their expertise and insight at your event.

Call Dearborn Trade Special Sales at
1-800-621-9621, ext. 4444,
or e-mail trade@dearborn.com

Dearborn™
Trade Publishing
A **Kaplan Professional** Company